Contemporary Indian Drama
astride two traditions

Festschrift for
Professor Santosh Gupta

Edited by
Urmil Talwar
Bandana Chakrabarty

RAWAT PUBLICATIONS
Jaipur • New Delhi • Bangalore • Mumbai

ISBN 81-7033-935-9

Published by
Prem Rawat for *Rawat Publications*
Satyam Apts., Sector 3, Jawahar Nagar, Jaipur 302 004 (India)
Phone: 0141 265 1748 / 7006 Fax: 0141 265 1748
E-mail: info@rawatbooks.com
Website: www.rawatbooks.com

Delhi Office
4858/24, Ansari Road, Daryaganj, New Delhi 110 002
Phone: 011-23263290

Also at Bangalore and Mumbai

Typeset by Rawat Computers, Jaipur
Printed at Chaman Enterprises, New Delhi

Contents

Preface

It is our great pleasure and privilege to put together this volume as a festschrift for Professor Santosh Gupta on the occasion of her sixtieth birthday. This is to honour her contribution towards teaching and research. Of the two of us, Bandana's association with Professor Gupta began in 1984 when she enrolled as an M. Phil student, later she did her Ph.D. under her supervision. Urmil's association with her began in 1980 when she joined the Department of English for her Masters. These associations have fondly continued in different ways.

Professor Gupta has been a warm and friendly person guiding us as and when required during our research and teaching. She has herself been a student of the Department of English, University of Rajasthan both for her masters as well as doctoral programmes. She worked on the theme of love in Iris Murdoch under the guidance of Professor Kashi Prasad. Later she joined the University of Rajasthan as a teacher in 1966. Since then she has been associated with the University in various academic and administrative capacities – Assistant Principal of Maharani's College, Head of the Department of English, Dean of the Faculty of Arts, and as member of various administrative committees. Despite her administrative preoccupations, she has been fervently engaged in the pursuit of knowledge and has generously shared it with her friends, students and scholars at all occasions.

During her tenure as a teacher she has taught and guided research on various authors, across centuries and across geographical boundaries ranging from Victorian era to the 20th century, on British, American and Canadian writers. Some of the writers on whom she has guided research are Joel Chandler Harris, George Gissing, Elizabeth Barrett Browning, E.M. Forster, Muriel Spark, Edith Wharton, Doris Lessing, Philip Larkin, Alice Munro, moving on from modernist and postmodernist analysis to the relationship between form and medium, as for instance films.

Her academic eminence can be attributed to her sense of commitment both to teaching and research. She has interacted with young researchers and teachers and has made a significant contribution to the area of British, American, Canadian and Indian Literature. Professor Gupta has published a number of research papers on subjects like Critical Theory, Feminist Theory, Poetics of the Novel and Postcolonial Issues. She has organised several workshops, refresher courses and seminars of national and international level. She has edited *Contemporary Indian Literature Positions and Expositions (2000)*, co-edited *The Utopian Imagination (1991)* with Professor Jasbir Jain and *Re-thinking Modernity (2004)* with Professor P.C. Kar.

For this festschrift we had requested for papers on contemporary Indian Drama in English and English translation from colleagues, friends and scholars who have known her. Some of our senior colleagues have responded warmly to our request and have contributed papers mapping the journey of Indian Drama and Parsi Theatre. We extend our heartfelt gratitude to Professor Jasbir Jain, Professor Nilufer Bharucha, Professor Sudha Rai, Professor Chaman Ahuja, Professor Ranbir Sinh, an active theatre critic, and Ravi Chaturvedi, a theatre director for their contributions to this volume. Our thanks are also due to all the contributors, friends, co-scholars and senior colleagues who have not only scripted the articles but have also enabled us to meet the deadline.

We take this opportunity to pay tribute to our dearly loved and respected teacher and colleague and to convey to her the deep affection and regard we have for her. She has always showered immense affection and generous hospitality on us. We wish her health and happiness in years to come.

Putting together of this volume has been a journey both of learning and pleasure as we have moved from plays to essays and vice versa, then to dictionaries and bibliographies, explored this comparatively less explored area, honed our skills and sharpened our critical knives as we have found our way in this labyrinth. We have moved from play to text and to translation. Learning, especially when it is a collaborative exercise, and more so when it is in honour of a teacher we care for, can be more than fun. It is the beginning of new journeys and relationships. We are happy to say that there are many who have shown us the way and many who have joined us. We thank every one who has been involved in this project in whatever way.

Urmil Talwar
Bandana Chakrabarty

Introduction

Contemporary Indian Drama: Astride Two Traditions traces the development of Contemporary Indian Drama specifically in English and in English translation. Drama, being a performative art, has an immediacy of appeal which poem or fiction may not need. Initially drama was meant only to be staged. It is of recent origin that the drama is written in the form of a text meant to be analyzed and interpreted by the academicians. Aesthetic theories which govern the writing and interpretation of drama are also different. Drama as a theatre has had a glorious tradition and in India it has been a popular folk entertainment. In various regions of India it has thrived in different forms as Bhavai, Yakshagana, Tamasha, Jatras, Ramlila, Raslila and the like. But the Indian Drama in English is of recent origin looking for its form and technique in the West.

The dramatists writing in English - Dina Mehta, Nissim Ezekiel, Gurcharan Das, Manjula Padmanabhan, Mahesh Dattani - have to work under diverse constraints. They have to capture the indigenous habits of thought and expression in the English language, cater to the demands of both native and foreign audience. They are conscious of their own culture and emotional life but have to work under a creative tension as they are burdened with the English poetic tradition. They are under constant fear of making their product imitative. The Indian English dramatist has to choose his own blend of tradition synthesizing both the Indian and the English form.

In the post-independence era regional theatre specifically in Marathi, Bengali, Kannada and Hindi was active and dramatists like Dharamvir Bharti, Mohan Rakesh, Vijay Tendulkar, Badal Sircar, Mahasweta Devi, Bibhas Chakravarty, Girish Karnad, Chandrashekhar Kambar were experimenting with bold innovations and revived folk forms and rejuvenated the language theatre. They have used myth, history, folk legend and religio-centric tradition to comprehend and reflect upon contemporary situations. Indian dramatists writing in English and in regional languages have both amalgamated the orient with the occidental traditions of theatre.

Some of the issues dealt with in this volume are – interpreting play as a performative art, history of drama and theatre, use of myth, history and mask in contemporary Indian Drama in English and English translation, the political and the socio-economic condition of India and the issue of cultural adherence in diasporic writers. Ravi Chaturvedi, theatre director, takes up the issue related to the performance of a play and questions the liberty of the director to edit the text for performance. In "Interpreting the Play" Tanuja Mathur takes up how the interpretation of a play is different from that of a poem or fiction. Jasbir Jain explores the beginnings of the writing of Indian Drama in English looking for form in the ancient folk theatre and Sanskrit drama in "The Curious Journey of Indian Drama in English". Her second essay "The Narrative of a Play: Cyrus Mistry's *Doongaji House*" stresses the need to evoke the stage while reading a dramatic text. Nilufer Bharucha traces the history of the Parsi Zoroastrians, in "Retreating into Tribal Mansions: Race and Religion in Plays Written by Parsi Zoroastrians in India." The plays by two Indo-Canadian dramatists and their focus on South-Asians minorities in Canada are taken up by Supriya Agarwal in "Immigrant Spaces: Uma Parmeshwaran and Sadhu Binning".

Sridhar Rajeswaran in "Tying Beginnings to Ends" works through the structure and meaning of Karnad's plays. Two other papers focus on myth as for instance. Ranbir Sinh's "The Bold and the Meek" wherein he compares Karnad's *Naga-Mandal* with Aspazija's The *Serpent's Bride*, a Latvian play. Bandana Chakrabarty discusses the use of history and myth to comment upon the contemporary social problems of the downtrodden in "Reconstructing the Past and Critiquing the Present: Mahasweta Devi's Plays" while Sudha Shastri and Amith Kumar P.V. in "Locating Bakhtinian Carnival in Girish Karnad's *Hayavadana* and *Naga-Mandala*" have situated the Bakhtinian carnival in Karnad's use of myth and folk theatre. Madhuri Chatterjee goes on to delineate the condition of women through the myth of Mira in "Gurcharan Das' *Mira*: Transformation to Transcendence."

Venkat Ramani, Nidhi Singh and Charu Mathur take up Mahesh Dattani's plays. Nidhi explores the problem of homosexuality in "The Not-so-gay 'Gay' Plays of Mahesh Dattani", Charu discusses the technique of open-endedness in "Dramatic Structure in Dattani's *Tara* and *Final Solutions*" and Venkat Ramani deconstructs Dattani's play in a postmodernist sense in "Meaning in Abyss: *Seven Steps Around the Fire*." The leitmotif of the essays by Neelam Raisinghani, Sonu Shiva and Nishi Upaddhayaya is violence against women. In "The Potential and the Real: Dina Mehta's *Brides are not for Burning*" Neelam illustrates the problem of bride burning for dowry and Sonu takes up the problem of gang rape and the role of society in her essay "Countering Darkness: Manjula Padamanabhan's *Lights Out*", while Nishi takes up the issue of women as a commodity in "Vulnerable Victims: Vijay Tendulkar's *Kamala*". Sudha Rai also discusses Tendulkar's women characters who negotiate gender crossings and emerge as change-agents in Indian society in *"Gender Crossings:* Vijay Tendulkar's Deconstructive Axis in *Sakharam Binder, Kamala* and *Kanyadaan*". In "Viewing Women: An Exploration of Ezekiel's Plays" Shaila Mahan analyses Ezekiel's women protagonists through the prism of male gaze and brings out the discordant man-woman relationship. Pranav Joshipura offers a postcolonial reading of history in "Gurcharan Das's, *Larins Sahib*". In "The Protean Self: Karnad's *Tughlaq*", Urmil Talwar uses the postmodernist notion of the divided self to comprehend the multiphrenic personality of Tughlaq. Preeti Bhatt moves on to Badal Sircar and brings out the absurdist dilemmas through the confrontation between reason and the silence of the cosmos in "Absurdist Dilemmas: Sircar's *Evam Indrajit*". Apart from these twenty-two essays we have a collection of fifteen poems jointly translated by Anju Dhadda Misra and Arti Sah in "The Fugue of Experience" and an interview with Girish Karnad by Chaman Ahuja, both of which enable the reader to move out of the play text and to share the processes of creativity as they occupy the creative artist's mind.

The papers have been organised in a manner so as to reveal the development of theatre in an historical perspective. Beginning with performance and interpretation of the dramatic text, we proceed to the history of development of Contemporary Indian Drama in English and the history of the plays written by Indian Parsi writers. Next we have essays which deal with more than one writer or more than one text. Then comes an interlude (in this two act book) consisting of translated poems and an interview and then we work according to the date of publication of the play under discussion.

The subject of contemporary Indian drama is far too vast and this volume makes no claims to being an exhaustive study, but it has opened up certain areas and raised several issues which reflect contemporary concerns and historical continuities and which await further investigation.

1

Play as Performance

A Circle of Theatrical Communication

Ravi Chaturvedi

I

When animals and humans play, they exaggerate and show off in order to impress playmates as well as non-players who are watching.... In most kinds of play, in order to play successfully, all the players must agree to play. Players send meta-communicative messages that say, "We are playing." In some ways, play is very much like ritual and theatre. Play is often an orderly sequence of actions performed in specified places for known durations of time. Much playing is narrational, with winners and losers, conflict, and the arousal and display of emotion. But there is also playing that is less formal – bursts of microplay that can loosen the tensions in a room or relieve the boredom of routinized work. Some play is "dark", making fun of people, deceiving them or leading them on. One group of play theorists sees playing as the foundation of human culture, art and religion specially. Others regard play as an ambivalent activity both supporting and subverting social structures and arrangements. However one looks at it, play and playing are fundamentally performative. (109)

Including the above conclusion drawn by Richard Schechner in his book *Performance Studies*, there are several other definitions and explanations of the term 'Play' and 'Performance'. Rather the act of performance in theatre begins with the act of 'playing' if we look at the origin of theatrical performance. However, the content of this essay does not intend to discuss the etymology of the word play, or the ethological approaches to play, or the philosophies of the play, it is more inclined to discuss the functions of the play and its performivity that appears in a performance as an end result.

Picking up the thread from Mr. Schechner's statement that, "Players send meta-communicative messages" that say, "we are playing", the statement sounds appropriate if it is limited only within the group of players. But if it is meant for a performance, the act which leads to the division of space between the group of players and the group of several other persons, that are watching the players playing, then the statement of Mr. Schechner should have read like "Players send meta-communicative messages to the group of people that is waiting to watch them playing." Considering the fact that Mr. Schechner in fact meant the same, as I mentioned, the communication or the 'communicavity' is an essential aspect of a play if it has to be 'a performance for an audience'. As we know that every communication has a meaning, an object and a definite purpose to be served, then the performance also has a definite purpose to serve.

For example, in the tenth Chapter of the Bhagavada Gita, Lord Krishna tells Arjuna, "Listen, as I recount for you in essence the divine powers of myself. Endless is my extent.... I am indestructible time, the creator facing everywhere at once.... I am death the destroyer of all, the source of what will be, the feminine powers; fame, fortune, speech, memory, intelligence, resolve, patience.... I am the great ritual chant, the meter of a sacred song... the dice game of gamblers..." I have chosen this example which reminds of a dreaded crime, that changed the face of the world in recent past. If we carefully study this passage, Lord Krishna right in the beginning says "Listen as I recount for you..." The sentence is divided into four parts; one – the act of drawing attention or listening; two – the player 'I'; three – the audience 'you'; and the fourth – the message 'recount'. In the science of communication, this performance involves the sender 'I', the receiver 'you', the 'message' and the process, or the medium of communicating the message, that is 'listening'. On this basis we can say that it is a play as performance of communication. In this case this play is not merely limited to the players only but it interacts with the audience. Here, one must not forget the scenario, that the performance is taking place in the midst of a huge army standing on both the sides, and in between the Great Performer is asking the audience in despair to focus their attention towards the performance. This is important, as the environment is not favourable for any kind of performance except the war, while the content of the play is of philosophical nature, and the purpose is to reactivate the disgusted warrior.

In another situation, J. Robert Oppenheimer, the head of the scientific team for making the atom bomb, quotes the same lines of *Gita* to convince himself, in July 1945, standing at dawn on the New Mexico desert, witnessing the first explosion of that awesome, terrifying, yet visually spectacular weapon, his own creation. This is a different story that a month later this 'visually spectacular' weapon was dropped over Hiroshima and Nagasaki, and the dejected creator rejected his own creation.

Coming back to the point, let us have a brief scientific look at the play transforming into a performance. Bharatmuni has discussed this transformation in detail. Interestingly, or may be amazing for some of the theorists, he does not use the word 'performance' in his entire book of 36 chapters. Rather, he very frequently and definitely uses the word 'prayog' or 'the experiment' for the act of playing. Almost every playwright of Sanskrit theatre in the beginning of his text followed the convention of using the word 'prayog' where the 'nati' asks 'sutradhaar' about the play to be performed. The word itself gives an indication of scientific understanding of enacting a play that he terms as 'kavya', the dramatic material. In this respect his concepts are totally different from the Aristotelian concept of acting, which he calls 'abhinaya'. According to Bharat the act of 'abhinaya' is an act of 'carrying in forward direction'. (*Natyashastra* Ch: 8, 6-7) In another sense this is a conveyance, which carries the dramatic material in progression instead of an act of mere 'imitation'. The dramatic material or the 'kavya' should grow further through 'abhinaya', and should reach to the audience in a developed form. With this explanation he underlines the importance of actor as 'abhineta'. The word is the composition of 'abhi', which mean 'in forward direction'; 'ne' means 'to carry'; and 'neta' means 'who carries' Bharat has laid down several rules, regulations and principles for driving this carriage and to handle the conveyance in a very scientific and logical way, however, he also underlines the importance of feed back, reaching back to the poet and the players.

This may sound like a ritual, but then every scientific act starts with ritual, which is essential for the act to follow. For example, a doctor has to perform a lot of things in a ritualistic manner before he actually starts an operation like arranging equipment, washing the patient, changing the dress, etc. They are essential for every operation, no matter how major or minor, it is not only for the successful operation but to create an environment also, which is the demand of the performance. The performers may change with each performance, the setting of the operation theatre may also differ according to the requirement of the operation but the rituals or the initial acts are the same.

Bharat has applied this principle in theatrical performance. According to him, the 'kavya', or the dramatic material needs to be 'encoded' through the 'prayog' for its success, which he calls 'siddhi'. This process of encoding the poetry is in fact the process of discovering the meaning, the philosophical layers, the interpretative depths, the emotional undercurrents of the poem in performance through experimentation. At the climax of the performance, the Rasa, or the taste is communicated in its saturated form to the audience; the poem is called 'de-coded' as the 'arth' in its real sense is communicated. The varied and balanced use of various parts of this experiment like assemblage, speech, body, spirit create an environment for the performance.

This brief analysis points out the play as performance from classical point of view. Nonetheless, if a play is considered in an etymological sense then there is no problem. In this situation the performance of the play is very simple, improvisational, spontaneous, with very relaxed rules. The space is normally fixed; the time duration is also fixed. If the players are playing football, cricket or volleyball, the duration may vary as it happens in a folk play which may continue the whole night, or any dance performance for inclusion in the record books. But the real problem arises when the play is in written form, set is fixed, rules are decided, interpretation is given in a ready text. An idea of the performance is also reflected through the stage instructions given in brackets. This is a challenge for a creative team of the performers, as well as a reason for the conflict on the other hand. All of us have witnessed such conflicts between the playwright and the performing team here and there. In such situations, the play text becomes a separate entity and the performance is seen as an effort to break that entity. It is a sort of rivalry forgetting the fact that a play takes birth twice in its life; first, when it is performed on the paper; and second, when it is staged. In its first birth, play can be read and the performance is imaginary but at the second stage the play is a moving imagery in respect of temporal sense and the performance can be visualized happening in front of your eyes in a theatrical form. The conflict arises during this transformation, when the narrative of a written text is changed or edited to the suitability of the performing team. The problem also arises in a different situation when the narration remains un-changed but the connotation is changed. To avoid this situation, the playwright started to write the detailed stage instructions within the brackets. The performing team under the leadership of its director started crossing over such instructions and writing his own, questioning the essential discipline of the duality of the birth of a play. Even the spectators are also found divided on this issue, some in favour of the sanctity of the written word and some with the visual interpretation and enjoyment of the performance.

Here are a couple of examples of such conflicting situations that happened during the stage performances of the written texts of the plays. In the last scene of Jaishankar Prasad's play *Dhruvswamini*, Ramgupt, the husband of Dhruvswamini is killed by a soldier in his court during the fight with his younger brother Chandragupt. The issue is Dhruvswamini herself, who is married to the King Ramgupt, but likes Chandragupt, the younger brother of the King. The King is impotent and coward, while Chandragupt is courageous, brave and handsome also. Dhruvswamini belongs to the non-Indian society, but her choice is denied in the name of traditions. The play ends on a happy note of union of Chandragupt and Dhruvswamini. The director was not convinced with the end as in his opinion, a lady who can dare to express her choice fearlessly in an ancient feudal society can also kill her impotent husband, with whom she has been married against her will. She cannot remain silent when the life of the person she likes is in danger. At this stage the director made a little change - when Chandragupt is fighting with the royal guards, Ramgupt, the King takes a sword and attacks Chandragupt. Anticipating the danger, Dhruvswamini herself takes out the sword of a soldier and kills Ramgupt before he is about to kill Chandragupt. The act of killing is committed by the bodyguard of Chandragupt in the original version. The play wraps to its end within few minutes after this scene. With this end of the play a bewildered crowd rushed on the stage and in the wings with loud protest as how such kind of change in a written text could be thought of. This is against the Hindu traditions as well as an unauthorized trespass in the territory of such a reputed writer, a misinterpretation of classics and so on, but there were few spectators also, who were in favour of such a change as this was a reflection of the self-respect of a woman and a realization of her identity and the inner power.

The second example is of the famous play *'Silence, The Court is in Session'* written by Vijay Tendulkar (a very possessive writer with his scripts). In the last scene of the play, Miss Benare is sitting inside the witness box turned into a cage, completely broken keeping her head down at the rim. Samant goes near her with a toy parrot in his hand, stops for a moment and calls Miss Benare but she does not answer, Samant puts the toy parrot over the rim of the cage and leaves Miss Benare alone and exits. The stage is almost dark, only one tight spot of light falls on Benare. In the background, the tune of a folk song is echoing. After some time Benare gets up and goes inside the room where all the actors have gone a little before. The director made a little change here – Miss Benare is sitting inside the cage, completely broken keeping her head down at the rim of the cage. Samant goes near her with a toy parrot in his hand, stops for a moment and calls Miss Benare, she looks at him for few moments, does not accept the toy parrot. Samant leaves the parrot on the rim of the cage, Miss Benare looks at it, then picks up her basket and leaves for inside with a determination in her cool eyes. The play ends here. Many of the spectators did not know the text of the play but some of them knew about it. In their opinion, this kind of end was also a possibility as why such a lively person like Miss Benare should surrender before the hypocrisy and double standards of the patriarchal society. She should fight for her unborn child, alone. Her unwed motherhood is a mirror of the social cruelty committed against a woman who wanted to lead her life in her own way.

In most of the cases directors and members of the performing team always safeguard the sanctity of the written word but they also expect a little space for communication of their own ideas and creativity through the performance. The situation was never so complex during ancient Greek and

Sanskrit, or in the Elizabethan period, as the territories of the play and the performance were not divided between the writer and the director since there was no director. But this is a modern period, full of complexities where every one wants his own protected territory and draws the boundary line. I close my paper with the words of Max Stafford Clark, the artistic director of London based experimental theatre group 'Out Of Joint' theatrical performance is not a game of tennis but a game of cricket, where every player has an important role to play but the success of each one depends on the success of the team.

II
Experimenting *Andha Yug*

Andha Yug, the poetic play by Dharamvir Bharti is an important play in the repertory of Indian theatre attempted by the major Indian directors. The play expresses the ethics of war and the eventual transmission of revenge and extremism into the human psyche. The contemporary atmosphere of war and antagonism in different manifestations, and the violence breeding in the psyche of human race has prompted almost every production of this play for more than the last forty five years. The central character of the play Ashwathama represents many, who are victimized to wander, armed with hostility and disgust. He is living beyond the epic of Mahabharata into an everlasting, ever living expression.

Briefly speaking, the play underlines the contemporary history of war, hatred and revenge, exposing the victorious and also the 'heroes', who silently spread the message and seed of violence. The blindness is a result of hatred of the victimised and the attacked, also of the manipulators who refuse to see into the future. The 'Brahmastra' of Ahwathama is the result of all such things[1]. Bharti calls it '*Andha Yug*' (The Blind Age) in which all human values succumbed and were submerged by a flood of all-pervading darkness born of hatred, greed, lust for power, false vanity and hypocrisy. Everyone, including Krishna himself, is afflicted with a kind of physical, mental or moral blindness which makes the victory not only more painful and frustrating than the defeat, but also more sinister and corroding, leading on to further disintegration, in fact to total collapse of civilization and culture.

Apart from the theme of the play, the other important aspects of the play, which inspire a director are the characters of the play as E. Alkazi says, "... these are not comprehensively and as easy to identify with the man-in-the-street. They are archetypes, symbolic representation of different aspects of the human psyche. The director needs therefore to develop an iconography of attitude and gesture" (*Enact*). Bharti has very intelligently carved out the linguistic idiom for each of the characters in such a way that they are easily distinguished from each other, yet they are part of the common thread. In fact, in the play, one can hardly find the stage instructions about the characters and the actors' movement except a few hints to underline the mood of the situation and the situation itself. However, the 'iconography and gestures' of each character is inherent in the language of the play itself, which decides the form of the play as Alkazi emphasized in his interview: "That is the sole function of the director: to release the form which already exists" (*Enact*).

It is true that the language constitutes a very important factor of the play, attracting a director to experiment freely, but, on the other hand, the strength of the visual pull cannot be undermined in any way. Although Satyadev Dubey does not agree with the idea of giving extra weight to the spectacular aspects of the play. In his opinion, the form should be allowed to emerge on itself rather 'be imposed' from outside, as he says:

> *Andha Yug* is not spectacle. It is a play, which should be done in close-ups, with the words modulated to the maximum effect, without any loss of vitality. The powerful, varied verse of the play suggests the physical movement of the scene and a director would do well to allow the form of the play to emerge rather than impose a ready-made form. *Andha Yug* may have borrowed

> a great many theatrical devices from the West but ... it requires an indigenous mind to project it. This is possible only if one can get intoxicated with the language of the play. Then one will find scenes, which can stand up to the best scenes of the world theatre. The case of Gandhari in *Andha Yug* is perhaps the most brilliant amongst them. (*Enact*)

This 'chauvinistic' approach may provide extra 'phillip'[2] to Mr. Dubey in theatre, but the visual pull of each act and scene of the play itself is so powerful and sufficient enough that the parallel language of spectacle is created in series accommodating the spoken language in its vast canvas.[3] For example, the visual environment around Ashwathama transforms him into a powerful bomb, ready to explode at any moment of time assessing all warmongers of the world and all those who watch and enjoy war from their drawing room:

> Listen all you heavenly hosts
> sitting each one
> and witnessing this battle.
> You will bear witness
> How Arjuna rendered me helpless
> Take this!
> This is Brahma's Weapon! (*Andha Yug* IV)

Another aspect of the play, which provides the ground for experiment, is its flexible craftwork. Almost every director has applied his own skill in mounting the production, making it different from the others. Alkazi placed the production in the background of the historical ruins of Tal Katora in Delhi in 1967. This was perhaps the first powerful exposure of the play, although, the play was produced by the Theatre Unit, Bombay (Mumbai) before Alkazi's production, but did not leave that impact, as seen in its later production of the National School of Drama at the open air environment of Tal Katora. Another important production of *Andha Yug* was directed by M. K. Raina, staged in Berlin and Moscow. Raina used some elements of Kabuki in his efforts to make it different, however, the play was not received open-heartedly in comparison to its earlier production in the National School of Drama. In fact, this was an experiment of mixing Indian-ness with Japanese flavour at the level of text and form, perhaps to make it comprehensive to the international audience, but could not draw the expected result.

Another production of *Andha Yug* at Bratislava (Slovak Republic) during Istropolitana Festival 2004 provided a unique experience to the non-English speaking audience of Europe in many senses by exploring its visual pull and the spectacular elements. Although, every director has taken liberty to edit the play suitable to his requirement, but in this production, the entire 'verbal chorus' was replaced by the dance movements mixed with modern and classical dance elements. English translation of the chorus was projected on the screen with the pictures of various wars fought in the different parts of the world. The effort was made to introduce an easy communicability to an alien audience but the interdisciplinary treatment provided freshness, which was not only communicable across the linguistic barrier, but also added an interesting visual element also along with an unconventional background of cotton curtains arranged in linear and curvy manner, crossing over each other suggesting the mythological background as well as giving an impression of disorder, confusion and chaos prevailing in the environment. A peacock feather was placed upon a white base against the black cyclorama, which was highlighted throughout the action of the play indicating the influence of Krishna on the epic war, but darkens with a jerk suggesting the beast like death of the Divinity followed by cave-hunter-dance type movement in a very dim light. The actors with small torches in their hands wearing uniform white masks with unequal foot steps and the faint flute sound easily communicating the after effects of a war, where the identity-less people are searching the meaning of their lives in a dark space – the space where values, faith and all other human elements have totally vanished. The unusual closing of the play was designed in a very meaningful way, as Ashwathama appears in the middle of the cave-hunter dance and speaks about his experiences of witnessing the death of Krishna. As soon as he starts speaking, the dancers run away from the stage with fear leaving Ashwathama alone on the stage, narrating the similarities of the blood oozing from his own wounds and the blood oozing out of the "deer-face like" foot of Krishna, as if both the "enemies" were facing the same experience of pain. With the death of Krishna, the pain of Ashwathama also disappears giving him relief. He puts a big optimistic question mark at the end of his dialogue, where other actors also join him – 'Is it belief?

> I was the only witness
> to his death,
> hidden in a cluster of palm-trees.
> The palm-fronds like sharp-edged rapiers
> cut into my pus-filled wounds,
> but I stood there holding my breath.
> (He stands transfixed and speaks piteously.)
> But, oh, what did I see?
> When the arrow struck his foot
> the same black, pus-filled, malodorous blood
> flowed out of the wounds
> as have flown out of my wounds.
> The same fester appeared on the wound.
> My enemy Krishna, listen!
> At the time of your death, did you wear
> on your foot this beastly hide
> and was your blood my blood?
> Oh, as when bad blood escapes
> the pain goes out of a fester,
> so I felt the passing of sorrow.
> This new feeling I have -
> is it belief?

Is it
belief? (Andha Yug V)

To sum up, as underlined in the earlier part of this essay, the theatrical communication lies somewhere between the balancing point of audio and visual elements of the play, which may not essentially appear in a written text of the play. The experiment to create this balance has multi-fold importance when the receptivity of the targeted receiver (audience) is in focus. Bharti himself draws the dramaturgical identity of the play from Sanskrit dramaturgy calling it 'drishyakavya' (visual poetry), but while writing this play, he was inspired by the performance traditions of Ram Lila, as he says:

> While I was writing it, I had in my mind the traditional Ram Lila performance. ... There are professional singers who sing couplets from Ramayana and then the actors come on the stage; between important scenes, there is again song narration. However, the original folk form could not be adhered to very strictly.[4]

Interestingly, on the other hand, N. C. Jain criticizing the text says, "Bharti is not quite certain about his theatrical design and his basic stage conception is one of Parsi – style roller curtains. He uses far too many devices, which clutter up and hammer the action. ... There is also an unevenness in his style which tends to become jerky because of frequent variation" (*Enact*). Nonetheless, the odds pointed out by Jain, certainly provided ground to make the production interesting at several occasions, for example, in the above mentioned production staged at Bratislava.

Notes

1. The word is indicative of atom bomb as well as of the circumstances and consequences of its use.

2. The word 'phillip' was used by Satya Dubey in his interview given to *Enact* 65.
3. Published in the brochure of Malayalam version of *Andha Yug* produced and staged by Lokdharmi Theatre Group of Kerala.
4. From the letter dated 3 May 1975 to Paul Jacob, the translator of the play.

References

Bharatmuni, *Natyashastra*, Trans. Shastri, B.L. Varanasi: Chaukhamba Sanskrit Sansthan, 1989.

Bharti, Dharamvir. *Andha Yug*, Trans. Paul Jacob, *The Blind Age*. In *Enact* 65, May 1972.

Paul, Rajendra Ed., *Enact* 65, New Delhi, 1972.

Schechner, Richard, *Performance Studies.* New York: Routledge, 2002.

2

Interpreting the Play

Tanuja Mathur

The present paper focuses on the issues significant in the reading, understanding and interpreting of a play. How should a reader of a dramatic text get started? The activity of reading a play can be very exciting if the 'signs' inherent are interpreted by its readers and recognised for what they are. We, as readers, should recognise the relationship between the 'script' and the 'performance'. Hence, the 'theatrical text' assumes significance. It is read by its readers from the stage just as the dramatic text is read by its readers from the page. It is difficult to separate the page (script) from the stage (performance). Both are read in their respective ways.

The first thing to realize when a reader sets out to read a dramatic text is that the words written are not designed to function in the same way as the words in a novel or a poem. The words are designed to become a performance in our minds, as readers. The words written convey a lot, which include the stage directions. They signify what is to happen on stage. It is at this point, that there are two sets of readings going on in the mind of the reader – for even in the absence of an actual stage, the dramatic text produces the sense of one.

The great 18th century German critic and theoretician, Lessing in his famous treatise *Laacoon*, defined the difference between poetry and the visual arts. He defined the visual arts as happening in space without extension in time, whereas the narrative poem moved in time alone without any spatial extension. Drama combines characteristics of both - the narrative poetry and of the visual arts. It has both a spatial and a time dimension. The dramatic space has a vital aspect as by its very existence, it generates a lot of meaning. It transforms the most ordinary and every day items of existence with carriers of significance. The dramatic action serves for a multiplicity of spaces. It can present venues which give it real dimensions or spaces infinitely larger than itself – spaces that may in reality be miles apart may in a play be supposed to be simultaneously present or may succeed each other within seconds.

Time is used both realistically and symbolically in a play. We, as conscious readers, should be able to understand the depiction of memory of a character. The play, in such circumstances, may violate the linear, sequential, forward motion of time. Events then would be depicted in a written play out of the chronological sequence. As interpreters of a play, it is very important to understand the use of dramatic space and time which are fundamental to the different theories, rules and aesthetics of drama. Martin Esslin in his book *The Field of Drama*, emphasizes, "Dramatic space and time are the axes along which the multifarious sign-systems of drama unfold themselves to its audiences" (42).

The Semiotic theory propounded by Umberto Eco helps us in understanding the Semiotics of Drama. We can sketch out a particular mode of analysis for reading and interpreting plays. The contemporary Semioticians distinguish three basic types of signs. The first and the simplest is the one that represents what it signifies by a direct image of that object, hence it is called an 'icon' – the Greek word for 'picture'. All dramatic performance is basically iconic, every moment of dramatic action is a direct visual sign of a functional reality. The second category comprises of signs which point to an object. They are 'index' or 'deictic signs', a Greek word for 'showing' or 'pointing'. We, as readers, can interpret if the word is accompanied by a 'gesture' which plays an important role in a play. The third category of 'signs' include those that have no immediately recognizable organic relationship to their 'signified'. This category of signs is called 'symbol'.

Signs, in the usual sense, are tools deliberately employed to establish communication, tools through which one person intends to convey a meaning or message to another. Any event or any object can, thus, become a sign to an individual who perceives it. The omnipresent signs that have no conscious originator, but are perceived as having meaning by those who 'read' them, are what Umberto Eco in his *Theory of Semiotics* calls 'natural' signs. In drama, this category of 'natural signs' which exist without anyone deliberately producing them or intending to convey a message, assume a special meaning. For example, dimming lights on the stage, or a shot of the setting sun are deliberately used to exhibit to the readers that night is about to fall. The mimetic representation of a darkening sky becomes an iconic sign of evening.

Thus, in drama, what are 'natural signs' without a conscious originator of their 'message' become deliberately produced 'icons'. Yet, these icons may assume symbolic connotations. For example, the darkening sky in a play may be used as a symbolic sign, interpreted for the ending of a love affair, or death. What in real world are 'non-intentional signs', in a play become deliberate 'iconic' representations of fear or embarrassment. In drama, as far as the human characters are concerned, there is no abstraction. For example, if a lady appears on the stage, she is shown as a completely concrete lady – as an 'icon' – the iconic sign for a fictional lady. The icon aims at suggesting a complete identity in looks, between the 'signifier' (the actress) and the 'signified' (the fictional character). These types of signs – icon, index and symbol, as well as the 'involuntary' (natural) iconic signs, without a deliberate originator, combine in drama in a multitude of 'sign-systems'. A knowledge of the 'grammar' and 'syntax' of different sign-systems helps us in the interpretation of a play, which on the printed page is a temporary stage between the writer's imagination and the reader's understanding of it.

The dialogue is a verbal communication which does a lot more than merely narrating a story. It creates images, movement and a stage world. An 'image' is a very important aspect in any work of art which contains a multiplicity of 'signs' what the Semioticians refer to as 'signifiers'. The images are significant because we remember them long after we have read a creative work. An image, according to Pound is that which presents an intellectual and emotional complex in any instant of time. An image, therefore, is not a pictorial reproduction but a unification of disparate ideas and emotions into a complex presented spatially in an instant of time.

Ezra Pound observed that the medium of drama is not words but persons moving about on a stage using words. Movement within a dramatic space is an important language. The distance between the characters, their movement towards or away from each other, their standing, sitting down and getting up are of a very expressive significance. Walking across, standing still, increasing or diminishing the distance between the two characters, the grouping of characters into significant patterns are instances of the signifying power of the movement in a dramatic space. The function of the dramatic set is an informational, iconic one. It pictures the environment against which the action of the play unfolds itself and provides much of the basic expositional information – by indicating its place and period, and the social and cultural position of the characters.

The literary 'sign' is powerfully over determined – that is to say it gathers sense through a variety of syntactic and semantic relations, manifest in the text itself. But it also takes on meaning from the historical and cultural contexts within which it is produced. This culture, itself, may in turn be interpreted as a global text, within which texts proper, within their different cognitive, communicative and expressive functions are generated (qtd *Alternative Shakespeares*, 123).

It is important to orient linguistic structures to non-verbal systems, such as those specific to the theatrical performance for which a play is written. The reader ought to deduce such codes or 'signs' through a play along with its verbal semiosis. The non-verbal codes such as light, colour, sound, objects, costume, gestures, movement, which are iconic as well as 'symbolic' signifiers have an extended connotation in a dramatic text. These function as 'objective correlatives', to use T.S. Eliot's term. It is through these 'sign systems' that the concrete page of a dramatic text becomes an abstract emotional stage in the mind of the reader.

The meaning of the verbal utterances by the characters in drama can never be merely analysed in isolation from the cultural context in which it occurs and the action it represents. The meaning of a dramatic utterance must also be understood in the light of the character from whom it emanates. The words spoken by a character are always the product of the individual character, his motivations, the situation in which he finds himself and the cultural context. Roman Ingarden points out:

> Drama represents its world by: (1) events that are indicated by visual and other means; (2) by elements which are indicated both visually and verbally; and (3) by events that are indicated only in words, for example, narration of events that have happened outside the spatial or temporal ambit of the action. (qtd Esslin 83)

The different sign systems therefore, become important in interpreting a play. These achieve universal connotations, crossing all language barriers. The individual signs and sign-systems constantly interact and reinforce each other or create new meanings. The full meaning of a play emerges from the total impact of these complex, multi-layered structures of interwoven and interdependent signifiers.

References

Bekerman, Bernard. *Dynamics of Drama: Theory and Method of Analysis*. New York: Drama Book Specialists, 1979.

Eco, Umberto. *Theory of Semiotics*. Oxford: Blackwell Publishers, 1995.

Esslin, Martin. *The Field of Drama*. London: Metheun, 1987.

Serpieri, Allessandra. "Reading the signs". Trans. Keir Elam in John Drakakis (Ed.) *Alternative Shekespeares*. London and New York: Routledge and Kegan Paul Ltd., 2000.

Styan, J.L. *The Elements of Drama*. London: Cambridge University Press, 1960.

Wallis, Mick. *Studying Plays*. New York: Oxford University Press, 2002.

3

The Curious Journey of the Indian Drama in English

Jasbir Jain

Contemporary drama in English presents a strange conjunction between at least three different categories: language, society and cultural tradition. It has today arrived at a point where the past and the present come into confrontation in a variety of ways. Where dramaturgy is concerned it has access to (and works under the influence of) three dramatic traditions: Sanskrit, folk and western. Another aspect is its choice of characters – from where do they come? Urban areas, metropolises, middle classes, immigrants, history and myth? Does this set of circumstances lead to an over-indulgence in abstractions as for instance myths? If the plays work at a realistic level then they may look for characters from regions or professions where English is the ordinary language of communication, a strategy, which even as it succeeds, confesses its own limitations.

It has had several interrupted moments of visibility and creativity, and has adapted itself to translated versions and ideas transmitted from one culture to another. The process of adaptations had begun as early as the nineteenth century for the benefit of the English-speaking imperial rulers, the foreign audiences abroad, specially in the universities there, and the college repertory productions at home. The play in English has also learnt to live at the level of the page, as purely a literary text. It is only now that it has found a breathing space in metropolitan centres. Thus in every way it is a circuitous and a curious journey which it has had to go and on the way acquire new roles and partners.

The dramatic form in India has always worked through different traditions – the epic and the folk, the court and the people – often dealing with similar themes (like the Ramlila) but different nuances. Chandra Rajan in her 'Introduction' to the plays of Kalidasa, is of the view that three avenues may be explored for tracing the origins and evolution of Indian drama – Vedas, epics and dance. The *Natyashastra* claiming a divine origin, 'styles itself as the fifth veda'. It also emphasises the need for pleasure (rasa) to be evoked by the creation of the proper mood (Rajan, 28-29). Spectacle is as much a part of the traditional Indian drama as of any other – for drama evolves and survives through performance, it needs an immediate connectivity between character and audience. There are references in the *Natyashastra* to the *natyamandapa*, which is a space for the theatrical performance. Rajan goes on to describe the *natyamandapa*, its various shapes, the minimality of props it advocated (33-35), but as the play itself paid attention to both language and dance it is apparent that performance was considered an integral aspect of the play to enable its full meaning to emerge.

And though as far as of plays and writers ancient times are matter of speculation, all available material points out that female roles were played by women. Despite this availability of women actors, classical Sanskrit drama does not come through as naturalistic. This may be due to the excessive reliance on the rhetoric of language and on the body language and gestures of dance. From that point of view the use of myths as play texts appears to be a natural fallout, enabling performances in public spaces like the public square or the courtyard of a temple, specially during festivals.

This tradition of transferring myth to the stage has survived from this classical heritage, as we find in the plays of the sixties, for myth enables a crossing over into the present, because the archetypal has the ability to move across language and culture. But of that later. It should suffice here to say that the languages in use were either Sanskrit or the languages of the various regions as we have in Kathakali, or in the various folk forms like jatra, tamasha, nautanki, nukkad-natak and other kinds of performances. None of these forms lends itself easily to English. Probably it was during the colonial period that drama in English surfaced primarily as a medium of reaching across or framing Indian culture for the benefit of the British. M.K. Naik's *A History of Indian English Literature,* dutifully lists several playwrights of the late nineteenth century, none of whom has survived in memory. The performance history of these plays also awaits research. The names are mostly from the south like A.S.P. Ayyar and Thyagaraja Paramasiva Kailasam. The Gandhian movement also generated its own crop of plays and in the pre-independence period the names of Bharati Sarabhai and J.M. Lobo-Prabhu stand out.[1]

Amongst the other writers at the turn of the century who wrote plays in English, one can count Sri Aurobindo and the translations of Tagore (some done by him as *Red Oleanders*, and other translations by other writers). The plays he himself translated have been almost always rewritten to facilitate cultural transference to an alien language. In the post-1947 period also the drama in English has had to continue the struggle. Poem plays or poetic plays have somehow managed to survive with or without performance. However, G.V. Desani's *Hali* was a poem play fortunate enough to merit a performance. Naik though doubtful about the mixed mythology of the play, records that it 'received extremely high praise from British critics, both for its thematic richness and its style' (Naik, 257).

A major writer of the post fifties period is Asif Currimbhoy, a Parsi business executive, whose passion for playwriting led him to a large number of plays on a wide range of subjects. His plays give us an idea of the difficulties which the Indian writer has to negotiate when writing in English. He chooses themes which can lend themselves to dramatic conflicts and are ordinarily focused on English-speaking characters. True, folk elements do not find a place in his work and the strength of his plays lies mainly in their documentary value. Several of his plays have been performed, amongst them are *The Dumb Dancer, The Doldrummers, The Hungry Ones* and *Goa*'. Two other plays dealing with armed conflicts are *Refugee* and *Sonar Bangla*. Despite a rich and varied output Currimbhoy died a disappointed writer. In 1993 when I met him in London, he was possessed by a sense of futility that his life's work had not been fully appreciated. The audience was just not there and he had failed to create one.

The above names do not make an exhaustive list. There have been several other writers, but in the main Indian drama in English has been slow to find a place in university courses till very recently. Works in translation by Tagore, Mohan Rakesh and Girish Karnad, may have found their way, but not the ones written originally in English. It is only now that Mahesh Dattani's work is being studied by the academia. This in itself is an indication of the slowness of the progress which drama has made, lacking a stage, an audience and also a critical public.

While the drama in English found it difficult to sustain itself, drama in other Indian languages was busy experimenting, growing and absorbing folk forms. Dharamvir Bharati, Badal Sircar, Mohan Rakesh, Girish Karnad, Vijay Tendulkar, Shankar Shesh and a host of other writers emerged on the dramatic scene in the post-1947 phase. The language theatrical scene in any case, had never been fully submerged.[2] It had continued in some form or the other even though the pace of development may have differed in different parts of the country. Women actresses entered the stage much earlier in

Bengal than in Maharashtra or Karnataka. Rimli Bhattacharya in her 'Introduction' to *Binodini Dasi: My Story and My Life as an Actress*, gives a fairly detailed account of the Calcutta theatre. But as Karnad's "In An Search of a Theatre" indicates, women performers were absent in the plays he watched as a young boy. Most amateur performance, including those of the 'mohalla Ramlilas' have an all male cast.

Of the writers emerging on the dramatic scene Dharamvir Bharati's *Andha Yug* (1953) laid down a pattern to be followed by several others. He took epic material, linked it to the contemporary political scene, and thus bridged the gap between the past and the present interlacing the play with a strong moral debate: the wrongs and rights of violence, the importance of the human will and the responsibility of the decision makers. Time and space are compressed as far as clock and calendar time are concerned but expanded through the argument and counter argument. It was first translated into English by Paul Jacob as *The Blind Age* (*Enact* No. 65, May 1972) and a new translation by Alok Bhalla has just appeared (in 2005). *Andha Yug* has played both in commercial and repertory theatre to appreciative audiences.[3]

The contribution of these new post-independence playwrights has been manifold. It placed a demand on the audience to be weaned away from classics, on the directors to explore the possibilities of realistic representation, on the critics to think in terms of relevance and ideology. Their success can be measured in terms of the controversies they raised. Tendulkar's play *Ghasiram Kotwal* was banned even before it was performed. The new language of the stage and its naturalistic trend, specially in Tendulkar's plays, was a source of embarrassment to the middle classes, but it was true to the class of people he chose to portray. And Mohan Rakesh, specially in *Aadhe Adhure*, chose to focus on an urban middle class couple with their fragmented desires as modern life with its bundle of temptations knocked at their door. The fragmentation was portrayed through the multiple love-relationships, all of which ended in a similar sense of incompleteness.

Tendulkar has, over the years, moved from one social concern to another and has experimented with shock tactics, chorus and folk forms like 'tamasha' to arouse public conscience. He writes in Marathi but his plays have been translated into other languages including English. But as he does not write originally in English, or aim at an English speaking audience, he is not limited in the choice of his subject matter, his characters or his idiom. Tendulkar has a strong sense of the stage and the dramatic. In fact, the prefaces, lectures and comments by these writers go a long way in defining the new Indian drama. Several of these essays are retrospective accounts of their experiences, struggles and conflicts, or are explanatory prefaces to English translations but they provide the reader with an understanding of the processes at work that were to shape the rationale on which contemporary drama sought to resurrect itself.

In 1997 Tendulkar delivered the Sri Ram Memorial Lecture "The Play is the Thing" (in two parts) where he emphasized the role of the writer's ability to inhabit different kinds of characters with equal facility, to think like them, get inside their mind, their language, even their body language. The actor has to work at an additional level but the writer's role precedes that of the actor. This role playing is important because character governs dialogue and the nature of the dialogue in a dramatic text is different, it has to function differently than the way it does in fiction. Dialogue in a non-performative text, even as it reveals character, is primarily a means of communication, not so in a performance play; specially not so in realistic drama where it has to play a much more active role and represent the character's location in society, the psychological mood, the emotional conflicts in addition to the communicative function.[4] Tendulkar is of the view that the form in itself makes no difference, it is the fluidity of language which becomes important when a writer chooses a different genre or form, 'the texture, the rhythm, the choice of words, the stance,' everything changes as the writer moves from one role to another. The writer acts as he writes (*Collected Plays* ix-x). The nature of theatrical writing is a reproduction, a total re-enactment, an imagined act staged even as the writer scripts it.

Creating a character is in itself a complicated process, it has to work through multiple contexts, get into the character's socio-psychological constructs and then work through language(xx-xxi). Despite language being its distinguishing feature, a play is not a book to be read alone by oneself (xxiv), the dynamics of performance are still needed for it to come alive. For this, as Tendulkar goes on to explain in his second Sri Ram Memorial Lecture, structure is the primary concern. It is structure which provides the framework, the placing, the action/narrative which leads to a continuity, tension and involvement of the audience, which with its move towards the next action pulls the audience towards it. But Tendulkar insists a 'performing structure is not static' (xxxii). What is one to understand by this, specially as earlier on he has used the word 'framework'?. My own interpretation discounts any fixity of event and consequences; it takes into account the unpredictability of human response and the possibility of some rupture. Thus the play, through the interaction between character and event, is constantly being propelled into a phase which the character is likewise controlling. The structure has to be fluid enough to allow this tension to surface. There is apparently no place for the cause and effect theory in Tendulkar's world, as there is none for supernatural forces or abstract mythical presences. His own journey as a journalist and the constant switching of 'writerly' roles, plunged him into a stark, real world even as the imaginative processes work overtime.[5]

Tendulkar has worked with enclosed spaces, with 'rehearsals' as the subject of a play and their sudden detonations which break the boundaries, and overflow into personal conflicts of the characters as in *Silence, the Court is in Session;* he has also worked with domestic spaces as in *Sakharam Binder* where moral norms become agents of disruption and the enclosed space no longer seems to remain closed. *Vultures* and *Kamala* handle space in yet an entirely way, different, though even in *Kamala*, it is the sitting room space which is extended into other directions and moves out into marketing places and media politics.

Girish Karnad's theatrical experiments however progress in an entirely different manner and work outside the realistic tradition. He does not necessarily focus on immediate social reality though ideology and history resurface both in *Tughlaq* and *Tipu Sultan* to connect with the present. They also do so in *Tale-Danda.* But by and large his preoccupation is with folk tales, myths and their retellings, character is not of that heightened concern with him as it is with Tendulkar. He works through abstractions and philosophical ideas, through questioning of tradition and traditional moral constructs and generates the conflictual element from this questioning. Is the imposition of individual will on the other moral as the imposition of the father on the son in *Yayati*? Does the mind govern the body or vice versa? Is perfection desirable? What is the nature of sexuality? of friendship (*Hayavadana*)? How do narratives come into existence, how do they survive and spread, and how does the human mind dodge social constructions, are some of the questions raised in *Naga-Mandala. Tale-Danda* and *Sacrifice* both connect the past with the present. He writes in Kannada but himself translates his work into English. Several of his plays have been first performed abroad. *Tipu Sultan* and *Sacrifice,* plays specifically commissioned by the BBC and the Haymarket Theatre Leicester, respectively premiered abroad. *Naga-Mandala* was written during his stay in Chicago and performed in the Guthrie Theatre of Minneaplities. Awareness of the specific kind of audience the play is meant for may not govern the choice of theme and subject, but does in several subtle ways influence the handling of the theme. Myths, even when culture specific, are able to transcend cultures. They problematise problems of philosophical dimensions and do not necessitate a specificity of language (governed by the idiom of the social role) or of locale as one finds in *Sakharam Binder* or *Kanyadaan*. Poetry also allows a further abstraction of ideas. Even in *Tipu Sultan* it is the dreams which contain both the narrative and the resistance (falling in line with the subaltern studies approach). Karnad in his preface to the play gives us the history of his long pre-occupation with the theme.

Tipu Sultan was written for a radio performance and later rewritten for a stage performance. Similarly Bharati's *Andha Yug* was written first as a radio play. The fact that these radio plays have had to be rewritten for the stage bring out the distinguishing element between the two. It is the 'spectacle' which makes the performative play what it is: not the spoken word alone. Tendulkar stressed the need for a visual image in the stage play (x). But when abstractions are written about the visual image rather than being a representation may become a parallel current. Very often, in Karnad's plays, the viewer works at two separate levels, one through a focus on the fluidity of movement and language and the second on the philosophical concept inhabits the play. This does not happen with Tendulkar's work because of its being firmly grounded in social reality. The image becomes a representation of the action.

Another writer the English and Hindi translations of whose plays impacted the growth of contemporary Indian drama is Badal Sircar whose work is largely in Bengali. Older than both Karnad and Tendulkar his major contribution has been in the collaborative assimilation of folk forms, the theatre of the absurd, and the 'happenings' of the sixties, into a common dramatic mode. He has succeeded in transmitting some of the Pirandellian uncertainties of human existence and value structures to the Indian scene. His plays explore the uncertainties and the incompleteness of the processes of life as well as of history. But Sircar, like Tendulkar, did not choose to write in English, and like him he already had a rich theatre in Calcutta whose theatrical language he could deviate from.

These writers of the fifties and sixties were instrumental in making the educated urban audiences aware of the theatrical form over and above the folk forms. They addressed the issues of the proscenium theatre, rather than the openness of the folk. At the same time they created space for folk dramatic forms within the stage-play. Their work spurred academic interest, their experimentation was vibrant and these plays were staged, talked and written about. Through the translations they prepared the ground for the reception of plays in English.[6]

The theatrical scene in Hindi was neither so localised nor so vibrant as in Bengali, Marathi and Kannada but Mohan Rakesh whose first major play *Aasadh Ka Ek Din* appeared in 1958 to be followed by another full-length play *Lahron Ke Rajhans* in 1963 also made waves. Rakesh humanises the legendary characters, an approach which the early audiences found difficult to accept as it went against the grain of hero worship. But it was a major step forward in the process of realistic presentations and meaningful debates about values. These two plays used semi-historical, semi-legendary situations but they also raised questions which went on to resurface in *Aadhe Adhure,* staged in 1969, and his first play to be located in contemporary life. The fragmented modern couple of the play is a continuation of the two sets of relationships portrayed in the earlier plays – Kalidas and Mallika in *Aasadh Ka Ek Din* and Nand and Sundri in *Lahron Ke Rajhans.* In all these plays his attempt was to free the past from myth and history and locate it in a real world of flesh and blood, of desire and unfulfilment and of pain and suffering and to bring out the multiplicity and elusiveness of truth and reality. Both character and structure are significant, except that conventional patterns are not adhered to. There is instead a character in the making, fluid and unformulated, while structure works through repetitions, contrasts and counterpoints.

Of his plays it is *Aadhe Adhure* which is relevant to our concern for it moves away from the kind of work Sircar, Tendulkar and Karnad were doing at that time.[7] The play carries an inbuilt sense of incompleteness and fluidity to support its title and theme and reinforces them through dramatic strategies. It dramatizes the incompleteness of man at multiple levels, through the gap between the dream world and the actual world, between the desired and the actual. Characters do not have names or identifiable tags to begin with. They live in their roles and are known by their clothes, gender or age – the 'man in the black suit', 'woman', 'girl' and other similar descriptions like Man One, Man Two, Man Three and Man Four. The role of the central male figure, the 'man in the black suit' is not only that of a character but also of the narrator. He is the *sutra-dhara* and begins straightaway by dialoguing with the audience, an opening speech which stresses his undefined role, the uncertain nature of the play and the questionable nature of reality. Later aggressor and victim switch roles, not once but several times and the sympathies of the audience fluctuate between the husband and the wife. As the play progresses, they acquire names, Mahendranath and Savitri. Mahendranath is unemployed, submissive, docile and wants to be helpful, Savitri is an overburdened housewife, additionally burdened by the name she carries, a name which has stood for marital fidelity and devotion. She is also the sole bread earner of the family. Mahendranath is weak and perhaps even lacks self-respect, hence the aggressive wife-beating and the latent homosexuality. Savitri betrays the label her name has imposed upon her and carries on several extramarital relationships – almost all of them fleeting and unsuccessful.

This 'ideal' family is completed by the progeny of this couple, a son and two daughters. Of these, the son is unemployed and an escapist, the older daughter elopes and lands herself in an unhappy marriage while the younger daughter has long outstripped the innocence becoming her years and has turned aggressive. As if this is not enough, other complications follow. The son-in-law is perhaps the mother's ex-lover. Other characters like Jagmohan and Juneja walk in and provide an occasion for further insight into the husband-wife relationship, Juneja's friendship with Mahendranath shuts out Savitri. He serves as Mahendranath's escape route and spokesman, his presence serves the function of a catalyst. Follows a confrontation between Juneja and Savitri which reveals their hidden fears, dreams and insecurities. It also reveals the ambiguous and often unconscious motives an individual has, and it reveals the conflicting emotions of love and jealousy, of friendship and hostility. It is not only the ideal relationship which is deconstructed but the idea of family, marital fidelity, sibling relationships, success, the nature of friendship and the nature of reality – all these are analysed, deconstructed and exposed and along with them the idea of the integrated character, the controlled structure, the continuity of tradition and the permanence of change. The play ends with the family together under the same roof but with all their equations upset and escape routes closed. There is an uncanny similarity in the men in Savitri's life hence the playwright's docketing them as Man One, Man Two, Man Three and Man Four. *Aadhe Adhure* has an importance for Indian theatre history comparable to Albee's *Zoo Story* for it deconstructs the very notion of the 'ideal' as well as the possibility of the 'real'. While locating itself in the present, it is able to move outside cultural constructs into psychological terrains. The visual image is also one of fragments flying all over the place.

In 1985, I had the opportunity to see two productions of *Aadhe Adhure* directed by the same person in close succession, November 20th and November 22nd. The director was S. Vasudev and the productions staged by Abhivyakti Natya Dal at Ravindra Manch. The very ideal of these two productions in close succession was to project the ambivalence of the play in its meaning and intent. Vasudev, himself played the role of all the five men and the change of roles was symbolised by donning a different jacket or cardigan. The play's incompleteness, which was part of the author's intent, still aroused a certain resentment amongst section of the audience (this came out in a post performance discussion). Plays, they were of the view, were meant to offer solutions or deliver morals. *Aadhe Adhure* did none of the two. In dramaturgical terms this was an effective method of bringing the structure and theme into consonance.

Mohan Rakesh's own reflections on art and the role of the intellectual are outlined by him in his book of essays *Bakalem Khud* (1974) and several of his plays carry prefaces as for instance, *Lahron Ke Rajhans.* Girish Karnad's lengthy preface to the Oxford University Press edition of *Three Plays* is titled 'In Search of a Theatre' and several of his other plays carry brief introductions. "A Search of Theatre" is an important statement for contemporary Indian drama. We have, in this essay, the doubts and uncertainties of a young man, his perception both of tradition and of the theatre scene as well as of the evolution of his dramatic method, the visits to the two theatre forms – the proscenium and folk – and then later the exposure to western dramaturgy(178), his respect for individual privacy imbibed through convention and his own unconscious questioning of the tyranny of convention. Apparently tradition marginalised the individual while his own conscious self was learning to think like an individual and not a unit. Here we have both conflict and character, the very beginning of drama. And later when debating this question of self or family, he found himself scripting *Yayati.* This is one reason for the resort to myth, to avoid the kind of exposure and fracturing which the viewer experiences in *Aadhe Adhure.* Myth then becomes a means of articulation as well as ordering of the rebellious human thoughts. It also served as a coming together of tradition and modernity, no matter how cliched the statement may sound; the narrative was traditional the structure western(180). There was also, in this return to myth, a getting away from predominance of incident. But traditional material like folk tales and folk dramaturgy were to prove equally relevant to Karnad in the years to come.

Where does all this relate to the Indian drama in English? First, it allows us to see that any drama which works in a cultural context has to work with it in mythical/historical and realistic terms; then it is obvious that theatrical strategies interact and merge, none ever retains its purity. Further the cauldron of the 60s and the 70s of this 'new wave' in experimental theatre created an audience. Translations of these plays into English further speeded this process. Indian drama in English cannot grow on any alien ground, it has to grow here and thus deal with myth, history and social reality. While translations are now being done overtime – Seagull has added its efforts to Oxford University Press – performances of the plays in English whether translated or in original are still rare and limited to metropolitan centres. Though in the case of plays translated from one language into another, a large, responsive audience and a fairly large readership has come into existence. Why? Is it that they are closer to the cultural reality? Or is it that their reception in the language of origin has whetted our appetite for them and there is a natural curiosity to know what they are about? Translated plays also make good export material. And when Indian characters from non-English speaking pockets (as slum-dwellers, artisans or historical characters) speak in English, their acceptance is easier than in a play written in English because it represents a constructed space, an enclosed world. The difference is demarcated clearly enough to allow the audience to suspend their disbelief. But plays written originally in English have yet to create their own audience, an uphill task with the electronic media not opening up much space and films making inroads into play texts. Dattani himself has turned film director for the filming of *Morning Raga.* His other play *Mango Souffle* had also been filmed. The best hope still lies in the universities and repertory groups.

The journey of the Indian drama in English has indeed been a curious one, rather circuitous, as in order to establish a direct relationship with its audience, it has had to concede space to translations. Writers like Mahesh Dattani have benefited from the experience of the language writers, have moved ahead of Asif Currimbhoy and Nissim Ezekiel and have learnt to use both language (with all its varied range of nuances and pitches) and structure (with its disruptive possibilities built in) and are now increasingly working with social concerns even if, at times, they choose to use fantasy or dystopia. This is a journey astride two cultures and across two dramatic traditions, yet it is an ongoing journey where, hopefully, form and structure will expand to accommodate cultural needs.

Notes

1. Also refer Sisir Das's 2 volume *History of Indian Literature* 1800-1910 (Vol I) and 1911-1956 (Vol II).
2. In the nineteenth century the rise of the Parsi theatre was an urban phenomenon. It cannot be dismissed as a hybridity, instead it has served a most useful function in establishing continuities and filtering influences. Karnad's reference to it is rather dismissive, but the Parsi Theatre's achievements are many. For one it brought into existence a public theatre, encouraged translations and adaptations of plays from the west, adopted rhetoric which went well with the audiences and was in itself an accommodation to the folk Ramlila style. Many of its writers and actors were Hindus. Ranbir Sinh has a full-length book on the Parsi Theatre which provides us with its rich history. These urban audiences were from all communities. Several of the earlier performances of the Parsi theatre were in Gujarati. Prithvi Theatres was an offshoot of it and we find in the acting style of actors like Prithviraj Kapoor and Sohrab Modi a continuation of the Parsi theatre acting style.
3. *Andha Yug* was a comment on the violence and anarchy of the post-partition period and is a poetic play. Poetry, songs and dance continue to form part of the Indian dramatic tradition. Karnad is another writer who uses them with effect. It is futile to try and trace T.S. Eliot's influence on the poetic plays in India, even though the writers of this period must have been exposed to his work. What is worth attention is the comparative ease with which poetry is accommodated even in the translated versions.
4. One can realise the importance of character through closely observing some TV serial for a stretch of time. As soon as a particular

actor is substituted the rest of the framing also undergoes a subtle change. Either the language or the narrative, the nuance or the relationships, or all of them undergo a change.

5. Another contemporary play, Mahesh Elkunchwar's *Autobiography*, elicits the plays's narrative and constructs character through an entirely different strategy. It is one long continuous scene, the stage is divided into three parts, in which the centre is empty. It is this emptiness, which becomes the central motif of the play as the aged writer who is contemplating writing his autobiography, reveals the lie. Memory, reality and truth all get merged into hallucination and self-deception. And the play shifts its focus from event and plot to existential issues.
6. One must also recognise the role of other agencies and institutions like the National School of Drama and the Sangeet Natak Academy. Further directors like Elkazi, Karanth and Tanvir also have their own share in stirring up the drama scene. The 60s, the world over, was an age of theatrical ferment.
7. Each one of the four major dramatists of this period stressed something different: Tendulkar stressed character and language; Karnad worked for universal patterns and through abstract representations, Sircar concentrated on experimentation and existentialism and Rakesh the fluidity of character and the flow of movement. Despite these different methods and priorities they were all interested in the theatre as a 'live relationship' between actor and audience and in the disruptive questionings which this rendered possible.

References

Bharati, Dharamvir. *Andha Yug* translated by Alok Bhalla. Delhi: Oxford University Press, 2005.

Bhattacharya, Rimli. "Introduction" to *Binodini Dasi: My Story and My Life as an Actress.* New Delhi: Kali for Women, 1998.

Currimbhoy, Asif. *Goa* (1970). Calcutta: Writers Workshop, 1982.

Das, Sisir Kumar. *A History of Indian Literature 1800-1910: Western Impact: Indian Response.* New Delhi: Sahitya Akademi, 1991.

—. *A History of Indian Literature 1911-1956: Struggle for Freedom: Triumph and Tragedy.* New Delhi: Sahitya Akademi, 1995.

Dasi, Binodini. *My Story and My Life as an Actress.* Translated and edited by Rimli Bhattacharya. New Delhi: Kali for Women, 1998.

Elkunchwar, Mahesh. *Autobiography* (Marathi original titled *Atmakatha*, translated into English by Pratima Kulkarni). Calcutta: Seagull Books, 1989.

Karnad, Girish. "In Search of a Theatre", *Creating Theory: Writers on Writing*. Ed. Jasbir Jain. Delhi: Pencraft International, 2000.

—. *Naga-Mandala* (1990). Delhi: OUP, 1993.

—. *Talè-Danda*. Delhi: Ravi Dayal Publishers, 1993.

Karnad, Girish. *Two Plays: The Dream of Tipu Sultan and Bali: The Sacrifice*. Delhi: OUP, 2004.

Naik, M.K. *A History of Indian English Literature* (1982). New Delhi: Sahitya Akademi, 1989.

Rajan, Chandra. "Introduction" to *Kalidasa: The Loom of Time. A Selection of His Plays and Poems* New Delhi: Penguin, 1989.

Rakesh, Mohan. *Lehron Ke Rajhans* (Hindi), (translated into English as *The Great Swans of the Waters. Enact,* May 1972). Delhi: Rajkamal Prakashan, 1978.

—. *Aadhe Adhure* (Hindi) 1969. (translated into English as *The Half Way House*) in *Mohan Rakesh Ke Sampuran Natak*. Ed. Nemichand Jain. Delhi: Rajpal and Sons, 1999.

—. *Aasadh Ka Ek Din* (Hindi) 1958. Delhi: Rajkamal Prakashan, 1985.

—. *Bakalam Khud* (Hindi). Delhi: Rajpal and Sons, 1974.

—. *Lahron Ke Rajhans* (Hindi) 1963. (translated into English)

Tendulkar, Vijay. "The Play is the Thing", Sri Ram Memorial Lecture, extracts in Sinh, Ranbir. *Parsi Theatre* (Hindi). Jodhpur: Sangeet Natak Academy, 1990.

—. *Collected Plays in Translation*. Delhi: OUP, 2003.

Venugopal, C.V. "Asif Currimbhoy's 'The Doldrummers': A Glimpse into Bombay Shacks", *Aspects of Indian Writing in English*. Ed. M.K. Naik (1979). Madras: Macmillan India Limited, 1992.

4

Retreating into Tribal Mansions

Race and Religion in Plays Written by Parsi Zoroastrians in India*

Nilufer E. Bharucha

Ethnicity has been defined by M. Blumer as "a collectivity within a larger society having real or putative common ancestry, memories of a shared past, and cultural focus on one or more symbolic elements which define the group's identity, such as kinship, religion, language, shared territory, nationality or physical appearance" (54). Ethnic identity is fundamental and composed of primordial affinities and attachments. At this point it needs to be noted that in any society, that ethnic group which becomes dominant, ceases to be "ethnic" and becomes the "norm". So British or American literature is not ethnic. However, Black writing within these countries is marked ethnic. Given the economic and political power enjoyed by Britain in the imperial period, its national culture, especially its literature, transcended its national boundaries and attained the status of a universal literature. The sole Superpower status of the USA today has guaranteed a similar privileged position for its culture and values. The ethnic marker therefore usually means the marginal or the subaltern.

---

* A longer version of this paper was first published in *Contemporary Drama in English: Race and Religion*, Vol. 6, 1999, Trier, Germany.

The politics of ethnicity also operates within postcolonial spaces. In such societies too the dominant group becomes the norm and the rest ethnically marked. So Postcolonial texts do not merely foreground resistance to the colonial past or resultant ongoing psychic traumas. As Arun Prabha Mukherjee has put it, 'Postcolonial discourse also offers resistance to domination and marginalisation within the national space.' Notwithstanding independent India's secular constitution, ethnic minorities in India in the post-Babri Masjid period, have been subjected to increasing domination by the Hindu majority. Current ethno-religious discourse in India is in direct response to her increasing engagement with Hindu fundamentalism. This has alarmed the smaller minorities in India who saw the nominally secular politics practised by the Congress Party as a protection and guarantee of their rights and freedoms. They feel threatened by the militant Hinduism of the BJP and even though they are currently not the targets of their anger, they do feel disturbed by their slogans of Hindu India and anti-Muslim rhetoric.

Even the Parsi Zoroastrians who number under 60,000 in India and a 1,00,000 worldwide, feel threatened enough to produce distinctly ethno-religious discourse. The history of Parsis in India goes back to circa 785 A.C. or 936 A.C. depending on which historical version you wish to privilege[1]. After the fall of the Persian Empire, the Parsis fled Iran to escape the religious and economic oppression of their Arab conquerors. In India, they came to be called Parsis after the Iranian province of Pars or maybe after the Farsi language they spoke. They landed on the Western coast of India and were given refuge and allowed to practice their ancient monotheistic religion Zoroastrianism, but had to give up their arms, language and Iranian costumes. So the Parsis adopted the local language, customs and costumes but fiercely protected their racial and religious identities. This was done through strict rules of endogamy and a ban on conversion to Zoroastrianism. You cannot become a Parsi, you can only be born one. The ban on conversion to Zoroastrianism, does not apply in modern day Iran which still has a small number of Zoroastrians – approximately 25,000. However, converts to Zoroastrianism in Iran or any other part of the world, cannot legally be defined as Parsis in India. The promises made at the time of refuge in India are today observed more for economic reasons than theological. Historically these promises and self-imposed conditions were a means of self-protection and self-definition. However today there are other, not often voiced, reasons for the ban on proselytisation. During the British colonial period the Parsis prospered tremendously in economic terms and today the Parsi Panchayat Trust Funds are very rich indeed in terms of property, bonds, shares and even liquid cash. Given the sky-high property prices in Bombay and other metros in India, conversion to Zoroastrianism would give the new converts the right to reside in the sprawling housing complexes owned by the Parsi Panchayats and claim rights also to their other welfare schemes. This is a scenario not too many Parsis would welcome with open arms.

The reasons for the wealth the Parsis amassed during the British Colonial period can be traced back to the fact that the Parsis became mediators between the imperial power and the Indian peoples. Hitherto they had been small land owners and merchants in what is today the state of Gujarat on the western coast of India. As a diasporic people they had kept a low profile and tried their best to please their Hindu hosts. With the conquest of Gujarat by the Muslims from Central Asia, the Parsis had further retreated into their ethno-religious shell, so as not to annoy their new rulers, whose co-religionists had originally caused them to flee from their homeland Iran. With the coming of the Imperial European powers, the Parsis who were unhampered by the caste taboos of the Hindus or the psychological trauma of the Muslims caused by their defeat at the hands of the British, surged ahead. They were among the first Indians to accept English language education and became one of the most westernised of Indian communities. However,

Liberal Western education which was meant to provide the East India Company with a battalion of clerks boomeranged badly on the Raj, when educated Indians became "infected" with notions of liberal humanism and even worse began to think of themselves as a nation.

So while the majority of Parsis continued to foster close links with the colonial rulers, a small but very powerful number of Parsis became active in India's anti-colonial freedom struggle. Dadabhai Naoroji and M.M. Bhownugree became the first Indian members of the British Parliament and represented India's interests there. Naoroji was also one of the founder members of the Indian National Congress. Phirozsha Mehta became the Mayor of Bombay and took the British administration head on in several well documented and colourful conflicts. Bhikaji Cama was a radical revolutionary who was exiled by the Raj. She had the distinction of unfurling India's first national flag at an international forum. Thus in the colonial period while many Parsis aligned themselves with the British, some began to image themselves as Nationalist Indians.

Among the latter group were the growing band of Parsi creative writers. In the pre-colonial times Parsis had not produced much literature. The only available piece from that period is the foundational text, *Kissah-e-Sanjan* written in Persian around 1600 A.C. by Kaikobad Sanjana. This text details the arrival of the Parsis in India and their settlement in the Kingdom of Sanjan. The oral tradition has the Parsi folk songs the Gujarati *garba*, which also tells the story of the Parsis' flight from Iran and their subsequent settling down in India. Also available are the *Rivayats* – religious tracts – which were written between 1478 and 1766[2]. So the extant pre-colonial literature, oral and written, is comprised of religious tracts and narratives of valour. These texts displays some of the classic features of diasporic discourse noted by William Safran, viz., the insecurity and a sense of alienation from the host country. However, this discourse lacks some of the other diasporic features detailed by Safran, particularly the belief in the restoration of the homeland and the definition of self in terms of this lost homeland. Instead as Eckhard Kulke has noted there is the shared history of flight from Iran, refuge in India and pride in the Persian lineage (the Parsi race) and Zoroastrian religion.

Colonial Parsi discourse was written mainly in English but there are also some texts in Gujarati. Prominent writers of this period were Behram Malabari, a bilingual poet, travel writer and journalist; Cornelia Sorabji a lawyer by profession who wrote short fiction and other autobiographical texts; Fredoon Kabarji and A.F. Khabardar who were poets and wrote poems in English and Jamshedji Petit and Jehangir Marazban who wrote poetry in Gujarati. There were also the Parsi playwrights, C.S. Nazir, *The First Parsi Baronet*, 1866, D.M. Wadia, *The Indian Heroine*, 1877, P.P. Mherji, *Dolly Parsen,* 1918. These Parsi playwrights founded the Parsi Theatre movement which had a major impact on Indian theatre and even the cinema. The Parsi Theatre in the late Nineteenth and the first quarter of the Twentieth Centuries operated mainly in Gujarati and Hindustani. None of these text displayed overt ethno-religious tones. The Parsi muse in the colonial period was happy with the newly emergent nationalist label of Indian.

With the end of Colonial rule, the Parsi writers once again went into a kind of hibernation. The independence of India was won at a high cost and the country was divided into India and Pakistan. The carnage of Hindus and Muslims on both sides of the new border, made the tiny Parsi community feel very insecure again, as it was spread out in both the new nations. So the Parsis withdrew into prudent silence. This silence was sometimes punctuated by stray stories and novels in English and plays in Gujarati, but was broken in a major way only in the late 1970s and early 80s. This Postcolonial Parsi literature was mainly in the form of novels and short-stories written by Bapsi Sidhwa, Farrukh Dhondy, Rohinton Mistry, Firdaus Kanga, Dina Mehta and Boman Desai. All these texts displayed ethno-religious attributes not evident in the writing of the colonial Parsis. Apart from the novelists, this period also saw the growth of Parsi poets and playwrights – Keki Daruwala, the poet, Gieve Patel the poet, playwright and painter, and Cyrus Mistry, the playwright. The feeling of alienation and insecurity experienced by diasporic communities is evident in most of these texts. By the 1970s India's engagement with Nehruvian secular politics had been brought to an end by Mrs. Indira Gandhi's practise of power politics and her initial abatement of Sikh Fundamentalists. These decades also saw the rise of Hindu revivalism, initially as a response to Governmental appeasement of the Muslim minority. This resulted in an atmosphere in which the tiny minority of Parsis began to retreat into their tribal mansion.

The post-colonial Indian Novel in English has many high-profile Parsi practitioners, especially Rohinton Mistry but the field of drama has fewer Parsis. This can also be attributed to the fact that drama in English is a rather low-key activity in India and there are very few Indian dramatists who write in English – Pratap Sharma, Gieve Patel, Gurcharan Das, Cyrus Mistry, Mahesh Dattani and Manjula Padmanabhan being the better known among them. It is extremely difficult for original plays in English to be staged in India and few producers are willing to put up the necessary finances. The audience too is very limited and even that limited number prefers to watch re-hashes of Broadway plays. Most of the Indian theatre in English is thus amateur. Moreover, theatrical activity is restricted to the big metropolitan cities of Bombay, Delhi, Calcutta and Madras. However, in the last three to four years there is a growing audience even in smaller cities like Bangalore, which is Dattani's home town.

Among the contemporary Indian playwrights, Gieve Patel and Cyrus Mistry are the only Parsis. All the three plays that Patel has written – *Princes* (1970), *Savaksa* (1982 but published 1989) and *Mister Behram* (1988) are focussed on the Parsi world. Mistry's first play, the Sultan Padamsee award-winning *Doongaji House*, was written in 1978, but was performed for the first time only in 1991 (it was also published in that year), since then it has had 25 shows in Bombay, Goa and Bangalore. In an interview with me Mistry displayed understandable bitterness about this long delay in the staging of *Doongaji House* and felt that the theatre company that gave him the award, the Theatre Group, should have also staged his play. He also said that they and other companies in India were not interested in original English plays as they feel they are not commercially viable. Patel on the other hand was more optimistic. In this interview he went on to say that the Indian audience response to original plays in English, has been growing and from 1970 to 1998 there has been an over 50 per cent increase in the audience for such plays. However, he felt that there should be more outlets for such plays. Patel would also like more newspaper coverage for original plays in English. Such plays are often ignored by the press in favour of the Broadway imports and Shakespearean plays put up by visiting British theatre companies, sponsored by the British Council. This of course strengthens the arguments put forward by postcolonial critics like Edward Said, Frantz Fanon and Ngugi wa Thiong'o who say that Colonialism breeds a slave mentality that often survives the end of empire.

Neither Patel nor Mistry write in the tradition of the old Parsi Theatre of Colonial India, which had tackled large, epic subjects from Indian history and was nationalistic in tone. Both these dramatists in fact actively resist the overblown style and melodrama of the old Parsi Theatre. They react even more strongly to any attempt to link their plays to those of another Parsi playwright, Adi Marzban, who wrote in Gujarati in the immediate postcolonial period. Marzban was a force to reckon with on the Gujarati stage in Bombay in the 1950s and 60s. His plays were the first ethnocentric dramatic texts written by a Parsi. They detailed Parsi society, customs, cuisine and above all humour. However, this humour often bordered on the farcical and his characters were caricatures and stereotypes rather than real people. He specialised in clownish old Parsi men and women – the *Bawajis* and *Maijis*. Like most Parsis today, Mistry and Patel disassociate themselves from these caricatures, but these clownish characters could have been clever ploys on the part of Marzban. They drew attention away from the Parsis' elite status in the colonial period. By portraying Parsis as a rather comic, harmless minority he made them objects of love and affection among the majority of the Gujarati Hindu community. In fact till date Gujarati Hindus are die-hard fans of Marzban's theatre and after his death have taken to reviving his plays, with a Parsi cast but with Gujarati Hindu directors.

Patel and Mistry's inspirations have been European and American dramatists. Patel's acknowledged influences are Ibsen and Racine, while Mistry has been inspired by Chekov, Ibsen and Eugene O'Neill. Neither acknowledge the Indian dramatic traditions, classical or folk. Both of them prefer the Western Nineteenth Century Realistic mode and do not, unlike the other Indian dramatists, Karnad or Dattani go in for Indian folk or Brechtian experimentation. Mistry has said that for him content is more important than form and that there should be very good textual reasons for experimentation. If there is to be a break from reality it has to come naturally (*Personal Interview*). In Patel's opinion taking on the folk tradition in contemporary metropolitan drama is like carrying artificial baggage. In his own words: "For me modern theatre is a metropolitan construct. You could call me a purist if you like but I stick to this view" (*Personal Interview*).

Patel is equally clear about the focus on Parsi race and Zoroastrian religion in his plays. He says that he has done this deliberately as he is most comfortable with that ethos and knows it most closely. However, he is quick to add that his plays are not just documents of the Parsi race and religion. In fact, Patel is not an orthodox Zoroastrian – he is a liberal who has married an Indian Christian woman – incidentally so has Cyrus Mistry. Patel says that he identifies with the Parsi ethos at the level of the social and cultural rather than the theological.

For him this ethos has been the filter through which he has explored the dramatic possibilities of life. He very strongly refutes the idea that writing about Parsis reduces his plays to the level of ghetto discourse. For him the ethno-religious nature of his drama is a means of reasserting the Parsi space within the wider Indian context. Patel also offers the interesting contention that all communities in India are ghettoised and not just the Parsis. In his opinion, Dattani's *Dance Like a Man* (1989), which is focussed on the South Indian Brahmin ethos, language, accents, culture, etc. should also be called ethnic discourse, rather than an "Indian" play (*Personal Interview*).

However, Patel's Parsi characters and backdrop have not been obstacles to the wider Indian acceptance and appreciation of his plays. Patel feels that "the more faithful a play is to its origins, the more universal it becomes. All three of my plays have been seen by a wide range of Indian audiences" (*Personal Interview*).

Patel, who wears four hats, simultaneously, medical doctor, poet, painter and playwright claims that he feels most complete when he is being all four of his selves. He practices medicine every evening and paints almost every day in his studio, where he also writes his poetry and plays. His late wife Toni was a theatre director with her own company called Stage Two. Most of Patel's plays as well as that of Mistry's have been put up by "Stage Two".

Princes written in 1970 was Patel's first performed play. It is set in a small village in Gujarat, with a large Parsi population. The play centres around the confrontation between two families over a male child. The boy dies at the end of the play so that neither family gets him. The play is not overtly biographical but Patel has drawn upon his family background. It is located in the village where his parents lived and the contested boy was his own elder cousin who died tragically young of rheumatic heart disease while the family squabbled above his deathbed.

In *Princes* as in *Savaksa* and *Mister Behram*, Patel has juxtaposed the Parsi race with the indigenous Warli race in Coastal Gujarat. The Warlis are tribals who are outside the pale of the Hindu caste system and live on subsistence farming and hunting. They were displaced from the margins of the Hindu villages where they used to live, by the newly arrived Parsis. The Parsis cleared the land, planted guava and chikoo orchards and became the big landlords for whom the Warlis worked as servants. So in Patel's plays one has him trying to work out the ambivalence of being at one and the same time the dominating, even oppressing class, and the ethno-religious minority which is anxious about the dominant Hindu community. Thus while on the one hand Patel's discourse is resistant to political and ideological domination, on the other it emerges from a socially and economically successful group. This raises the same questions that Sander L. Gilman has asked: "In a culture of victims, does being ethnic mean being oppressed? Can successful ethnics be considered ethnic? Do ethnics have to be subalterns?" (*PMLA*, 113, 1:23). Homi Bhabha has related ethnicity to anxiety. He has quoted Freud to strengthen his argument, "As Freud writes, anxiety, like ontopology is an archaic, atavistic, cathexis of longing...a defensive reaction to the left loss (or displacement) of the object (*Inhibitions, Symptoms and Anxiety*). Anxiety keeps visible and present both the moment of birth as a trace and the displaced state and in that sense constitutes a transition where strangeness and contradiction cannot be negated and must be continually negotiated and worked through. Anxiety is a culture's longing for place and its borderline existence..." (*PMLA* 113, 1: 35).

The anxiety and borderline existence in the context of dominance in the Postcolonial Indian context is tackled more centrally in *Savaksa*, while the guilt *vis a vis* the oppression of the Warlis is sensitively worked out in *Mister Behram*. *Savaksa* revolves around the eponymous ageing landlord and his passion for a young girl called Perin. Savaksa who is 64 wants to marry Perin who is only 20. Savaksa's wealth outweighs his age in the minds of Perin and her mother Khorshedmai. So Khorshedmai along with Perin and her elder daughter Hutoxi pay a visit to Savaksa's home. This upsets Savaksa's grown up children and his daughter-in-law. Matters become further complicated when Hutoxi in a cunning and calculated move decides to seduce Savaksa's younger son Adersar, who is somewhat mentally retarded.

The daily routine of a Parsi household, the cuisine and customs as well as colourful Parsi Gujarati idiom, translated into English, provides ethnic particularity to the play. Patel has said that he writes in English rather than in Gujarati because that is the language he is most familiar with. However, it is an English he has "moulded" to suit his Parsi characters. In the interview with me Patel had said: "It is often ungrammatical, it is not correct English" (*Personal Interview*). However, he is not interested in merely reproducing the errors that Indians normally make when they speak English. "I wanted to recreate a language. The language of theatre is an artifice, but it is not artificial. It is something created and so I would change the syntax. I would change the grammar in order to get the right rhythms of the characters" (*Personal Interview*).

The character of Savaksa is the most colourful one in the play and so is his language: "Put courage inside your husband Jermai", he says to his daughter-in-law. "He is frightened by colours." "My son, some red colour on a flag must not frighten you" (77), he continues, this time directly addressing his son with reference to the red flags carried by their striking labourers. Khorshedmai's language is equally interesting: "I won't talk now. My mind is free. I can see from you face that all my worries were wrong! No, don't go away, I am telling you I have cleaned all these thoughts out of my brain..." (79), she says to Jer, Savaksa's daughter-in-law, in relation to the acceptance of her own daughter by Savaksa's family.

The red flags which Savaksa dismisses so airily are signposts of the declining power and prestige of the Parsi landlords in rural Gujarat. The political jockeying for power, outside the home is duplicated within Savaksa's family as his son Dorab aspires to become the dominant force within the family by displacing his father. The decline in the fortunes of the rural Parsis is mirrored in an even more intense fashion among the urban Parsis. The object of Savaksa's attention, Perin and her sister Hutoxi are aware that unless Perin manages to marry the rich old man, their financial situation would be extremely precarious. Jobs for not so well educated Parsi girls are not available as easily in Postcolonial India as they were during the colonial period when such girls would have been snapped up as secretaries thanks to their Westernised looks and good English.

However, Savaksa's own glory days are coming to an end. His position as head of village Panchayat, is challenged by a tailor. This would have been inconceivable in colonial India. As his shocked son Dorab puts it: 'Pappa I have found it all out! He sits on a machine all day, he bites thread and talks. And our workers sit on the ground around him – and they listen! Imagine it!" (103). The tailor thus not only hopes to replace Savaksa in the Panchayat, but he also instigates his workers against him. Savaksa's troubles come to a head when his beloved Perin runs away from him and his ambitious son Dorab squeezes more and more concessions out of the old patriarch. At the end of the play, the stage directions indicate Savaksa 'with his head down, looking around him with the tormented, restless eyes, like a snared bull" (146).

Mister Behram which is set in late Nineteenth Century India is a play that fits in very well within the framework of resistant postcolonial discourse. *Mister Behram* also fits into what Edward Said has called the "second stage of Postcolonialism" (*Culture and Imperialism:* 252-53). When a country wins its freedom from its colonial masters, its first priority is to consolidate its political sovereignty and to secure its external and internal boundaries. This is the first stage of postcolonialism. In the second stage the political sovereignty becomes a given and the delineation of borders more or less accomplished, the postcolonial society turns its attention to asserting its distinct cultural identity. At this stage the erstwhile colonised subjects begin mapping their cultural territories and repossessing their histories. When *Mister Behram* was written in 1987, India was well into the second stage of postcolonialism. The wars for authoritative borders it had fought with Pakistan and China were well in the past and with the exception of Kashmir, the external borders were finalised. India had now moved into the age of self-definition and the conquest of its cultural domains which included the repossession of its histories. That this is happening in the time of globalisation and what some have called neo-colonisation, lends this stage an even more intriguing edge. At such times it becomes very important to recall the colonial past and repossess it rather than shun it, as is usually done, in the immediate aftermath of decolonisation. This is essential as the impact of European domination does not automatically cease with the end of Empire. It continues to be felt in postcolonial societies at all levels – social, cultural, literary and economic. Vast sections of Postcolonial India continue to "image" themselves in the mirror of Eurocentricism. They still see themselves as a mirror image of the West – "the other" of Europe.

In *Mister Behram*, the titular hero images himself in the mirror of the colonising West. A product of English language education and a lawyer who practises in the courts of the British Raj, he is what Salman Rushdie in *The Moor's Last Sigh*, calls "Macaulay's Minutemen" (165). By the end of the Nineteenth Century, Imperial educational policies, supported by British institutions of law and administration, had ascertained what Antonio Gramsci has termed the complicity of the colonised in their subjugation. At that stage what the Raj needed were collaborators to ensure a smooth functioning of the colonial administration and an uninterrupted flow of the colony's wealth, into the Imperial coffers. The Raj at that point, however, had to be vigilant against people like Behram who could at any time cease being collaborators and move into more autonomous nationalist spaces. It was Behram's reputation as a powerful, independent-minded lawyer, sympathetic towards his countrymen that became a threat to the power of the Raj and hence had to be sabotaged by the District Collector Mr. Watts.

Behram is not just a challenger of the Raj, he is a very complex character. The complexity arises from the fact that he is obsessed with his adopted son Naval. Naval is a Warli tribal who was taken into the Behram household as a young orphan and then educated to become a fine lawyer in his own right. Naval's tribal name is Nahnu and in re-naming him Naval, Behram tries to assimilate him into the Parsi Zoroastrian fold. To further validate this adoption, Behram marries Naval off to his only child, his daughter Dolly. Lurking under the surface of this play are several tensions and conflicts that deal with not just the colonial backdrop but also concern the Parsi race and Zoroastrian religion.

Behram's projection of Nahnu as Naval refers to the dilemma among Parsis in India on whether or not to accept converts to Zoroastrian's as Parsis. The fact that powerful Parsis like Behram flout the laws against conversion and adoption, is an indirect comment on how in the past several Warli tribal youths like Naval/Nahnu and common law wives from among other tribes too, had been smuggled into the Zoroastrian community. This of course makes a mockery of the present day Parsis' contention that allowing converts to Zoroastrianism would despoil their "pure" Persian lineage.

Another area in which Patel's plays offer challenges and resistance is that of Gender Equity and Alternative Sexuality. Behram is an unabashed Patriarch and though he sends his daughter to England to acquire an education in law, he doesn't allow her to complete her degree. When he is pressurised by Dolly, he does let her join him and Naval in court, but treats her like a junior clerk rather than as a legal assistant. Dolly imputes this behaviour not so much to his patriarchal values as to his obsession with Naval. Here we have the piquant situation of a father and daughter who are rivals for a young man's attentions. Behram's interest in Naval has definite homosexual overtones, but his pride in Naval's mind and body could also be seen as the ultimate involvement of creator with his creation – a Pygmalion admiring his Galatea. One of the most powerful scenes in the play is when Behram makes Naval strip off his Western clothes and put on his tribal loincloth. This is done to show Naval's body off to the visiting British District Collector Mr. Watts: "See that body Mr. Watts! A repository of secrets! Under trousers and suits and lawyer's gown is that essential Warli body. Our bodies Mr. Watts, yours and mine, are dull dough before this vision" (22). It is ironic that Behram here aligns himself with the Westerner in reducing the tribal man to an object for study and aesthetic appreciation, thereby possessing him in much the same way as Western Orientalists appropriated Eastern lands, people and cultures. This is also a marker of how elitist groups in colonised countries internalise the coloniser's notions of the civilised and the savage.

Behram's fascination with his protégé horrifies his daughter. She cries out to her mother Rati: "He is snatching my husband from me...for himself!" (71). She confronts her father who very proudly claims that Naval means everything to him- "To me there is no part of him that is not a source of rapture...I could enter his entrails and eat the foul wastes of his bowels! Can you claim a commensurate devotion?" (83), he challenges her. Dolly hits back with "I can see now father, why you consented to our marriage in the first place. It was to retain Nahnu securely by your side. You are no different from men who nurture little infants over the years, waiting for the unspeakable pleasures that will be theirs when their charges have ripened" (83). Naval, however, rebuffs Behram's final advances and as a result Behram suffers a paralytic stroke. The play ends with Naval and Dolly leaving Behram's house.

Cyrus Mistry's *Doongaji House* could be seen as a metaphor for the Parsi community. Doongaji House is a dilapidated building full of old people and ageing single women. All the young people and families have left. As the main protagonist Hormusji says: "First our Rusi went away to Canada. Then Fali went to Chikalwadi. The Bogdawalas and their children moved out lock stock and barrel. Who is left in the building now? Only old people" (1-2). "When I think of the old times, I feels so brittle. I feel I could pluck the fingers off my hand and toss them away. Then my toes, my nose, my ears, my tongue...till nothings remains.." (8). This feeling of disintegration is further intensified when Hormusji once again sees the ghost of his old neighbour Dhanjisha Bapasola, who had died when Hormusji was still a boy. The ghost is in a sense the moral conscience of the Parsi community which has fallen upon bad times and forgotten its old Zoroastrian ethics.

In addition to this focus on the disintegration of the Parsi community, the play is also full of ethno-religious details. The characters speak of the Parsi *Roj*, i.e. the day of the week according to the Parsi calendar. There is also constant reference to Parsi food.

Mistry's language too is in the tradition of the colourful Parsi Gujarati. Piroja says to her husband Hormusji when he comes home smelling of alcohol: "This is poison for you, poison! Dr. Lalkaka has warned you thousand of times. When you are flat on your back, your liver all chewed up and rotted, then don't expect me to bring the bedpan to your cot" (4).

The increasing socio-political tensions between the Indian minorities and the Hindu majority is also focussed upon in this play. Hormusji's son Fali brings the old people the news that "Last night two Maharashtrian (Hindu) boys were stabbed in a fight. Some political thing. They were members of that group – Yuvak Sangh or something. So their gang retaliated. Some shops in Null Bazaar were looted. Some Muslim fellows were beaten up. That's all" (19-20). He assures them, 'No one's going to bother you' (20).

Hormusji however is not convinced. "This is serious. No laughing matter. In 1921 when the Prince of Wales came to Bombay, the same thing happened. Parsis Vs Hindus. Soon we were fighting to save our lives. What a licking we gave them" (20). But he soon realises that "those days are gone...This is a generation of sissies. The blood has been polluted.' – a snide reference to Parsis marrying outside the fold. There are also many other statements by Hormusji about the changed status of the Parsis – "Snatch, snatch! Maharashtra for Maharashtrians indeed! After the Parsis have built the whole city! Now if the British were here, they would have just flogged one or two in a public place" (26).

Hormusji's feeling of being under siege in a wider socio-political context, is exacerbated by his daughter Avan turning against her father and aligning herself with her cousin Cavas. This wounds Hormusji deeply as he and his brother, Cavas' father, had been estranged for a very long time. The problem ostensibly had been business and property related but in actuality was the attraction between Piroja, Hormusji's wife, and his brother.

Even as Hormusji's life is falling apart and his building is becoming more and more dilapidated by the day, riots break out in the city. He is caught up in the violence and returns home in a bloodied state.

The last act opens with the chanting of Zoroastrian prayers in the ancient Avestan language. The prayers are being chanted for the soul of one of the oldest residents of Doongaji House, who had been killed when the roof had caved in and fallen on him as he lay asleep in his bed. This results in the evacuation of the building. The man who is in charge of relocating the residents in a sanatorium – a temporary shelter – advises them to get rid of most of their old and heavy furniture. Hormusji is distraught and rages, "Leave me here alone. Let these walls collapse on me. I'd rather be buried alive under Doongaji House, then found dead in some rat-ridden gutter" (58). Yet, Piroja is able to persuade him to leave with her and as he follows her he says: "Slowly Piroja...I'm not so young as I used to be. You'll have to help me" (62). This could be the exit line of the Parsis in India too. The question however is will

India "help" its minorities assimilate into the mainstream or will it push them further into their tribal mansions.

Ethnoreligious self-esteem does not preclude interaction with other ethnic groups. As Werner Sollor has put it, "after deconstruction, ethnicity can no longer be an essentialising truth. It must be something constructed, potentially multiple, hybridized and interstitial?" (xi). However, this presupposes that the dividing lines of anxiety and fear that "enclose" give way to the hybridising, interstitial seepage. This can happen only when the dominant spaces expand and become more inclusive. Then ethno-religious minorities' existence need not stop at the edge of their skins.

Notes

1. For details on the controversy regarding the dates on which the Parsis sought refuge in India, see J.J. Modi, *A Few Events in the Early History of the Parsis and their Dates,* Bombay, 1905, pp.9-10; K.N. Seervai and K.B. Patel, *Gazetteer of the Bombay Presidency,* ed. J.M. Campbell, Bombay, 1899, IX, Part II, p. 185; S.K. Hodivala, *Parsis in Ancient India,* p. 31; D.F. Karaka, *History of the Parsis*, London, 1884, Vol. I, p. 30.
2. Khan Bahadur Bomanji Byramji Patel in a paper contributed to the *Cama Memorial Volume,* in 1900, has written how the Parsis in the year 1478 had sent one Nariman Hoshang to Persia to ascertain the authenticity of their religious practices and rites. More emissaries were sent between the 15th and 18th centuries to Iran and the resultant data was collected in the *Rivayats* – codes of usages and rituals. For more details see *Zoroastrian Theology*, Dr. M.N. Dhalla, New York, 1914.

References

Bhabha, Homi. "On the Irremovable Strangeness of Being Different". *PMLA* 113, 1 (1998): 34-39.

Blumer, M. "Race and Ethnicity". *Key Variable in Sociological Investigation.* Ed. R.G. Burgess, London: Routledge, 1986, 54-75.

Dattani, Mahesh. "Dance Like a Man". *Final Solutions and Other Plays.* Bombay: Manas, 1992.

Eckhard, Kulke. *The Parsees in India: A Minority as Agent of Social Change.* Delhi: Vikas Publishing House Pvt. Ltd., 1978.

Fanon, Frantz. *Black Skin White Masks.* Trans. Charles Lam Markmann. New York: Grove, 1967.

Gilman, Sandra. "Ethnicity-Ethnicities-Literature-Literatures". *PMLA* 113, 1, (1998): 18-27.

Gramsci, Antonio. *Selections from the Prison Notebooks.* Q. Hoare and G.N. Smith Eds., London: Lawrence and Wishart, 1971.

Isaacs, Harold R. "The House of Mumbi." *Washington Monthly* 3, 1971: 37-49.

Mistry, Cyrus. *Doongaji House.* Bombay: Praxis, 1991.

Mistry, Cyrus. *Personal Interview*, 15th March, 1998.

Mukherjee, Arun Prabha. "Whose Post colonialism, Whose Postmodernism?" *World Literatures Written in English.* 30.2, (1990): 1-9.

Ngugui wa, Thiongo. *Decolonising the Mind.* London: Heinemann, 1986.

Patel, Gieve. *Princes.* Unpublished script, 1970.

—. *Mister Behram.* Bombay: Praxis, 1988.

—. *Personal Interview*, 3rd March, 1998.

—. *Savaksa. The Bombay Literary Review*, No. 2, 1989.

Rushdie, Salman. *The Moor's Last Sigh.* New York: Pantheon Books, 1995.

Said, Edward. *Culture and Imperialism.* London: Vintage, 1994.

Soller, Werner. *The Invention of Ethnicity.* New York: Oxford University Press, 1989.

5

The Bold and the Meek

Ranbir Sinh

In literature, it is interpretation which is important and not the plot. Let us take the two folk tales one from Karnataka and other from the distant land of Latvia, and analyse them as to how the two playwrights Girish Karnad and Aspazija have dealt with them respectively in their plays, *Naga-Mandala* and *The Serpent's Bride*. Both the plays are based on the snake cult. In the Latvian play the snake is the king of the underworld and lives in the lake, while the snake dwells in the forest in the Kannada tale. In both plays the heroine is married or abducted by the snake.

The Serpent's Bride

Aspazija and her husband J. Rainis, the great poet of Latvia were both closely and actively involved in the freedom movement of Latvia. The Nationalistic fervour had entered the Latvian theatre in 1870. Aspazija wrote the play *The Serpent's Bride*, based on the Latvian fairy tale *Zaltis Per Precinieku* (The Serpent's Suitor), after she returned from a long exile, suffering the trauma of revolution and the effects of the World War I. To subvert the laws of censorship playwrights all over the world have used mythological themes and folk tales as vehicles to communicate their message to the people. Aspazija used the fairy tale to its great advantage.

The total rejection of one's very essence became the central theme of her poetry and plays, and she expressed it through her two plays *The Silver Veil* and *The Serpent's Bride*. She expressed her sentiments that if women are bound by marriage to men they do not love; get rid of the marriage laws. Her play *The Serpent's Bride* echoes both these feelings, the rejection of one's essence and arouse the National feeling among the oppressed.

Dedzikle, Virpule and Ziednese are out in the forest. Dedzikle and Virpule are playing a game of throwing wreathes on the top of the trees. Anyone who succeeds will marry first. Both of them have failed. Ziednese is sitting beside the lake in a pensive mood staring into the deep water.

Dedzikle: Ah! she always sits like that
Sits and stares into the deep
As if someone pulled her down. (I i 258)

Virpule mysteriously discusses that the lake is enchanted:

Virpule: This deep lake, they say's enchanted:
The green Serpent, the king himself
Dwells below down in the water.
In his castle made of glass. (I i 259)

In *The Serpent's Bride* everyone is in the know of the fact that there lives a snake in the lake who is the powerful king of the underworld, and is a threat to the freedom of the earth bound people. The people are constantly trying to kill the snake. Saulgaitis who is engaged to be married to Ziednese has gone with the hunters in search of the snake to kill him. Aspazija has made the snake the symbol of the Tsar of Russia and the German nobility which controlled most aspects of Latvian life.

The innocent girls do not understand why the people are searching for the snake king elsewhere when he is supposed to be residing in the lake. Ziednese with a firm and strong character recklessly proclaims that she will go to the lake and ask the snake king to come and dance with her.

Ziednese: I will go and call the serpent
Ask him if he'll dance with me.
Hear me call you, dearest snake
Come at once and play with me
Since you have stolen my white garland
I shall hit you with this stone. (I i 260-261)

She throws a stone into the lake disturbing the water and this leading to an exodus. One day Ziednese, without caring about the dangers, swims naked in the lake. The Serpent takes away all her clothes and Ziednese is unable to find her clothes. Faced with the dilemma as how to go home she wonders as to who has taken her clothes. At this moment the serpent appears and demands the engagement ring which she is wearing in exchange for her clothes. The helpless Ziednese gives him the ring but hides the fact. She pretends that she has hurt her finger and ties a bandage.

Ziednese: Did you steal all my clothes?
How can I go home naked?
Everyone will laugh at me.

Serpent: Why does a bright and shining star
Need to hide beneath the clouds?
Why must a fully opened rose
Still be covered up with leaves?
You are now most beautiful.

Ziednese: Pity me – give me my shirt.
Give it to me ... I shall die...
How can I go home naked?

Serpent: You no longer have a home
Where I am there you must live.

Ziednese: Have you come to ravish me? (I viii 269)

Serpent desires that Ziednese will have to pledge something to get back her clothes and demands "The ring which encircled your white finger" (I viii 271).

When Saulgaitis comes to know that Ziednese has lost the ring, he expresses his fears in these words.

Saulgaitis: When a bride's ring is lost
Lost will be her love as well.

Ziednese: No, No, Saulgaitis! Love's not lost
Love cannot be bound in circles.
Love flows like a mighty river
And breaks through all narrow banks. (II ii 279)

Equipped with the engagement ring the Serpent King appears in full glory in the presence of the villagers. Ziednese is afraid and pleads to be hidden and saved from falling into the hands of the serpent.

Ziednese: He is coming! Hide me! Hide me!

Saulgaitis: My dear love. I am with you
Fire and water cannot touch us
Love is stronger far than these.

All: The serpent! It's the serpent!
He will swallow us alive! (II ii 282)

When the people shout to kill the serpent Auglone, the mother of Ziednese, who is more practical and can see into the future, says:

Auglone: Ha! you can't kill him any more
He comes to rule us in full strength.
He will kill us with one stroke. (II vi 282)

Aspazija points out as how the Super Powers dominate the smaller and developing nations, and subjugate them. When Saulgaitis and others attack to kill him, the Serpent King lifting the scepter threatens the village folks that he will ruin everything of theirs.

Serpent: Who will dare to fight with me?
My wrath will turn into storms.
And flood you like the autumn rains
I shall uproot your trees by force
And flatten all your houses down.

When Saulgaitis opposes him and tells him that Ziednese is engaged to him and he will never allow him to take her away, the Serpent King tells him that Ziednese is engaged to him, and he has the ring with him. On being questioned by Saulgaitis, Ziednese confesses that she did give the ring to Serpent. No one allows her to clarify her action. Serpent forcibly takes her by hand and drags her to his boat.

Serpent: Fate has ruled over you
You must leave your home on earth
And must follow where I lead you. (II vi 284)

Ziednese is now imprisoned in the palace of the Serpent King. She is nothing more than a mere slave to the Serpent. However much she may dislike, resent, and be sad she is fated to live with the powers of horror. She moans and says:

Ziednese: I'm in darkness, blackest darkness,
The Sun, the last bright light of earth
Is vanishing from my sight
I have entered death's dark cave.
And aim in the power of horrors. (III ii 288)

It is through Ziednese that Aspazija speaks to the people of Latvia about the bondage of slavery, sorrow of the soul, the painful existence, no opening for escape, the craving for sunlight on earth, and the deep longing for freedom.

Ziednese: Where is the Sun? Give me my Sun
Lead me back to earth again.

Here my flesh will turn to ice
My breath blows like a ghostly wind
Opening and closing doors.
Here I shall be lost forever...
Even heavens eyes the stars
Could not find me in the darkness. (III ii 289)

When the Serpent asks Ziednese to wear the Royal garments and the jewels, she refuses and says:

Zidenese: Of what use are clothes of gladness
When my soul is dressed in sorrow
Many years have come and gone
And still in slavery I smother

Serpent: Amber urns and treasure chests
Are laid full of precious stones
But you haven't looked at them.

Ziednese: Cold and mute are those stones
They don't hold the warmth of life
Everything I touch is ice. (IV i 296)

Ziednese even spurns the advances made by Serpent:

Serpent: You won't die, but live with me.

Ziednese: Don't! Don't come near me!
I don't like all your splendour,
And I cringe from your cold touch.

Serpent: I realise I must seem strange
But come to me, I'll give you life.

Ziednese: No! No! No! as a human I was born
Please, Now let me die as one. (III ii 289)

Ziednese tells him that no amount of kindness can weaken her desire for freedom.

Ziednese: Serpent, all your words are useless
All encouragement you give me

Only increase my pain.
It awakens my deep longing
To return to earth again.

Serpent: Is the earthly life that good?
Why are there so many tears
Wept by people on your earth?
Gather up all their tears
Lock them into cold sea shells
Hold life's misery before you. (IV i 297)

To this Ziednese replies:

I weep enough tears of my own
Which will not turn into pearls,
But as living parts of me
They will burning fall on you. (IV i 298)

The Serpent tries his best to win over the love of Ziednese. He tells her that although she does not like him, yet they are man and wife, and another tie that binds them are their children. Ziednese even refuses to accept the children.

Ziednese: I can't stand to look at them
Constantly they remind me.
Of your slippery embraces,
Of your wet and slimy lips.
Atleast on your wedding night
You could have turned into a man;
Perhaps then our children would be human
Instead of being half bred beasts. (IV i 298)

She further says,

Ziednese: No, I don't I feel no love
I am neither wife nor mother.
My true love lives on the earth.
If I can not ever see him,
Lock me up in your dark caves.

Feed me to your hungry beasts!
'Tis better to cut off life quickly
Than to die in slow torment. (IV i 298)

Enslaved as she is Ziednese does not wish to turn into a beast. She wants to remain human. Serpent tells her that once he was also human.

Ziednese: Reveal yourself in human form!

Serpent: I shall lesser be when human,
Prone to injury and weakness.
I shall die in human form....

Ziednese: You must die if you turn human,
But I shall die if I turn beast.
Here we stand as opposites
That can never be united.
We shall both destroy each other. (III ii 290)

Ziednese tries to escape, but she is captured and imprisoned. The Serpent himself sets a judgement and frees her. He tells her that as you still cling to the earthly life, "I make you free". He pulls off the ring from his finger and gives it to Ziednese who puts it on. At the last moment of separation Serpent wants to fulfill one wish of Ziednese that he should take the human form. He appears in human form. It is in his human form that Ziednese understands him and his love.

Ziednese: You gave so much love to me,
Now I understand your love.

Serpent: Only now when it is gone?
We are strangers to each other.
Go and walk earth's dusty roads!

Ziednese: Is there no real love on earth?

Serpent: For the earth love is too fragile,
Unreachable it floats away.
As a sunbeam breaks 'gainst clouds,

So love breaks from contraries,
Ever reaching, never grasping
Those destined for each other
Can unite through death alone. (IV xi 310)

Ziednese is freed from the miseries of the underworld, but she is in two minds, she does not know whether it is joy or sorrow. On earth people are anxiously waiting for the Serpent to emerge once again from the lake. They are all ready to kill him. At the same time they long for the return of Ziednese. But Auglone emerges with the two children of Ziednese, Gints and Gina. People are horrified to see them. They enquire about the welfare of Ziednese. Auglone says that she is the Queen, but "A prison is always just a prison", Auglone tells them that she tried to escape but was caught and imprisoned again in the palace. Saulgaitis does not accept the children and wants to kill them.

Auglone: You, big, bloody thirsty brute!
Get away from these children!
What if Ziednese returns,
How could you embrace her then
With your bloody, murderous hands. (V v 320)

Saulgaitis has lost hopes of Ziednese's return.

Saulgaitis: She won't come back! There is no hope!
I want to keep her in mind
Beautiful, white, and pure;
I want to purge her image
Of this dirty, ugly trash.
I don't have time to stand and argue. (V v 320)

He kills the children. The lake swells up again. Ziednese emerges, the people are jubilant. Saulgaitis meets Ziednese and wishes to take her in his arms, when Auglone comes and stops them. She takes Ziednese and shows her the grave of her two children. Ziednese is surprised as to how the children came to the earth. Auglone tells her that since she did not care for them, she brought them with her. Ziednese admits that she did not love them.

Ziednese: Ah – I remember, I did not love them
They were ugly and repulsive
Mother, how could I have loved them. (VI i 329)

Auglone: A mother's love overcomes all things:
A mother loves her helpless child
He may be crippled, blind, and deaf,
Broken out with open soars,
Sick, rejected by all people,
An outcast in his own land:
A mother's love will always find him,
A mother's look will comfort him;
A mother's kisses like the stars
Will turn all ugliness to beauty,
And her tears like sweetest balsam
Will wash away all evil stains. (VI i 329)

Aspazija once again brings the nationalistic fervour in the play. The speech of Auglone is directed to Ziednese and evokes the love of mother for her children, but at the same time it is the call for the sons of Latvia who had gone abroad to distant lands to escape the misery of being enslaved in their own lands, to return and also to Latvia that as mother she must accept them with open arms and with love. When Ziednese comes to know that Saulgaitis has killed her children, she rejects him.

Ziednese: Murderer! I see their blood
Still sticks to yours treacherous hands,
Don't come near me with those hands. (VI ii 332)

She screams at Saulgaitis and tells him that they are separated for ever.

Ziednese: Stay away from these graves!
Stay away from my children!
I don't know you anymore:

Red blood rivers break between us.
We are separate forever. (VI ii 333)

Saulgaitis declares her a witch and tells the people that she must be judged by law. It is decided that Ziednese will have to walk barefoot on the hot rocks beside the lake. As Ziednese starts walking towards the rock trumpets are blown and a silver boat approaches in which sits the Serpent with his guards. He now appears as a man, dressed in the same way when he freed Ziednese from the underworld. He tells Ziednese that he has come to save her and if she wished she could come back to him. But at this time Saulgaitis shoots him. Serpent sinks in the lake colouring it red. Saulgaitis tells Ziednese,

Saulgaitis: Ziednese, you are free from judgement;
The chains of witchery are broken
Which like a nightmare held you fast.
You have been returned to earth
And forever will be mine!

Ziednese: I am neither yours nor the earth's!
Serpent, my beloved king,
I shall follow you in death
And shall rise with you to life!
The earth is dark, all hearts are cold,
There's more darkness here than light,
Much more hatred than true love. (VIII vii 347)

Ziednese then turns to the People and implores them,

"It is time for all to Change"

She then jumps into the lake and gives up her life.

Naga-Mandala

Let us now have a look at the play *Naga-Mandala* based on a Kannada folk tale, written by Girish Karnad. It is interesting to know that as the characters of *The Serpent's Bride* are described as Ziednese (one who brings blossom), Virpule (a fast moving object, here symbolic of Joy), Dedzikle (a burning object, here symbolic of envy), in the same manner in *Naga-Mandala*, the characters are Appanna (which means any man) Kurudavva (which means the blind one) Kappanna (which means the dark one) and Naga (which means the cobra).

The Prologue itself lends to the play a touch of mystery and an aura of fantasy. The hero of the play Appanna means any man, which does not give him any tangible character. The heroine is Rani, a meek, doll like girl who has been taught not to ask any questions but to obey. She does not have a lover. She is married to Appanna most probably without even having seen him before marriage. He brings her to his house and assures that they have brought in all their luggage.

Appanna: Have we brought in all the bundles?
Rani: Yes.
Appanna: Well, then, I'll be back tomorrow at noon, Keep my lunch ready. I shall eat and go. (I, 6)

This becomes a routine. Appanna comes only for lunch and locks Rani in the house for the rest of the day and night. Between them there is no relation of man and wife. Being alone she is frightened the whole night. She pleads to Appanna but in vain.

Rani: Listen (fumbling for words) Listen – I feel – frightened alone at night –

Appanna: What is there to be scared of? Just keep to yourself. No one will bother you. Rice!

Rani: Please you could –

Appanna: Look, I don't like idle chatter. Don't question me. Do as you are told and you won't be punished (finishes his meals, gets up) I'll be back tomorrow, for Lunch. (I, 7)

Don't ask questions – do as you are told – or you will be punished. This is what Rani meekly surrenders to. Kurudavva and her son Kappanna come to the house of Appanna, but find the house locked from outside. Kurudavva meets Rani and enquires from her if Appanna is at home.

Rani: No.
Kurudavva: What is your name?
Rani: They call me Rani.
Kurudavva: And where is Appanna?
Rani: I don't know.
Kurudavva: When did he go out?
Rani: After lunch yesterday.
Kurudavva: When will he come back?
Rani: He will be back for lunch later in the day.
Kurudavva: You don't mean, he is home only once a day, and that too only for lunch? And you are alone in the house all day? Does he lock you up every day like this?
Rani: Yes, since the day I came here ...
Kurudavva: Does he beat you or ill-treat you?
Rani: No.
Kurudavva: Does he 'talk' to you?
Rani: Oh, that he does. But not a syllable more than required. 'Do this', 'Do that', 'Serve the food'...

Kurudavva comes to know that Appanna and Rani do not have any relation of man and wife. She promises to help Rani. She gives her some root and gives instructions – make a paste and feed Appanna with it. Girish Karnad probably adhering to the main folk tale does not make any change in the character of Kurudavva or Rani. He does not make Kurudavva strong enough to accost Appanna and force him to behave decently towards Rani. He neither makes Kurudavva to give wise lessons to Rani to be strong and demand her right of a wife. She gives Rani a love potion. Rani prepares the potion, gives it to

Appanna, who after partaking of it, faints. When he recovers he drags Rani into the house and locks it from outside. Kurudavva returns to see if the medicine has had any effect. Rani wakes up and goes to the window.

Rani: Who is that?

Kurudavva: Me.

Rani: Who? Kurudavva. This time of the night.

Kurudavva: What happened, child? Why is the lock still there. Did you feed him the root.

Rani: Yes.

Kurudavva: And what happened.

Rani: Nothing, He felt giddy. Fainted. Then got up and left.

Kurudavva: That's bad. This is no ordinary infatuation then. That concubine of his is obviously –

Rani: Who?

Kurudavva: Didn't want to tell you. There is a woman, a bazaar woman. She has your husband in her clutches. Squeezes him dry. May be she's cast a spell. There is only one solution to this.... Feed him this larger piece of root. (I, 15-16)

Rani prepares the medicine, but the colour red frightens her. Afraid of the horrible consequences she pours the curry into the anthill. She is slapped by Appanna and is again locked in the house. Girish Karnad has dutifully kept himself entrenched in the folk atmosphere. He makes no efforts to give strength to Rani or to voice her feeling of revolt against the male dominated society as Nora in *The Doll's House* or Ziednese did before her. Rani accepts everything that comes in her life without questioning. The cobra takes the shape of Appanna and seduces Rani. Appanna in the day and cobra in the night keep on visiting the house. Rani without questioning accepts both of them. She only feels that she may be dreaming. The visits of the day and night becomes a riddle for her and when she wants to know the secret of the riddle she is again told by the cobra (Naga).

> Naga: I am afraid that is how it is going to be. Like *that* during the day. Like *this* at night. Don't ask me why. (II, 23)

Rani submits meekly and agrees not to ask any questions. Rani is like a bird who is hypnotised by the cobra who later strikes her. Rani relates the story as told to her by her father.

> Rani: I don't feel afraid anymore, with you beside me. Father says: "The Cobra simply hooks the bird's eyes with its own sight. The bird stares – and stares – unable to move its eyes. It doesn't feel any fear either. It stands fascinated, watching the changing colours in the eyes of the Cobra. It just stares, its wings half opened as though it was sculpted in the sunlight."
>
> Naga: Then the Snake strikes and swallows the bird. (He kisses Rani). (II, 24)

The nocturnal visits continue. Rani has a little doubt when Naga says, "I'll be back again at night".

> Rani: Only at night? Not for Lunch?
>
> Naga: Of course. There's always that (Pause) Listen Rani, I shall come home every day twice. At night and of course again at mid-day. At night wait for me here in this room. When I come and go at night, do not go out of this room, do not look out of the window-whatever the reason. And don't ask me why. (II, 25)

.....

Rani: No, I won't. The pig, the whale, the eagle none of them ask why so I won't either. (II, 26)

It is only when Rani becomes pregnant that she realises that she was not fantasizing. But she does not know the reality, who is the father, Appanna or Naga. Naga tells Rani to keep it a secret. Rani asks from whom?

Naga: From me.

Rani: What are you talking about? I have already told you. How can it be a secret again? And how long can it remain a secret? Another fifteen days? Three Weeks?

Naga: I realise, it can not remain a secret for long. That is why I said, as long as possible. Please do as I tell you.

Rani: Yes, I shall, Don't ask questions. Do as I tell you. No, I won't ask questions. I shall do what you tell me. Scowls in the day. Embraces at night. The face in the morning unrelated to the touch at night. But day or night, one motto does not change. Don't ask questions. Do as I tell you. (II, 32)

But Rani realises that her pregnancy is not a dream. She says:

> But this is no dream now Dreams remains in heads. This one has sent roots deep down into my womb. (II, 32)

When Appanna comes to know of the fact he declares that he is not the father and threatens to take the issue to the elders of the village. Rani pleads helplessly.

Rani: Why are you humiliating me like this? Why are you stripping me naked in front of the whole village? Why don't you kill me instead? (II, 33)

Rani does not have the courage to face the elders and to tell them frankly about the visits in the day and night. She remains an embodiment of the typical weak, oscillating, confused, dumb, suffering Indian woman. Never does she muster courage to speak out. The village elders give options to Rani to prove her purity and faithfulness. To prove her chastity she has to put her hand in the boiling water, or hold a red hot iron rod, or she could swear by King Cobra by putting her hand in the anthill. Rani as previously told by Naga agrees to take oath by King Cobra. Hesitatingly she puts her hand into the anthill and pulls out the Cobra who is coyly curled around her hand. Rani in the court of the elders declares:

Rani: "Since coming to this village, I have held by this hand, only two...

Appanna: (Triumphantly) There. She admits it. Two she says. Two! Who are they!

Rani: My husband and ...

Appanna: And – say it – who else.

Rani: And this Cobra. (II, 39)

It is now for the first time that Rani speaks out boldly and with complete confidence.

Rani: Yes, my husband and this king Cobra. Except for these two, I have not touched any one of the male sex. Nor have I allowed any other male to touch me. If I lie, let the Cobra bite me. (II, 39)

Instead of biting, the Cobra slides up her shoulders and spreads its hood like an umbrella over the head. The people in full awe declare her to be a Goddess – Appanna when he combs the hair of Rani a dead Cobra falls from the hair, he also proclaims Rani as a Goddess. Rani does not ask any questions – and is destined to live the rest of her life as a Goddess.

Conclusion

Here are two plays based on similar folk tales. It is the interpretation which differs. The difference between *The Serpent's Bride* and *Naga-Mandala* is that of the bold and the meek. Rani is the picture of Indian womanhood, who meekly submits to fate. She does not ask questions, she sleeps with Naga who appears in the form of Appanna. The nocturnal visits make her happy, while in the day she is cursed, beaten and made to suffer. Yet she does not ask any questions, as she has never been allowed the freedom to do so. She remains imprisoned. But when the King Cobra spreads his hood over her head in protection, she is proclaimed as the Goddess, and once again she silently accepts her new fate without asking questions. Similarly, she accepts to live with Appanna. *Naga-Mandala* is the product of the folk oriented theatre. It has the popular old belief of the folk people, the blind faith, the mysterious elements, the norms of the old decadent society which does not allow women the freedom of expression.

While, *The Serpent's Bride*, which had its premier in 1928, at Riga (Latvia) was the product of the national movement, of which Aspazija was an active member. She as a poet and playwright used her pen as a weapon to inspire the people to rise against the foreign powers, change the society and demand their inherent right to live in freedom. She was aware and talked about injustices that society and individuals impose upon women. *The Serpent's Bride* raises the question that it is only love which can bind men and women, and not the law. It is a play about love, expression of longing, passion and pain, conflict and exquisite beauty. Ziednese is strong and bold. She rejects the laws of society, breaks away from the false and deceitful love. She rejects the offer of Saulgaitis to return to his arms. She, at the end, chooses death, as death to her was far better than prolonged torture, she proclaims:

The Earth is dark, all hearts are cold
There's more darkness here than light.
Much more hatred than true love.

Before departing she implores to the people "It is time for all to change".

References

Aspazija. *Her Life and Her Drama*. Translated from the original Latvian by Astrida B. Stahnke. Lahab: University Press of America Inc. 1984.

Karnad, Girish. *Naga-Mandala*. New Delhi: Oxford University Press, 1992.

6

Immigrant Spaces

Uma Parameswaran and Sadhu Binning

Supriya Agarwal

When one talks about an immigrant what comes to mind is not just individual psyche, history and narratives of belonging but certain collective issues as well. While settling down requires surrender, change, and self annihilation, there are several other elements which one has to come to terms to – as difference in terms of appearance, race, faith, ritualistic practices, language and political power. Immigrant spaces are not homogenous, they depend on how an immigrant adjusts and adapts to the new environment and nation. Education, qualification, usefulness to society, economic status and one's rootedness to one's culture – all factors effect settlement. The diasporic Indian today, views this process in several different ways. Their views are based on individual experience, which interfere with the whole process of belonging and adjustment.

Uma Parameswaran believes that belonging is a transplantation and one needs to nurture the feeling – home is where the heart is. As pointed out by Jasbir Jain in her essay "Identity, Home and Culture Through Dislocations" different diasporic writers have expressed varied opinions on this theme. Bharati Mukherjee has addressed the issue of belonging by distinguishing between the immigrants and the expatriate.[1] She believes that one should feel part of the community one has adopted and try to grow roots there and for this one has to face the trauma of self-transformation. Neil Bissoondath in his work *Selling Illusions: The Cult of Multiculturalism in Canada* talks about Canadianness, reflects upon ethnicity in the article "The Uses of Ethnicity" and says that "despite the attention of the past, the changes wrought by immigration and radically different circumstances must be recognized, assimilated and accepted" (111). Ashis Gupta is of the view that usefulness to a society leads to acceptance[2] while Avtar Brah in her essay "Diaspora, border and transnational identities" delineates specific features, which serve to distinguish diaspora as a theoretical concept from the historical experiences of diaspora. In fact the instinct for survival is always the ultimate moving force in migration but as time passes there are a series of mergers and divisions between the older and the newer set of values. In the case of minorities, from developing countries to developed, especially non-whites have to fight for both the erasure of a negative identity pre-given by the power groups and the forging of a positive identity. Parameswaran's plays move around the problems faced by South Asian and other visible minorities in Canada.

I want to problematise this issue further by bringing into my paper two specific factors which effect immigrant spaces – they are exclusion and exploitation – these force a sense of rejection on the immigrant. For this purpose I have taken up two plays – Uma Parameswaran's *Rootless but Green are the Boulevard Trees* and Sadhu Binning's *Lesson of a Different Kind.* Play is the medium of conveying more than the story and through stage setting, dance and music it becomes a living epitome of culture and tradition. Parameswaran's plays link epic India with modern Canada through myth and dance. The situations in the drama have been so structured as the real happenings in Indo-Canadian families. Drama has been called "speaking prose" by Parameswaran herself in her introduction to her work written in 1996.

Parameswaran who writes from her own experience of migration focuses in the play on the life of an average Indo-Canadian family which migrated to Canada for better prospects. Several factors related to the recognition and acceptance of the immigrant have been raised in this play, as the change called for, affects a total reconfiguration of memory, history and cultural values and at times the individual immigrant has to work within polarities between the question of belonging and not belonging. Savitri who is staying at Winnipeg in the year 1979 with her husband Sharad and who is the mother of teenagers – Jayant and Jyoti, goes to the office clad in a pant suit but once back home puts on a saree and kumkum. She is also very much worried for her daughter who is in love with a local Canadian boy, Andre. Savitri's Indian moral values about love, marriage, sex and family guide her consciousness and she experiences a clash in allegiance. We understand that there cannot be a total severance of ties or a complete transference of values and past cannot be done away with. Thus absorption cannot be total and immediate but there is an ongoing involvement with reality and there is an emergence of a new self.

The author has portrayed the dilemma of the Indian community whose effort is to transport an ancient culture, which is theirs to their new homeland. They do not want to give up Indian values, morals, mythology and other cultural links but want to reestablish the same in their new homeland. Inspite of a compromising attitude, the emptiness of the new self continuously troubles the immigrant, making him question his identity. Parameswaran enables the reader to understand the agony and trauma they are subject to and bring home to the reader the feeling of emptiness and exclusion felt by the characters. As Sharad says:

> It upsets me profoundly to find myself in a crowd. All those alien faces staring at or through you. It makes me wonder, makes me ask myself, what am I doing here? Who are those

> faceless people among whom my life is oozing away. Each so self contained, so complete, looking at me as though I shouldn't be there. It's a strange eerie feeling, all those discreetly questioning eyes that make me ask endless questions. (82)

Belonging does not have an individual or a collective dimension only, but also a generational one; there are people who are born in the country which their parents had adopted or been brought to. The generation which chose to displace itself has reasons of its own to feel happy in the new land but the effect of displacement becomes more acute in their children. No doubt dissatisfaction with one's situation is a common human trait but here it becomes more intense in the face of unequal treatment and injustice and the constant reminder of differences between the native and the alien. The next generation is caught between two worlds, two cultures and there is a struggle to carve one's own identity and find space. An anxious sense of dislocation is characteristic of the next generation. On the one hand is the pain of being a second-class citizen and on the other there is an impossibility of going back. Children feel the sting of racism in their school environment and most choose the survival technique of downplaying it but all react to it individually. Some feel dislocated and ghettoized between tradition and values given to them by their parents. In the sub-textual domains of the play the pressure exerted by parents on their children of imposing Indian values and morals has also been worked out. As Jayant tells his sister:

> Don't you come at me with all that crap about morals and Hindu values. I have had an earful from dad nineteen fucking years. He and his pipe dreams about India. Why the hell didn't he stay there? An atomic energy scientist he was right there from the beginning... Trombay, planning the whole bid. He'd have been a director by now. Instead he quits the place to be and rots here selling houses, Jesus, a crappy real estate broker, just one step better than an encyclopaedia salesman...(27)

The play gives expression to a vocabulary of resistance especially to that of the younger generation. In this dimension the parents bear the pangs of criticism because perhaps they did not have enough cause to support their shifting nor are they able to convey to their children a clear set of values. The parents are themselves confused whether to align themselves with the old or the new set up. The younger generation feels frustrated of racism. Jyoti, the twenty year old girl says to her brother Jayant "I sure hope it get into that thick head of yours that we are different and no matter what we do, we are never going to fit in here. Take to the road, get high, sleep around but still and all" (27). The play sensitizes us to the issue of oppression, subjugation, discrimination and also to the dilemma of the immigrant families who feel the pangs of dislocation but the questions that arise here: Is an amalgamation of all culture possible or has one culture to be displaced for the other and how long will the assimilation of minority groups or communities into nation state take?

Although the younger generation feels the vulnerability of their position they seem to undertake the question of multiculturalism and try to adopt a compromising attitude as Jayant comments, "Dad there's no our people and no old country for anyone in the world, anymore, least of all for us. This is our land and here we shall stay" (34). Parameswaran's play presents the mindset of the new generation that is grappling with the problem of dislocation and discrimination. Like their parents they do not have memory and nostalgia to fall back upon, nor do they cherish the comforts of the present life, as they have not known the discomforts. They experience a state of turmoil and pain because they are still searching for a cause as the mind cannot stay in a void and needs to anchor on something, on which it can thrive. There is a resistance expressed in the conversation of teenagers who do not have a political agenda, nor seek any sexual, social or religious politics. They are individuals with their own psychology and biography, reacting to situations in their own individual manner. Vithal who is

Veejala's son and Sharad's nephew unlike others condemns the merging and assimilation and says, "They want us out, we will be squashed like bugs soon. They've never wanted us and now we are a threat, we have to stay separate from them and stay together within" (54), expressing the fear of the minority. He wants that Indians should build a temple and that would help them to assimilate but in fact an outward manifestation is not what is needed to develop a sense of belonging and create a space for the immigrant. It is a gradual absorption, a coming together of opposites and as Savitri points out "Someday I hope Vithal and all of you will realize that we have already built that temple because we carry our Gods within us and with us wherever we go" (59).

The problem of exclusion faced by the immigrant and the need to create space has been worked out subtly by putting together the question of homeland and lost identity. Veejala, Sharad's sister, who is an assistant professor of Astronomy in Winnipeg quits "her position from backwoods of Canada for backwoods of India" (64). She believes that nothing of significance could be achieved in Canada as she never bothered to push herself politically and when asked if she had been discriminated against because of her sex, Dr. Veejala Moghle points out that she happens to be of the wrong colour as well. She feels that if life is to be wasted it might as well be in her native country than in Canada. Uma Parameswaran has very strongly addressed the problem of exclusion and discrimination meted out to the South Asian immigrant and the settling of the Indian community in Winnipeg is compared by the writer to the planting of Ontario poplar trees in Manitoba, all set up overnight around the new apartment block, appearing green and flourishing but which gradually take roots. An immigrant also has to adopt the organic process of gradual growth to carve space for oneself.

Sadhu Binning, born in Punjab and settled in Canada has problematized the exploitation of the doubly marginalized immigrant in his play *Lesson of a Different Kind.* Falling in the category of Canadian morality plays it deals with social, sexual, ethnic, racist and economic evils. Being an issue oriented drama it connects the Punjabi community with the larger community portraying the neo-colonial exploitation whereby the system employs middlemen who exploit the members of their own minority. Resham Gill, the protagonist is a student who has carried on a research on a work place and needs help to resolve a problem. The play reveals the system of work in an office and every comment the workers make is double-edged, sometimes overtly and sometimes ironically. Workers have got job through personal recommendation, the old woman is the aunt and the young female is the daughter-in-law of friends known to the "Boss". Nobody gets overtime and the boss treats them like family – meaning he deviously tells the worker's spouse or mother if he has a complaint about the worker. Daljit, the second female worker, is an activist who wishes to form a labour union. She is aware of the neocolonialism at work. She says:

> The employers here know that the best way to exploit immigrant labour is to do it through their own people and as a result you get this contracting system. And your poor cousin is only a link in the chain. The real villains are the people who keep this system in place. (93)

Every line of the play reflects a real-life situation and hints at injustices in the system and the community. Not only are the workers doing menial tasks of cleaning and serving but their condition of work is also pathetic. They sit on stolen chairs in a storage room amidst chemical containers, with no light or air anywhere. They have no freedom to take leave or speak against the system and when Resham wants to support the female worker in her protest against unreasonable firing, those who appreciate the report refuse to join, preferring to go for skiing or to a concert. There are categories of characters in the play – exploiters, exploited, rebels and some passive acceptors. At the same time they can be classified into three kinds of positions –

before and after migration. The original deplorable situation that forced them to migrate. The second position is the present one in which the living conditions are better than earlier ones but there is a compromise in the working situation and exploitation involved but there is third world of fantasy as also desired by the characters. Binning's play has the uneducated class of workers for whom earning a living is the main criterion of survival and they are bound by circumstances to accept what is being given to them as they have no choice. An old female worker says "Thanks to my wonderful nephew, I was working in the farms – very hard and dirty work in the farms – you know – this here is nice with good pay too and you get it every two weeks. This is like heaven, my son" (87). They live through their memories and dream and believe in their destiny. At another point the same character says:

> What I like is not possible. I want to sit in the winter sun on the rooftop of my home in the village and watch the little children play. That's what I like to do, not cleaning people's ashtrays and toilets – but everybody eats the fruits of their Karma – nobody can change that. (87)

Both the plays take certain common issues but the class of characters differ on one hand is the educated group who can voice their resentment and even have the choice to go back to the homeland as Veejala – the professor does in Parameswaran's play. Whereas Binning's characters are forced by circumstances to accept their condition. The very setting of both the plays is different. One has a greener aspect attached – there is openness, while the other is cramped. The place chosen is an enclosed factory room with no space for movement, thus presenting the ghettoized condition of the immigrant. Indian diaspora as reflected in these plays touches on various differences and hierarchies – linguistic, religious, and ethnic – that these groups of immigrants carried in their cultural gunnysacks as also the memories in their heart. Factors that also affected the character of the diaspora were whether the immigrants were from rural or urban backgrounds, whether they were blue or white collared workers.

The narrative of belonging expresses a self of loss, seclusion and dislocation felt not only by the characters but also by the writer and we observe that both Binning and Parameswaran have handled it differently, we can discern in their work a search of new identity, a loss of home and memories of past. The inner conflicts felt by common minority group has been worked out and the writers have suggested several ways of self-assertion and belonging. The migrated class banks upon their individual memories which to some extent hinder them from settlement but also renders strength to express their feelings. Vijay Misra has very subtly equalized the memory for lost land to mourning and in his essay "Diaspora and the Art of Impossible Mourning" observes "Without Memory, without a sense of loss, without a certain will to mythologies, life for many displaced people will become intolerable and diaspora theory would lose its ethical edge" (46). In fact belongingness is an adjustment which requires a bringing over and relocation of culture and a forward looking attitude and the process of belonging is finally culminated in the fact of acceptance.

Notes

1. Bharati Mukherjee "Two Sisters and Two Ways to Belong in America", *Times of India,* October 8, 1996. Made available by Professor Jasbir Jain as part of the Refresher Course Material on *Expatriate Writing: Theory and Practice.*
2. See Ashis Gupta's piece, "The Extraordinary Composition of an Expatriate Writer" and the interview given to Veena Singh titled "The Fragile Self Image of an Immigrant Writer", both in *Writers of the Indian Diaspora.* Ed. Jasbir Jain, 1998. Also see Uma Parameswaran, "Home is where your feet are, and may your heart be there too" in the same volume.

References

Binning, Sadhu. "Lesson of a Different Kind", *Saclit Drama Plays by South Asian Canadians.* Ed. Uma Parameswaran. Bangalore: IBH Prakashan, 1996.

Bissoondath, Neil. *Selling Illusions: The Cult of Multiculturalism in Canada.* Toronto: Penguin, 1994.

Brah, Avtar. "Diaspora, border and transnational identities", *Cartographies of Diaspora: Contesting Identities.* London: Routledge, 1996.

Jain, Jasbir. Ed. *Writers of the Indian Diaspora.* Jaipur: Rawat Publications, 1998.

Jain, Jasbir. "Identity, Home and Culture Through Dislocations". In *Dislocations and Multiculturalisms.* Ed. Jasbir Jain. Jaipur: Rawat Publications, 2004.

Misra, Vijay. "Diasporas and the Art of Impossible Mourning". *In Diaspora: Theories, Histories, Texts.* Ed. Makarand Paranjape. New Delhi: Indianlog Publications Pvt. Ltd., 2001.

Parameswaran, Uma. "Rootless But Green are the Boulevard Trees", *Saclit Drama Plays by South Asian Canadians.* Ed. Uma Parameswaran. Bangalore: IBH Prakashan, 1996.

7

Re-constructing the Past and Critiquing the Present

Mahasweta Devi's Plays

Bandana Chakrabarty

> We, being one-eyed deers, have not used the vast legacy of myths, social laws, ballads and songs. The folk material and the common people's version of events are assets to literature. In using them ...I have found my salvation.[1] – Mahasweta Devi

A social activist with an acute sense of Indian history makes Mahasweta Devi one of the most celebrated (Bengali) writers of recent times. She is engaged in portraying the inner lives of the tribal communities and landless labourers in her novels, short stories and plays. Less of a feminist and more of a humanist, Mahasweta Devi asserts that her text is a part of the discourse of class rather than gender. Her writing is known for giving 'voice to the voiceless' section of Indian society.

This essay is an attempt to evaluate Mahasweta Devi's dramatic achievement, which has long been ignored. Her plays, set in contemporary India, are an expression of her deep concern about the sufferings of the downtrodden. She has been a long time champion for the political, social and economic advancement of the tribals whom she characterises as "suffering spectators of the India that is travelling towards the 21st century" (Devi 1993: iii). To bring the message nearer home she dramatises her own novels and short stories, which are translated into English. She has chosen the medium of drama as E. Satyanaryana says, "She believes that plays can reach the large illiterate audience" (2000: 21).

In the second phase of her play writing in 1976-77, in the dramatisation of her short stories – *Aajir* (Slave), *Bayen* (Witch) and *Jal* (Water), Mahasweta Devi has reconstructed history and myth and brought them into contemporary setting using songs and rituals.

Devi has a penchant for interweaving tradition, myth and history with the present condition of tribal lives and shows how their lives are being so manipulated by society so as to perpetuate the subjugation of the marginalized people and prevent them from becoming fully human. In an interview in April 1983 she told Samik Bandyopadhyaya "A writer should document his own time and history. The socio-economic history of human development has always fascinated me.... So I chose to resurrect older periods in history in their immediate physicality, as if they were nothing less than contemporary." In the three plays under discussion. *Aajir, Bayen* and *Jal* Mahasweta Devi has made use of history and myth to bring to the surface a legacy of the exploitation and subjugation of indigenous peoples and attack the foundation on which contemporary corrupt society stands.

The play *Aajir* is about a slave, enslaved by an ancient bond, who discovers too late that the bond had turned into dust years ago and he was actually a free man. In the Preface to *Shrestha Galpa* Mahasweta Devi writes:

> I got the idea for *Aajir* from a slave bond executed by a slave who sold himself into slavery, reproduced in the family history of the Mustafis of UloBirnagar.... To capture the continuities between past and present, I bring legends, mythical figures and mythical happenings into a contemporary setting and make an ironic use of them. (qtd. *Five Plays* xii)

Bonded labour is an outcome of the socio-economic system prevalent in India. In an interview with Gayatri Chakravorty Spivak, Devi says, "In 1965, I started going to Palamu. The British took away tribal land and converted the tribals into debt bonded slaves. The Government of India had to introduce in 1976, the Bonded Labour System Abolition Act" (1993: iv).

But we know that this social evil still exists and persists in many remote rural areas. The tribal people are forced to mortgage their belongings and even themselves to the landlord who in turn provides for generations "oil for their hair, clothes for their bodies and rice for their stomachs" (36).

When the play opens, a voice is heard saying: "The term 'Aajir' stands for one who has sold himself into slavery for a paltry sum" (35) and then the stage light illuminates Paatan, the protagonist, who addresses the audience directly.

Paatan: I am an Aajir ... Ages ago in the hoary past there was once a terrible famine in the tracts of our Ayodhya hills. And then.... (35)

Paatan is conscious of his dehumanised condition and can do nothing but follow the tradition initiated by his ancestors. Paatan's forefather, Golak Kura 'born in a land of famines, nurtured by famines,' had doomed his descendants to the lives of Aajirs. The dramatic significance of this opening is reinforced by the transformation which Paatan undergoes on the stage, when he appears as Golak Kura, his forefather.

Paatan: Watch gentlemen, how a man becomes a slave from birth. Please allow me to become my forefather, Golak Kura. (He leaps to the centre of the stage)

By using the same actors to perform dual roles across time, class and status, the dramatic method underlines the commonality of humankind.

Samik Bandyopadhyay is of the view that Devi's use of the dramatic device of a character in the present enacting a happening in the past "is a metaphor for the continuities in the process of exploitation" (1997: xiii). She uses contrasts and parallels in her plays to concertise the life she knows best. The name Raavan Shunri in *Aajir* is suggestive of the mythological Raavan of the Ramayana epic who held Sita captive. By using the same character play the role of Raavan and Maatang as villains, Mahasweta Devi shows us the similarities as well as differences between them. Raavan, the ancient villain, buys the pair of Golak and Gairabidasi for a sum of three rupees, which is an exorbitant sum for the poor Golak and his wife. The present day Raavan in the form of Maatang is impotent, lusts after whores and 'filches' money from the government relief.

Paatan, the present day bonded slave is a step ahead of his ancestor Golak Kura. Whatever is handed down from generation to generation undergoes a change. Golak had resigned to his fate whereas Paatan revolts against the traditional constraints and wants to marry. But he realizes that there is no escape from his present situation. In the final scene of the play Paatan becomes defiant and says:

> Paatan: You bastard, Golak Kura: for a paltry three rupees you signed an Aajir's bond and left generations enslaved for life. I'll bring your line to an end. If there's no death for the Aajir's bond I'll finish it off with my death. (48)

Irony is the hallmark of Mahasweta Devi's plays. When Maatang, the master, discloses to Paatan that the Aajir's bond 'had turned to dust long ago in this *gaamcha* in which it had been once upon a time ...' (50), he is shocked. The man who always wanted to be free was actually a free man. For having killed Maatang's wife he finally offers the mob his hands and utters: "Come, bind me, do whatever you like to me" (51). Paatan laments, "Like everyone else in the world I was a free man and I alone didn't know" (51). The voice of the chorus sounds ominous. The Chorus epitomizes the fate of a bonded slave.

An aajir, you! An aajir you!
No life for you! No world for you!
An aajir you! No escape for you!(50)

Mahasweta Devi once again uses the dramatic device of recall/enactment and interweaving the past and the present in the play *Bayen* (Witch). Space is often used to indicate character changes and transformation. Devi resorts to an unusual use of transformation by presenting two characters in one being simultaneously on the stage. Roles are changed but the central image is one of enslavement. The two characters played by one-character represents the presence of the past in the present. Her use of myth, which deals with the curse of bondage, underlines its contemporary relevance for a society. As E. Satyanarayana observes, "The device of a character in the present performing an incident in the past by changing roles right in front of the audience not only allows the playwright to present different situations without any recourse to superfluous scenic displays but also assures the smooth flow of action, touching the play with an element of authenticity" (2000: 86).

The protagonist, Chandidasi Gangadasi, the gendered subaltern, buries dead children and guards the graves during the night as she belongs to the family of the illustrious Kalu Dome[2] who had been assigned to look after "all the cremation grounds of the world" (78). The play revolves round the predicament of a woman who is disposed of, discarded, rejected and subjugated. Here tradition and superstition are used as means to an exploitative end. As Jasbir Jain comments, "Gender continues to govern the individual's interaction with society and gender is both a social and cultural construct" (2002:54). Socially Chandidasi has to fulfill the role of a good mother at the same time she is culturally bound to fulfill the "job handed down to (her) by (her) ancestors" (82) though her hands rebel and yet she has to go on doing it.

Narrating the story of Kalu Dome to his son Bhagirath, Mahasweta Devi once again uses Malindar, Chandi's husband, as enacting the role of his ancestor, Kalu Dome. The stage direction says:

> Malindar: (He comes to the centre of the stage, turns his back to the audience, raises his face and shouts) what have you for us? For my community? (78)

Mahasweta Devi uses the story of the mythological king Raja Harishchandra, who had sold himself to an untouchable, an undertaker of the burial ground. Harishchandra worked as a watchman of the cremation ground. Malindar, narrating the story further says that when Harishchandra became king once again, he had gifts for all and sundry and when Kalu Dome asked for his share he was given "all the cremation grounds of the world" (78). Malindar makes a scathing attack on the inequalities prevalent in society when he explains to his son, Bhagirath, "The Brahmans, the Sadhus, the Sanyasis get cattle, land and gold and we get all the cremation grounds of the world" (79).

Malindar also tells his son that rules have changed and there are new laws laid down by the government but it is ironical that for untouchables nothing has changed. The cremation undertakers in Varanasi are called Dom Raja because they consider themselves descendants of Kalu Dome who employed Raja Harishchandra. The Doms of Kashi consider themselves as Rajas of the kingdom of the dead. Doms are scheduled castes who purview the burning ghats. Kalicharan, a dom, at Harishchandra ghat says, that although they come under the scheduled castes there is no job reservation for them. Their children will have to take up the same profession." In *Bayen* Malindar, though a dom, had learnt to write and sign (his) name, so the government gave him a job in the morgue. Even his son, Bhagirath, is sure of winning the district scholarship and of going to high school.

But the actual thrust of the play is not simply the father-son relation or the myth of Kalu Dom but the eternal conflict raging in the mind of Chandidasi – the loving mother as opposed to the professional gravedigger. When the play opens Chandi appears all alone on the stage wearing a filthy red sari, her hair dishevelled, she wears no jewellery. She has become a Bayen, a witch, who has been debarred entry into human society. Chandi has not only been ostracised by society but also by the family. The son when he grows up wants to do something for her. She had been branded as 'witch', primarily due to her maternal concern for the dead infants. Her anxiety to protect their shallow graves had been seen as an attempt to feed on the bodies. And she is punished by this forced separation from her only child.

Bandyopadhyay has observed, "Mahasweta touches the larger space of the social forces that separate mother and son in a male dominated system" (1997: xiii). The redemption comes for her when at the end of the play, she lays down her life in an attempt to avert a train accident. When the train guard demands from the mob the identity of the dead woman, it is her son, Bhagirath, who comes forward and owns her.

> Bhagirath: my mother, the late Chandidasi Gangadasi (suddenly breaks into loud weeping)... sir, Not a Bayen. She was never a Bayen, my mother (91).

The inhumanity perpetrated by the superstitious people, in reducing a fellow human being to the level of an animal, speaks volumes about the social ostracisation of the marginalized, the subaltern. Malindar tells his son:

> Malindar: They set up a hovel for her beside the railway track, every Saturday they leave a hamper of food for her at her doorstep. Once a year they give her two saris and two *gaamchhas* ... she couldn't let me out of her sight for a moment. But now she's been all alone for all these years. (87-88)

Bayen becomes the medium through which the nature of woman's subordination within the patriarchal structures of family, religion and society are examined. In "*A Literary Representation of the Subaltern*" Gayatri Spivak says that Mahasweta

Devi has always been 'gripped by the individual in history'. She writes of what may be called 'history imagined into fiction...' (95) The plausibility of Kalu Dome and Maghai Dome is that they could have existed as subalterns in a specific historical moment imagined and tested by orthodox assumptions. The term 'subaltern' is used to denote the entire people that are subordinate in terms of class, caste, age, gender and office.

The play *Jal* (Water) deals with the subaltern as class-subject. At the same time *Jal* is a new variant of the Ganga-Bhagirath myth. Myth and history flow into each other and in India, "myth finds a continuity in history while history constantly intervenes with myth" (Jain 2002: 12). Ganga, the holy river of the Hindus, is associated in myth and history. It is at once a river and goddess with a myth that Ganga would take on all the sins of the world.

The play *Jal* (Water) first appeared as a short story published in *Agnigarbha* and then collected and reprinted in *Shrestha Galpa* in 1985. The nine-page story has been transformed into a play covering over fifty pages. Though very little of the original story is contained in the play, yet it is all but about a battle over water rights. New characters have been introduced; it has a pro-woman angle and it also has the beginnings of a peasant rebellion. In *Jal* Maghai Dome, a traditional water diviner is entrusted by godly sanction to locate water. In Schwarz' opinion, "Through him Mahasweta Devi illustrates how Hindu religion and textual authority conspire to regulate contemporary oppression." Maghai believes that his ancestors had been chosen by Ganga – the river-goddess – to bring her hidden source to the surface in exchange for worship.

The ancient legends about the origins of the Ganga still structure contemporary rural society. It is believed that Ganga descended from Shiva's matted hair at the behest of King Bhagirath to save sixty thousand sons of Sagar. Devi has used as well as subverted the legend in this play. She shows that Maghai Dome has been enslaved since times immemorial. The water-diviner, the modern Bhagirath is an untouchable and religion has always been used to legalise and legitimize oppression and exploitation in India. Though he locates the spots where wells are to be dug for the Panchayat and other upper-caste people the irony is that he has no right to touch that water. Instead the untouchable women have to dig at the sands near the Charsa River for a 'cupful of water'. Maghai tells Santosh Babu:

> Maghai: I'm one of the Dome caste. We have been told that there's no untouchability in our sub-division and yet Santosh Babu you, your caste brothers and your relations won't let us draw water from any well. (104)

Maghai further accuses Santosh, the representative of the government thus:

> Maghai: Santosh, you won't give us the kerosene due to us against our ration cards and because of that our people die of snakebite. You hoard and trade in the drugs that the government sends for us. (104)

Critics like Shachi Arya feel, "The historical phenomena of exploitation, subjugation, dehumanization, poverty, alienation, has driven Mahasweta Devi to concentrate on the lives of the 'wretched of the earth' and give 'voice to the voiceless' " (63). In the original legend when Ganga, on her way to the nether world, asks King Bhagirath at what spot his sixty thousand relations were lying whom she was to deliver, he could not inform Ganga about the location. Ganga, before entering the sea, divided herself into a hundred streams so as to ensure the salvation of the cursed wherever they might be lying. In the play it is ironic that when the government sends officers to blast a new well, they are unable to find water. Ultimately Maghai's 'knowledge' comes in handy. The 'modern' Bhagirath performs a divining ritual, makes offerings to the goddess and is successful in locating the exact spot of the water. Jiten Maiti, the school teacher speaks on behalf of Maghai and tells the incredulous officers:

> Jiten: You blast the earth to divine water. He draws on the knowledge that he has inherited from his ancestors to divine water... Someone like Maghai can have both knowledge and culture. They have a mind like a continent that no one has dared to explore. (117)

The 'knowledge' and 'culture' of Maghai has been suppressed since ages. The landlord and the local authorities collude to guarantee that government relief and money will continue to pour into the district to end the drought conditions. The system of caste and class function in such a manner as to keep Maghai poor.

At the behest of the school teacher, Jiten Maiti, when the villagers build the dam it is a re-enactment of the scene from the epic Ramayana when the monkeys each carried a boulder to construct the bridge to Lanka to help Ram. Here the uncivilized villagers build the dam to help themselves. The song sung by the villagers is:

> Hei Lanka, Hei Lanka
> A boulder on your backs,
> A boulder on the ground,
> We're building the bridge to Lanka. (136)

The relationship between Maghai and his like and the people like Santosh, the SDO and the police is not a reciprocal one. The poor villagers cannot grasp the intricacies of modern social and economic organization and thus have to depend upon intermediaries who can easily exploit them. Veena Das comments upon the oppressive 'contract' that the tribe, caste or village is compelled to make with the modern institutions of domination. The police, SDO and Santosh connive at distorting the simple demand for water; blow it out into a cover-up for terrorist activity.

In the play and elsewhere in her work Devi questions the epochal history of caste and class exploitations in India. The police firing kills Maghai, the modern Bhagirath, and Jiten and Dhura, Maghai's rebel son, are captured by the police and imprisoned. The play ends with the dead body of Maghai, swaying on the 'crest of the wave' of the Charsa river. The water-diviner becomes one with the water.

Maghai's servitude may have little to do with the British but as Schwarz states, "What the British created were the conditions for the existence of agricultural capitalism, a system that facilitated the exploitation of greater numbers of Maghai Doms in whatever local terms were used to ideologically regulate it" (9). The independent Indian Government has made matters worse.

Rooted in history and myth and blending songs and rituals as well as contemporary reality with socio-economic milieu Devi's plays offer a view of India rarely seen in literature and help her in her working for her dream, "Fight for the tribals, downtrodden underprivileged and write creatively if and whenever I find the time" (Guha 2).

Notes

1. Mahasweta Devi: *Untapped Sources, Seminar.*
2. In the translation of *Jal* (Water) Samik Bandyopadhyaya uses the word 'Dome' whereas in *Subaltern Studies* the spelling used is Dom for the untouchables.

References

Arya, Shachi. *Tribal Activism: Voices of Protest*. New Delhi and Jaipur: Rawat Publications, 1998.

Das Veena. "Subaltern as Perspective". *Subaltern Studies VI*. Ed. Ranajit Guha. New Delhi: OUP, 1989.

Devi, Mahasweta. *Five Plays*. Trans. Samik Bandyopadhyaya. Calcutta: Seagull Books, 1997.

—. *Imaginary Maps*. Trans. Gayatri Chakravorty Spivak. Calcutta: Thema, 1993.

Guha, Ranajit. Ed. *Subaltern Studies* X. New Delhi: OUP, 1998.

Jain, Jasbir. *Writing Women Across Cultures*, New Delhi and Jaipur Rawat Publications, 2002.

Satyanarayana, E. *Indian Drama: The Plays of Mahasweta Devi*. New Delhi: Prestige, 2000.

Schwarz, Henry. "Postcolonial Performance: Texts and Contexts of Mahasweta Devi." *Sharp* Issue 2. University of Sussex, 2002.

Sen, Asok. "Subaltern Studies: Capital, Class and Community." *Subaltern Studies V*. Ed. Ranajit Guha. New Delhi: OUP, 1987.

Spivak, Gayatri Chakravorty. "A Literary Representation of the Subaltern". *Subaltern Studies V*. New Delhi: OUP, 1987.

8

Gender Crossings

Vijay Tendulkar's Deconstructive Axis in *Sakharam Binder*, *Kamala* and *Kanyadaan*

Sudha Rai

Vijay Tendulkar's plays persistently probe the operations of power, the hidden seams of violence in Indian history and the obstacles that stand in the way of social change and modernization. By examining three plays – *Sakharam Binder* (1972), *Kamala* (1981) and *Kanyadaan* (1983) I illustrate the concept of 'gender crossings', of masculinities and femininities, in the context of caste and family structures, pivotal to the deconstructive dramatic axis of Tendulkar.

In each of the three plays mentioned above, Tendulkar takes up a family situation, an existing set of relationships and roles. This domestic and private space is gradually propelled into a vortex of turbulent conflict belonging to the public space of communalism or secularism, politics and power. In *Sakharam Binder*, Sakharam's masculinity overrides his much valorized friendship with the Muslim Dawood, whom he has earlier defended against his 'wife' Laxmi over the issue of her excluding Dawood at the Ganesh Chaturthi aarti in their home. *Kamala* (based on a real-life media expose of the flesh racket), makes transparent the journalist Jaisingh's selfless 'protection' of the adivasi Kamala, as only a career-boosting ploy. By the time we move to the testing ground of *Kanyadaan*, conservative brahminical patriarchy is rejected in plain speech and through actions by Jyoti, a young, educated Brahmin, when she marries a Dalit poet.

Tendulkar places the so-called champions of a caste-free society and egalitarianism on the pinhead of a powerful deconstructive moment, where their limits are exposed. The onus of the deconstructive moment (effected through a networking of situations, opinions and emotions) ultimately rests as I argue, with Tendulkar's women protagonists who negotiate masculinities and femininities at these gender crossings, emerging as change agents in Indian society.

The deconstructive moment is shaped by Tendulkar as one wherein individuals transcend the strategies of systemic manipulation, choosing to stand by their own values of humanity/womanhood. Masculinity is thereby constructed as a weak and regressive force, prone to violence and corruption. The charge of the deconstructive moment of theatre, lies in the fact that what is achieved at the level of women's consciousness is a realization that is not only personal, but pierces through the system as a whole.

The subtle psychological process in the passage from an essentialized self (of the woman or Dalit character) to an awakened self is given concrete expression on stage in the charged and poised momentum of a deconstructive moment. The new existential awareness pierces the blindness of the social condition. At the level of a theatrical experience, the impact of deconstructive aesthetics can be summed up as the propelling of the audience into self-awareness and "deconstructive thinking" about the institution of marriage and the play of masculinities in denying women selfhood.

Sakharam, the binder who has run away from home when only eleven years, protagonist of Tendulkar's controversial drama *Sakharam Binder*, is in his own eyes, a rebel against the Brahminical system. "My mother used to say, the brat's shameless. He's a Mahar born in Brahmin home." Laxmi his current mistress, is his seventh woman. The violence in his personality, (which he expresses through verbal and physical abuse with his current mistress Laxmi), is probably a reaction to the frequent beatings he has received at the hands of his father. Sakharam's defence of his male sexual needs, euphemistically referred to as "the itch" in the play, obstructs his sensitivity to the impact of such masculinity upon the body and mind of women. Tendulkar penetrates the so called honesty of Sakharam as a desired value, by interrogating it with Laxmi's silences, her cowering and whimpering and finally her outburst against Sakharam's aggressive masculinity, when he orders, "You'll have to be a wife to me". "But I must be respected in my own house. I am the master here" (126), he proclaims, even more offensive when drunk. "We're not saints. We're men" (127), he opines. Sakharam berates the hypocrisies of husbands who frequent prostitutes on the sly. He condemns their violence stating "for them the woman's just dirt that's all" (129).

Friend to Dawood Miya, with whom he puffs his ganja, Laxmi's anti-Muslim feelings about Mian on the occasion of Ganesh Chaturthi when she doesn't want him to join Aarti, sends Sakharam into a tearing rage. Sakharam controls Laxmi's emotions, even her sense of playfulness, when he catches her in conversation with an ant. Possessive to the core, he has the traits of a sadist; he inflicts pain on Laxmi and orders her to laugh, "Laugh or I'll choke the life out of you" (141).

Tendulkar deconstructs the universalisms that originate from Sakharam's masculinity, questioning Sakhram's essentialization of truth. "They recognise only one sin in God's court. That's falsehood. It is the worst possible sin" (142). Act I concludes with a parting between Sakharam and Laxmi (who leaves to live with her nephew), both parties exasperated with the year long association. Act II presents Sakharam with a new mistress Champa. More self-confident than Laxmi, she orders Sakharam around. He repeats his formula of himself being the master of the house and she a mere wife. Tea making is in his view "a woman's job." He says the women must always speak with restraint. "She has to carry out all the duties of a wife" (159). Champa who has walked out on her drunken husband Fauzdar Shinde, is a strong women who retaliates with physical blows and verbal abuse for all the physical abuse her husband did on her. She is the other to the 'pativrata nari', Laxmi. As a strategy of characterization, Tendulkar also uses Champa as a female mirror of aggressive masculine behaviour; she drinks, swears, beats men and is an idler rather than the angel in the house. When Laxmi returns, thrown out by her nephew's wife, Sakharam too throws her out of his house.

In Act III the binaries of traditional masculinity and femininity are collapsed, with the establishing of the courtesy and caring relationship of the two 'mistresses' Champa and Laxmi. These women, as a subversive counter discourse to patriarchy, slight male impotency. However the female bonding that has the potential to fracture the supremacy of the male, is thwarted when Sakharam murders Champa by squeezing her neck, after Laxmi leaks out Champa's infidelity with Dawood, Sakharam allows himself to be guided by her and they burn Champa's body in their own courtyard.

Tendulkar locates the violence in lower class Indian society in patriarchal, caste bound family structures that have seared the consciousness of men like Sakharam. Women with religious faith like Laxmi, emerge as stronger individuals. The play ends on a note of domesticization of the male by the combined onslaught of the 'benign' and 'terrible' aspects of female power in Indian culture. It is Sakharam's mother's insult in childhood, where she 'labels' him as a Mahar untouchable that scars his identity, so that he chooses to become a social deviant, an outsider by choice. Despite a caste-based explanation, Tendulkar drives home with irony that a man like Sakharam can never be outsider to his own masculine choices.

Orthodox attitudes and practices in Indian society such as castigation of the female for male impotency, the stigma attached to the 'barren woman' blamed for not upholding male honour and family pride by bearing a child, and hypocrisy within the patriarchal institution of marriage are developed within the middle-class family structure of Tendulkar's *Kamala*.

In Tendulkar's *Kamala* the theme of the purchase of an adivasi girl Kamala by the journalist Jaisingh, moves beyond the social problem of trafficking in women, to deconstruct and subvert the sexism within marriage. Sarita, a role model, as Jaisingh's wife, makes a radical interrogation of the slavery of women within marriage. Her consciousness is awakened by her dialogue with Kamala, who is an exhibit, a mere pawn in the power game between media and society.

Kamala's frank and innocent description of her understanding of man-woman relations through the idea of 'purchase' 'sale' and 'slavery' and her willingness to be Jaisingh's 'kept woman' and the womb that will bear the children he and Sarita do not have, bring Sarita face to face with her own exploitation and bondage.

The mirror self of Kamala underlines Sarita's marginalisation within marriage and it is as if through a single, powerful leap of consciousness, she crosses over to the new feminist ground of reality:

> I was asleep. I was unconscious even when I was awake. Kamala woke me up. With a shock. Kamala showed me everything. Because of her, I suddenly saw things clearly. I saw that the man I thought my partner was the master of slave. I have no right at all in this house. Because I'm a slave. Slaves don't have rights do they, Kakasaheb? They must only slave away. Dance to their master's whim. Laugh, when he says laugh. Cry, when he says, cry. When he says, pick up the phone, they must pick it up. When he says, come to a party, they must go. When he says, lie on the bed, they...(46)

Kakasaheb, her uncle defends marriage, and Jaisingh, from a masculinist essentialist perspective. "That's why he's a man.

And that's why there's manhood in the world" (47). Even though Sarita capitulates to Jaisingh's immediate crisis of being thrown out of his job (because he has stirred a hornet's nest by exposing the flesh racket), the play's conclusion grants Sarita emancipation at the intellectual level. "But a day will come Kakasaheb when I will stop being a slave. I'll no longer be an object to be used and thrown away, I'll do what I wish and no one will rule over me. That day has to come, and I'll pay whatever price I have to pay for it" (52).

The impasse that the nascent Dalit identity creates in the modernization of the Indian nation, is the subject of Vijay Tendulkar's drama *Kanyadaan* (1983), while focusing on the dynamics of gender and caste in the context of family relationships and transmitted family values. Implicated in caste and gender discourses, these values are subjected to critical self-scrutiny when Jyoti, the daughter of a Brahmin family, decides to marry a Dalit writer, Arun. The family members namely the father Nath, a socialist MLC, his wife Seva, a social worker, Jyoti their daughter and Satyaprakash, their son, are equally, though with varying degrees of intensity and honesty forced to confront their stereotype beliefs, and prejudices about caste. The journey of understanding and disillusionment each of the four members of the family takes in the process, intertwined, yet separate, is Tendulkar's structure for mapping the volatile issue of a Dalit awakening that resists their condition of 'objugation' (objectification and subjugation) (Raj: 1998) and its consequences for the Brahmin middle class. Tendulkar also relates the violent oppositional clash of Brahmin and Dalit to the less visible fabric of gendered attitudes, constructions and stereotypes.

Though the educated middle class woman of the eighties has made headway in her interrogation of the masculine givens, set ways of social thinking or apparently logical formulations of experience, the rise of Dalit identity as Tendulkar suggests, may precipitate the birth of a new traditional masculinity. Modernity therefore brings with it the challenges of eroding a patriarchal masculinity, and yet, in an 'emasculated' community like the Dalits, make acceptable the release of an aggressive masculinity. Similarly, the erasure of stereotypes of femininity by the middle class educated working class women at one level, may involve the recovery of a subjugated sacrificing model of femininity (which may be rationalized as romantic love), when a woman of the upper caste like Jyoti surrenders herself to the Dalit masculine identity of Arun.

The first act of *Kanyadaan* interrogates Nath's ideological masculinity that imposes a 'centre' on family and nation that is only seemingly democratic. Self absorbed in his own routine as an MLC, he travels frequently to chair meetings and make speeches. His wife Seva leads a similar existence, responding to her duties as a social worker. Nath and Seva barely live under the same roof for length of time, and even when they do, are found hooked to their telephone. Nath brags about the open culture of his home: "We have a democracy in this house and we are proud of it. Democracy outside and dictatorship in the home, we don't know these two-timing tricks" (4), but his summations are interrogated by others in his family.

The act concludes with Nath urging Jyoti to stick to her resolve to marry Arun and "not run away from the challenge." Clinically weighing the pros and cons of the proposed marriage on an intellectual, abstract plane, Nath makes his daughter the scapegoat of his socialist commitment, congratulating himself for "having broken the caste barriers in the real sense for the first time." He is oblivious of the pitfalls of the cultural divide between Dalit and Brahmin that his wife Seva considers as virtually impossible to bridge; She warns Jyoti, "You have been brought up in a specific culture. To erase or to change all this overnight is just not possible. He is different in every way. You may not be able to handle it". She also adds, "later there is no chance for a woman to hide or to run away" (13).

The tussle between husband Nath and wife Seva boils down to his fixation with translating an ideology and risking the experiment of the inter caste marriage and Seva's resistance on the grounds of motherhood and the possible violation of her daughter's female self. "Does it means that my daughter's life is to be used for an experiment", Seva asks indignantly. "You may have your views. I cannot accept them. I am her mother" (28). Jayaprakash, Jyoti's brother, is reserved when it comes to approving his mother's decision. As he points out, Nath's approval of Arun as a husband, is on the grounds of caste (i.e. because he is a Dalit whom the Brahmins have betrayed for generations). This self-consciousness about caste is for, Jayaprakash, itself a form of casteism.

The second act of the play concludes with Nath's idealism turned upside down, the shattering of his centre captured in the stage directions which describe his breaking down and collapsing on the sofa, as much as in the sound effects as of "huge buildings hurtling down". As Jyoti points out to him; "Bhai, the way you talk, it's as if you have been specially appointed for the task of reminding all the people in the world of their duties" (2).

Nath laments the post-independence decline of India, pointing the finger everywhere but at himself. "The visions we had of the future of this nation before independence", he exclaims, "And what we are forced to see today!" In the same breath he asks Jyoti whether she has cleaned his lime juice flask and whether she has put in his shaving brush and towel.

However, Tendulkar undercuts complacent, uncritical observations like these, with behavioural patterns that follow, making clear to the reader/viewer that the rigid core of patriarchy is somewhere intact. Jyoti for example, needs to pick up her courage before initiating dialogue on a matter as important to her as her marriage. Not much love is lost between Nath and Seva. As he states "the call of the nation is far more important than the call of a wife" (5). Husband and wife are preoccupied with their own lives and Jyoti's announcement of her decision to get married to Arun meets with varying reactions. For Nath it is a coup since his socialist agenda is ratified through the inter-caste marriage. Seva however responds with practical anxieties about the success of the marriage. Tendulkar examines, through the interplay of thoughts, emotions and responses amongst the five lead characters of *Kanyadaan*, the subtle ways in which Dalit diversity is rejected or applauded, historicized and judged, and in the second and final act of the drama, disowned by the so called custodians of 'diversity' and an egalitarian society.

In a decisive closure to parental arbitration in the matter, Jyoti who has been subjected to physical violence by Arun after their marriage, even kicked in the stomach, when Arun is in one of the drunken states, finally walks out of her parent's home, which she now perceives to be a citadel of spurious values of egalitarianism. Defiantly she asserts:

> I have my husband. I am not a widow. Even if I become one I shan't knock at your door. I am not Jyoti Yadunath Devlalikar now, I am Jyoti Arun Athavale, a scavenger. I don't say harijan. I despise the term. I am an untouchable, a scavenger. I am one of them. Don't touch me. Fly from my shadow, otherwise my fire will scorch your comfortable values. (70)

In its rewriting of a patriarchal social text, *Kanyadaan* debunks the segregation of the politics of the domestic space from the politics in the world 'out there'. In the opening scene of the first act of the play, Seva, rebukes her husband for constantly imposing distorted meanings on the words she uses. Attributing this to his work as a politician, Seva tells her husband, "Don't thrust your politics into this house." Seva's desire that the political spaces should be segregated from the domestic space is defeated through multiple ironies that structure *Kanyadaan*, as the manipulations of a caste and power-governed society make inroads into their home.

The marriage does not only upset the societal divide between Brahmin and Dalit communities, as Tendulkar shows us, the marriage unleashes the dormant political currents waiting to capitalize on the new nexus between caste and power. The marginalised too not only seize the opportunity to mobilize their claim to status and power but practise covert forms of revenge.

The release of the suppressed Dalit voice becomes instrumental in deconstructing caste identities, social values, political ideologies, splintering role models of patriarchal or parental identities hitherto taken as givens. Jyoti and her brother Jayaprakash as much as the Dalit Arun as the new generation of India, make radical interrogations of the reformist cultural mission of the contemporary leadership (both politicians and social workers), whose acceptance of the margins is only a form of tokenism. Tendulkar's contribution as a dramatist is to bring into confrontational dialogue, Brahmin and Dalit voices and the charged silences that punctuate their encounters, capturing the tension and the undissolved mistrust between the two sides. Masculinities and femininities are constantly deconstructed and also reconstructed to represent the complexity of relationships between the marginalised and the power centric, drawing out into the conscious domain the hidden threads of the web of codified cultural existence in India.

Jyoti marries Arun, suffers his anger and violence, and finally rejects the parental home as a symbol of failed idealism. The crystallization of her understanding of the complexity of Dalit consciousness, which must be accepted at any cost, is the play's transcendence of the divide between the 'self' and the 'other' constructed as I have argued, in two central oppositions – the first between Brahmin and Dalit identity, the second between masculinity and femininity.

Seva brings an ambivalent cultural feminity to Jyoti's decision to marry. It contains maternal concern, pragmatism and a middle-class feminist consciousness that urges Jyoti to be aware of her own rights as a woman. Nath's masculinity concedes intellectual approval to Jyoti's decision but cannot participate at the emotional level, in the consequences of her choice. In this sense, he has precious little cultural critical awareness as insider to understand the grassroots hurdles of an inter-caste marriage.

In its construction of a subversive counter discourse, which undermines Brahminical attempts to easily appropriate and domesticate it, *Kanyadaan* invites us to study and probe the issues of Dalit anger. Centuries of abuse of the Dalit right to humanity are thrown up in Arun's dialogues so as to create embarrassment and discomfort, and confusion and failure on the part of the Brahmin intelligentsia to deal with it. Arun says, "At times a fire blazes – I want to set fire to the whole world. Strangle throats, rape and kill. Drink up the blood of the beasts, your high caste society" (18). He makes a conscious attempt to shock Jyoti's parents by projecting her life with him in its most debased form, claiming her (albeit jokingly) as the subjugated wife of a downtrodden Dalit, whom society has left with no option but to make a living, by brewing illicit liquor: "It is a first class profession for two persons. The man bribes the police and the wife serves customers. People call her aunty. The more striking the aunty's looks, the brisker the trade...." (21).

Tendulkar stirs many embedded issues of caste and gender identity, caught in essentialisms of one kind or the other, cemented by the elites in Indian society, and internalized by the subjugated too. Before a further set of essentialist stereotypes are consolidated though the inexorable demands of utilitarian politics. Tendulkar makes visible the power politics that appropriate the "old center" and the "old margins" to perpetuate divisive mind sets, to reignite the hostilities of caste politics. It is perhaps only Jyoti who takes a conscious decision to surrender privilege, status, the security of her parental home, and puts at risk even the body, whom Tendulkar posits as a conscious agent of social change. As Jyoti tells her father, "I have to stop thinking and learn to live." Jyoti makes a progressive choice, by destroying an imbibed caste consciousness while, ironically Arun to constitute his own requirements of a Dalit masculinity. The message she leaves us with is a clear one it is not communities that are superior or inferior, but individuals who are so.

The male critics of the system or establishment values in Tendulkar's dramas such as the binder Sakharam, the MLC Nath and the journalist Jaisingh are exposed as male chauvinists who exhibit aggressive and/or conservative masculinities. The real liberation of consciousness in the direction of modernity takes place in varying degrees for the women characters in these plays, namely Laxmi and Champa (Sakharam's mistresses), Sarita (Jaisingh's obedient wife) and Jyoti (Nath's daughter who marries the Dalit poet Arun). Tendulkar pointedly directs our attention to the closed domestic, private spaces, of marriage and family as volatile sites for conflicting masculinities and femininities where there is more urgent need for social change.

References

Raj, M.C. *From Periphery to Centre:* Analysis of the Paradigms of Globalization, Casteism and Dalitism. Tumkur: Ambedkar Resource Centre and REDS, 1998.

Tendulkar, Vijay. *Collected Plays in Translation.* New Delhi: Oxford University Press, 2003.

—. *Kanyadaan.* Translated by Gowri Ramanarayan. New Delhi: Oxford University Press, 2002.

9

'Viewing' Women

An Exploration of Ezekiel's Plays

Shaila Mahan

Nissim Ezekiel, one of the pioneer Indian English poets, was also a playwright who wrote as many as six plays in an era when drama was distinctly a 'Cinderella' like figure in Indian English writing. His plays have escaped critical scrutiny primarily because of the sporadic nature of Ezekiel's dramatic output which makes it verily impossible to consider seriously his development as a dramatist. In one of his interviews, Ezekiel himself admitted: "I have not yet written plays substantial enough to be considered in terms of good, better, best and worst – *Nalini* (1969) and *Marriage Poem* (1969) – I consider worth staging" (Reddy, 15). This paper attempts to focus on the delineation of women characters in these plays in order to reflect the significant gender issues that Ezekiel raises and analyses, the depiction of women as the object of the 'male gaze'. Although the discussion will be centred mainly around the dominant theme of man-woman relationship and the portrayal of women as victims of the pressures of gender code, the theatrical devices employed by him are in themselves important as means of framing the character projection.

Feminist theories have revealed how 'sex' is a biologically determined entity but 'gender' is essentially a socio-cultural construct. Simone de Beauvoir in *The Second Sex* points out how men regard women as the 'other', "She is the incidental, the inessential as opposed to the essential. He is the subject, he is the Absolute, She is the other" (Beauvoir, 16). As this view emphasizes, traditionally 'masculinity' is seen as the behavioural norm, while 'feminity' is an aberration or distortion. Critical writers draw on two main strands of theoretical research in treating themes related to femininity and its construction. The first focuses on the oppressive aspect of gender stereotyping. Theorists such as Betty Friedan, Kate Millet, Elizabeth Janeway and Ann Oakley paved the way for this approach which represented women as sex objects, wives and mothers. These roles restricted women to the private sphere of sexual relations and family life while preventing their entry into the professional field. The other approach has been the philosophical and psychological strand of research which has influenced women's writings and is chiefly associated with French feminists and their contestation of Freudian ideas and responses to Lacanian and Derridean theories. Helene Cixous, Julia Kristeva and Luce Irigaray building on Simone de Beauvoir's portrayal of women as the 'other' of men have examined the part played by the set of binary opposites produced by the patriarchal culture leading to identification of man with mind and culture and woman with body and nature. This identification of woman with nature and the body gives rise to the dominant theme of the 'male gaze' and the circulation of rather negative/oppressive images of women which it promotes in turn.

It was Laura Mulvey, a feminist film theorist who coined the term 'male gaze' and first used the concept in her article 'Visual Pleasure and Narrative Cinema', wherein she made use of the psychoanalytic theory (in a version influenced by J. Lacan) with reference to cinematic spectatorship. She revealed how men as active, controlling subjects usually treat women as little more than passive objects of desire for them and do not allow women to be desiring sexual objects in their own right.

The 'gaze' is in possession of men who do the looking; women in this view exist merely to be looked upon. This notion is extended in the frame-work of feminist theory, where it can deal with how men look at women, how women look at themselves and other women, and the effects surrounding this. The male gaze is used in feminist theory whereby a man gazes at a woman. Such feminist theorists posit that since it is almost always the females who are being gazed upon by the male, the male exhibits power over the woman. Laura Mulvey identifies the action of possessing a gaze as being intrinsically male and identifies the action of being gazed upon with the female. These point to the binaries of male/active, female/passive.

The present paper explores different manifestations which the identification of woman with body and nature can assume and will view woman's position as the object of the 'male gaze' through a close reading of Ezekiel's plays.

A comedy in three acts, *Nalini* is the story of two men, Bharat and Raj, who are both advertising executives and a woman, Nalini, who is a budding painter. Depicting the everyday milieu of the art world and the publicity media, the play revolves around Nalini's desire to hold an exhibition of her paintings and Raj, who knows her, approaches his friend, Bharat, to organize the publicity for Nalini's show. As the play progresses, we find that both men, particularly Bharat, have a set, stereotyped image of Nalini, as they do of all women. As a result, a major undercurrent of the play seems to demolish these stereotypes by presenting the 'real' Nalini as a woman of greater intelligence and substance than either Raj or Bharat. At this level, one might feel that the playwright is striving to liberate Nalini from the "male gaze" and the effort seems virtually a feminist statement in theatre.

And yet that will be too simplistic (or shall we say idealistic?) a reading of Ezekiel's play. Raj who approaches Bharat and requests him to plan the publicity for Nalini's exhibition, is hardly interested in paintings or artistic creations; he actually sees them merely as a vehicle for getting closer to Nalini (that too only physically, not emotionally). The Nalini as imagined by Bharat that is truly revealing: for him Nalini is "slender and sweet, tall, fair, completely mod, in style, her hair done up in a bee-hive, her choli short, low cut and backless, revealing a figure of some splendour. She wears her sari like a tight skirt and walks in it with casual elegance" (*Nalini*, 25). He conceives her as a vulnerable, "arty" woman who would be an easy "conquest". Ezekiel projects Bharat seeing Nalini basically in a physical, sex object form: this Nalini is an archetypal male conception of the female.

The dramatist even makes Bharat envisage his response to Nalini in a characteristic fashion. Ezekiel conceives a whole episode in the play where Bharat has a lascivious daydream in which Nalini becomes what "he" expects her to be; he enacts with her an entire sequence of disrobing and love-making in exactly the way that Bharat [and most men like him] would want Nalini to respond. The author employs a clever stage device, employing multiple settings of darkness and music to create a strong dramatic impact through this fantasy.

Ezekiel, however, also counterposes a "real" Nalini who emerges into light to continue the conversation about publicity for her exhibition and her paintings. While she is more or less similar in physical appearance to Bharat's dream girl, the 'real' Nalini is shown to be considerably less attractive. She is shorter and less slender and is soberly dressed but there is a strong hint of sensuality even in her persona. But it is in her attitude that the real Nalini is a contrast to the hyper-fantasy that Bharat has created about her. She seems a modern woman with a mind of her own; an independent woman who does not want to be dependent on anyone, including her own parents. When Bharat makes advances and puts his arm around Nalini, she shrugs him off coldly, making it amply clear that she is not available. Although she admits that many women would fall prey to his empty charms, Nalini herself rejects Bharat's advances. To his suggestion that she is a prude, Nalini retorts: "Prude? For not surrendering to your empty charm, your hollow ideas. You expect me to consider you honest because you admit your weakness. It's sheer hypocrisy!" (36).

Ezekiel also echoes in the play another subtle but rarely explored issue, namely the male inability to accept being rejected by any woman. Bharat and Raj picture Nalini as being readily available but find it deeply unsettling when she turns them down. After Nalini's rejection, the responses of her suitors are not only subtle theatre but also an expose of male chauvinistic ideas and attitudes. When she bids him goodbye, Bharat utters "Damn, Damn, Damn" and smashes his and her glasses! (43).

Later in the third act, the confused Bharat and Raj try to figure out which Nalini the woman, object of their sexual fantasies or the actual person who refuses to be objectified is the real Nalini. They discuss Nalini and their encounter with her, they (especially Bharat) cannot reconcile to the reality of Nalini, as Bharat tells Raj, the real Nalini is "serious...She has ideas...You can't fool her....She provokes, she challenges, she questions, she contradicts...She's an independent woman....she is a living insult to me and to you, to all of us. Damn her" (45).

Clearly, Ezekiel uses Bharat's character to ridicule men who cannot see woman as a person, for men like him, the second Nalini is not to be found anywhere. As Bharat remarks towards the end of the play, the real Nalini, "hasn't yet been born. Someone has imagined her. She doesn't actually exist" (52). In fact one is tempted to suggest that Ezekiel's essential achievement in the play is to reveal how most men [especially frivolous ones like Bharat and Raj] are unable to cope with "woman as a person", and how they tend to view 'women' only as a general category. This point is brought out vividly through a sharp exchange between Bharat and Nalini. When Bharat claims "I understand women", Nalini is quick to retort" I am not women. I am a woman". She accuses him. "You have a formula; you can't imagine an individual woman. You can't believe that a woman may want to create a world of her own just as a creative man does, a woman with the will to explore herself and the world around her" (38). These words seem to suggest that women too have an identity of their own.

The dramatist satirizes the superficial lifestyle of his male characters and in doing so exposes the traditional male/social attitudes towards women. Bharat is one such example who is a typical male chauvinist and makes derogatory remarks about women: "Has it struck you that we have a valuable equation there: "The less women talk, the less nonsense they talk?" (13). A little later he says: "Women just love words.... No action, no trouble. Just big words" (18). At another place he remarks: "What do you mean by freedom and adventure and experience? For most of us abroad, it only means encounters with women" (14).

The play reflects a considerable degree of imagination as Ezekiel makes a constant and clever use of the interplay between the imaginary and the real. The character of Nalini itself is tinged with fantasy. There is a double vision of Nalini – one imagined by Bharat in his day dream and the other – a real one. The dream character is smart and pretty but possesses no talent for painting; the other 'real' Nalini is a genuine artist and serious challenger of human predicament. In the course of the play, Nalini admits to Bharat that she sees herself as being divided into two persons; one is the ordinary everyday unimaginative Nalini and the second is the creative Nalini "who suffered from some unimaginable upheaval within her." This is how she talks about her identity crisis, "How long can I keep this other woman at a distance? Her experience is necessary to me. Without it I am nothing. I can never become an artist" (42).

There is skilful use of ironical fantasy in the play. The playwright uses fantasy for creating an alternate reality. By contrasting two or more visions of reality projected in the play Ezekiel drives home an important point. In the final act, Raj and Bharat wonder which of the two Nalini is real. They realize that none of them is real perhaps both Nalini are a figment of their imagination. The contrast between the real and the phantom Nalini of a dream serves to expose the philistinism of these business executives. Moreover, the projection of the contrasting features of the real and the imaginary Nalini blur the distinct identity of the two giving the impression to the spectators that the second Nalini is as unreal as the first. Bharat and Raj are confused: "She did upset me but she is not quite real. It is the first Nalini who is real. She is already on the scene. She is to be found everywhere. But the second Nalini is not to be found anywhere" (52).

The circulation of images of women produced by the media, particularly the advertising industry, are so oppressively pervasive that some men tend to view women only as a 'spectacle'. Cleverly, Ezekiel has set the present play in the advertising world, a world that he personally knew well and where the objectification of woman is a common feature. The dream Nalini is a perfect example of such a stereotypical representation. Ezekiel projects Bharat and Raj seeing Nalini simply as a physical sex object. In the third act addressing the first Nalini Raj tells her "We've read about you in Femina – We've read about you in Eve's Weekly – You are 35-24-35" (48).

If all this is not enough, the male protagonists also express a very poor opinion of the talents or intelligence of Nalini or indeed of any woman aspiring to be an artist. Ezekiel permits Bharat to debunk women authors in a really sharp manner, "The female writers are the most insufferable of all. Most of them write only middles for *The Times of India* and articles about their foreign junkets and intimate revelations about their quarrels with their husbands and difficulties with their children, all in a coy, giggly manner as if saying all the time, Look I can write too, I'm sensitive, I have feelings" (13). Given this sharp tone, one wonders which side the playwright himself stands on. It is true that Ezekiel is ridiculing the frivolity and pretentiousness of men like Bharat and Raj who fail to comprehend women as individuals. But one feels bewildered about the playwright's own attitude towards women. Its tough to miss the point that Ezekiel himself has a rather poor opinion of the intellectual and creative abilities of women.

In this context, it may not be inaccurate to suggest that Nalini encapsulates perhaps Ezekiel's own fundamental dilemma of portraying women. One gets the distinct feeling that the conflicting images of Nalini represent a fundamental tussle in the mind of Ezekiel, himself. The debate in this play is never resolved adequately. Woman at the same time fascinates and repels not just Raj and Bharat but also their creator.

The complex husband-wife relationship forms the subject of the second play, *Marriage Poem*. A one-act tragi-comedy, it reads more like a comedy than a tragedy. The play deals with the common theme of monotony in married life and presents marital disharmony in a fairly straightforward manner. But in doing so Ezekiel explores the psychological tensions inherent in married life and goes on to develop our perception of a failed marriage through several devices. The stage directions are occasionally elaborate and wordy but generally brief and precise and leave little room for ambiguity in one's visual conception of a scene. The drama revolves around the central couple – Naresh and Mala. Besides them, there is another couple – Malti and Ranjit – bringing out the frustrations and weaknesses of the primary couple. While the wife craves for Naresh's attention and affection, the husband is depicted as a philanderer who is cold towards his wife. The intentional melodrama is reinforced by continuous background music which, as the opening stage directions say, is 'heard softly – when the dialogue is going on and – loudly at every pause.'

Mala holds on to her husband and does not wish to give him up; Naresh continues to live between dream and reality without perceiving the gulf between the two. In his mind, he continues to live the fantasy life he shares with Leela with whom he has secret meetings on a weekly basis. Mala resents the affair deeply and finds it particularly galling that Naresh not only pays little attention to her but even forgets to post her letters nor does he remember her birthday and anniversary. Poor Mala does not know what to do with her husband's affairs till Mrs. Lall, a neighbour, comes and consoles her.

Besides his weekly trysts with Leela, Naresh even flirts with a socialite friend, Malti when she drops in to meet him with her husband Ranjit. In fact, Naresh is so fond of the 'other woman' that he gets poetic in their presence. He starts valuing the freedom of the individual though characteristically, this freedom is regarded as the prerogative of men only. Thus, Naresh gives a lengthy poetic speech in the presence of Malti but the speech completely mystifies his wife.

Structurally, *Marriage Poem* is a series of shifting scenarios and has all the nuances of a dream sequence as there is no chronological sequencing of events. As in *Nalini*, this dramatic device is used effectively in this play also. The existence of Leela, the other woman is real or merely imaginary is intentionally unclear, as she appears in the dream like sequences fading in and out. This theatrical illusion is maintained right till the end. Here, Ezekiel makes excellent use of the interplay of dream and reality. We find Leela entering slowly, dream-walking towards him and their dialogue is revealing:

> Naresh: You! I thought you would never come back.
>
> Leela: I'll always come back whenever you need me.
>
> (*Marriage Poem* 80)

This dream is interrupted only when Naresh and Mala wake up to the reality of the arrival of their two children. The binding factor in their marriage is only their children.

Overall, there are four women characters in this play but except for Mala they are all flat characters. In fact, Naresh the male protagonist is the only character that has some flesh and blood; all the women, in contrast, are mere caricatures. Mala is introduced to us as a middle aged, but not an unattractive woman. She is portrayed as the characteristic suffering wife who continues to nag her husband as he indulges in extra-marital affairs. But as she cribs and nags, Ezekiel reduces Mala to just a stereotype version of the conventional Indian housewife, despite always cribbing and nagging, she is keen to attract her husband's attention and is shown to want constant displays of his non-existent affection. Mala is shown to be constantly complaining to the omnipresent Mrs. Lall but the husband is shown to turn to Leela for sympathy. When such contrasts are built up regularly, the women characters clearly come off second best.

The portrayal of other women characters is even more stereotyped. The depiction of Mrs. Lall, their neighbour is also conventional. She is keen to advise Mala to accept her husband's follies but when it comes to her ownself she says she'll do everything within her means to make his life Hell if he ran after other women. As she remarks: "I would make a terrible fuss. I would harass my husband night and day till he gave her up ... I'll complain to the Home Minister. What's the use of being Home Minister if he can't guarantee the sanctity of the home? I'll take out a procession and shout slogans against him. We'll gherao the other woman. She'll have to agree to give him up..." (65).

Leela's character is also thinly etched, she remains the classic outsider, the 'other woman' coming off and on in the life of husband and wife but we are told virtually nothing about her personality or her individual traits. Similarly, Malti is also depicted just as a stereotype persona of the glib socialite who readily responds to Naresh's advances.

In contrast, Ezekiel displays greater sympathy for his male character, Naresh. While he is the philanderer, there is hardly any overt mention of his responsibility for the failure of his marriage. Instead, the author verily projects him as a 'victim', as a man who has made a disastrous marriage, the unstated implication being that it's the wife Mala who is the disaster. It's also interesting to note that even in this play, Ezekiel allows his male characters to mouth several chauvinistic statements. For instance, when Naresh remarks, "For every ten minutes of talk, there should be twenty minutes of silence", Ranjit quickly adds, 'That may be possible for a man, *not for a woman*' (72, emphasis mine).

In *Nalini*, the attitude of the playwright is rather ambiguous as the play is eventually left open ended. But the colourless, stereotypical representation of women in *Marriage Poem* leaves us with little doubt about the bleak outlook of Ezekiel towards women. Ultimately, all the women remain little more than caricatures in his creative hand. Though the play depicts a crucial marital situation – the husband's romantic involvement with another woman who gives him the sympathy and companionship he does not (or thinks he does not) find in his wife – what is disappointing is that the situation is delineated almost entirely through the eyes of the husband. The wife and the 'other woman' both remain peripheral players. But perhaps the stereotypes serve a dramatic purpose, allowing us to see the 'wooden' figures which men make of women. One needs to dwell a little more closely on both the title and the play's classification as a 'tragi-comedy'. One gets the impression that despite the seemingly comical situations being created, there is in reality an underlying tragedy – in the fact that human relationships which can be mutually enriching can be so self-centred that they gnaw at the strange abstraction of happiness. 'Marriage' which is a 'poem', an emotional, sensual and responsive relationship has fallen on disharmonious notes – the music has begun to jar.

In addition to dissecting the man-woman equation, his plays explore a wide range of gender related issues like power relationships in the family, sexual politics, gender inequality, and men's inability to accept rejection by women, and several others. Ezekiel makes an attempt to sensitize his audience to the problem and predicament of women and he deserves special credit for tackling these subjects much before the International Women's Year in 1975 after which India saw a proliferation of writings on gender themes. To that extent, the articulation of these crucial issues at a time when they were rarely raised underlines the significance of Ezekiel's achievement.

It needs to be emphasised that for Ezekiel, marriage and the man-woman interaction within that relationship was really the central concern. As *Marriage Poem* reveals [which a later play, *Don't Call it Suicide*, was to reaffirm], it's the marital bond that intrigues, stimulates and agitates Ezekiel's creative mind. While he captures the humdrum of married life with subtlety and finesse and reflects the boredom and routine that kills countless marriages, it is striking that he never mirrors the essential joy or balance that is the pillar of a successful life-partnership.

The cynical view of marriage in his plays seems to have a base in Ezekiel's own troubled marriage. While it is not possible to delve deep into his autobiographical details here, it needs to be noted that Ezekiel's own marriage had been shattered according to his authorized biography (R. Raj Rao 95-124), by a lack of common interests, his frequent affairs, bohemian lifestyle and finally his relationship with an American woman scholar. So deep was the bitterness in his personal life, that neither his wife nor any of his children, except one, even bothered to take care of him during Ezekiel's final years when he was engulfed by Alzheimer's disease.

This brief digression into his personal trauma is not to gossip but merely to comprehend why despite his intellectual awareness of the inequities that women suffer; Ezekiel seems unable to support the women's cause. Inevitably, despite his psychological prowess in understanding human nature, his insights into social concerns, Ezekiel's plays reflect women characters that are little more than stereotypes. No wonder, Vrinda Nabar is 'not at all happy with the uneven roles Ezekiel allots his male and female characters' and remarks "it's hard to believe that women are as drab, stereotype and unimaginative as they are made out to be" in Ezekiel's plays (76).

The stereotyping projected in his plays is, at times, reinforced by the treatment that women have frequently been meted out even in Ezekiel's poetry. One is tempted to quote from one of his poems, where the 'male gaze' is striking. In his poem 'At the Hotel', Ezekiel explicitly states the real/male motive for visiting hotels is:

Our motives were concealed but clear,
not coffee but the Cuban dancer took us there
the naked Cuban dancer,
On the dot she came and shook her breasts
all over us and dropped
the thin transparent skirt she wore.
Was it not this for which we came? (*Collected Poems* 112)

To cite a few instances, these are some of the phrases and images that Ezekiel employs for women in his poetry: 'frightened virgins', 'burnt out mothers', 'sacrificing mothers', 'women of semi-bare bosoms', 'wives of India who do not talk, drink, kiss and sit apart', 'wooden wives', 'lonely wives and whores', 'demons, temptresses, prodigious human flesh to feed the eye and the mind', 'beasts of sex, women locked in a cage....women as erotic art objects at the art gallery'. In a nutshell, it is tough to ignore that in Ezekiel's writings, there is a clear 'othering' of women that is in operation; women are represented as the exotic/erotic 'other' almost on the same lines as Western colonialists looked through their hegemonic 'gaze' on the native as merely an 'object' that needed to be subjugated. In Ezekiel's creations, of course, the 'gaze' is in possession of a male author and that deprives women of power and denies them any significant subjectivity.

It may well be argued that his plays depict women simply as they actually were; that in the India of the 1960s and 70s, women's status was indeed 'inferior' to men and they were regarded primarily as 'objects' of sexual desire. But it's tough to accept that a man as cerebral as Ezekiel is just a neutral spectator and like the *Sutradhar* in classical Indian dramas, only wants to report faithfully whatever happens around him. For plays to be truly meaningful, they need to move beyond merely descriptive representation to an inclusion of the causes that make things as they are, though obviously this needs to be done in not too overt or didactic a manner. Such insights and commentary could not only extend the range of dramatic theme and help in a balanced delineation of characters but might well create a theatre movement that finally assists in ensuring the justice and equity that eludes most women even today.

References

Beauvoir, Simone de. *The Second Sex*. Penguin, 1982.

Blackwell, Fritz. "Four Plays of Nissim Ezekiel". *Journal of South Asian Literature*, Volume 11, Nos. 3-4 Spring, Summer 1976, pp. 265-272.

Ezekiel, Nissim. *Collected Poems*: 1952-1988. New Delhi: OUP, 1989.

—. *Three Plays*. Calcutta: Writers Workshop, 1969.

—. *Don't Call It Suicide*. Madras: Macmillan, 1989.

Mulvey, Laura. 'Visual Practice and Narrative Cinema'. In *Screen*, Volume 16, 3, Autumn, 1975.

Nabar, Vrinda. "Domesticity and Drama: An Analysis of *Marriage Poem* and *Don't Call it Suicide*". In *Contemporary Indian Drama*. Eds. Pandey and Taraporewala. New Delhi: Prestige, 1990, pp. 75-81.

Palmer, Paulina. *Contemporary Women's Fiction: Narrative Practice and Feminist Theory*. London: Harvester Wheatsheaf, 1989.

Rao, Raj R. *Nissim Ezekiel: The Authorized Biography*. New Delhi: Viking, 2000.

Reddy, Bayapa P. *Studies in Indian Writing in English*. New Delhi: Prestige, 1990.

10

Girish Karnad

Tying Beginnings to Ends

Sridhar Rajeswaran

Girish Karnad's first play *Yayati* written in 1961, when he was in his early twenties, is about the bondage of youth to age. This play was written when Karnad was in England on a Rhodes Scholarship. At that time he had wanted to be a poet but what emerged from the English sojourn was a play. Karnad then refashioned his dreams and although upon his return to India he joined the Oxford University Press and later scripted, directed and acted in several films, it was as a dramatist that he has made his best mark in the world.

Yayati is based on a story borrowed from the *Adiparva* (in Sanskrit the first canto) of the *Mahabharata*. A carefully constructed play in four acts and a prologue in the Aristotelian vein, it possesses a balanced beginning, middle and end, follows the unities, has a lofty theme and an exalted hero, and achieves a catharsis of sublimated emotions. The dramatic action consists of the interaction between eight protagonists – four male and four female. The male protagonists include Yayati and Puru, while the female are Devayani, Sharmishtha, Swarnalata and Chitralekha. Chitralekha is Puru's wife, Devyani Yayati's, Sharmishta is her 'other' while Swarnalata exists as a foil. Of the two male protagonists not mentioned above, Sukracharya does not actually have a 'speaking' presence though he is integral to the action; the remaining one is his celestial counterpart, Brihaspati, also his absent 'other'. He too is integral to the action, though subcutaneously – under the skin of the play.

Yayati begins with a prologue. The wayfarer in the prologue is lost in the darkness of a huge cavern. The wayfarer himself too is blind, thereby intensifying the metaphor of blindness. As he gropes around in the cavern he dips into a bag from which he brings out old forgotten modes of existence from the past. The play is constructed in four acts and is focussed on the conflict between youth and age and the dreams of both. At the centre of the action is the pair of a father and son. Though the women protagonists are an integral part of the action, reiterated by the responsibility vested in a woman, by virtue of the curse that unfolds the very action, they occupy space silently and are voiceless even in matters concerning them. Indeed, they are not allowed a point of entry later since events once initiated, by the sheer force of their magnitude, while encompassing the women, contrarily allows only the male protagonists the felicity of negotiation. In contrast to the male protagonists, the feminine spaces shrink progressively, as if to make us conclude that gender lacks agency and women have no part to play in the world of cause and effect and in the larger order.

The conflict itself seems to dramatise the thesis that knowledge is located at the intersection of power and desire. Such knowledge fructifies pursuits as coming to nought, a point made through the sardonic resolution that marks the ending of the play. Being a cultural hybrid, Karnad dips into both Indian as well as Western scholarship in the construction of his plays. His Western sources are Camus and Brecht in particular, and the entire existential and absurd schools in general. Although impressed by the naturalistic plays of Shaw and Ibsen, he looked to them only for methods of depiction. Indian sources include the *Natyashastra* which decreed that the choricity of utterance be punctuated by action that is dance-like in movement and ritualistic. At the level of performance and stage the folk theatre of *Yakshagana* and *Bayalata*, the local, traditional/folk drama of Karnad's Karnataka is another influence (*Yakshagana* = celestial drama, with the word *gana* privileging music, *Bayalata* = is a generic term for movement as also game). The device that predominates at this stage though is the use of masks. These masks had their location in different worlds, they were loaded masks that did not depict merely an 'other' but could bear the weight of an antinomical engendering.

When the Prologue and four acts are read together creatively, the cavern in the play becomes the nation symbolically and the entire play, a transcendent drama of life defined by a search for a knowledge that would enable the negotiation of spaces, public, private and more importantly nation spaces. The "O God in heaven! What does all this mean?", which epitomises the ending of this play can be linked to the cry of anguish in *Tughlaq* – "God, What's this country coming to!". Taken together they indicate that the exhaustion of passion will continue to be underscored by a sense of bafflement, and will continue to see the artist inserting himself into the action.

The confused morality that marks the ending of *Yayati* reappears at the beginning of *Tughlaq* (1964) and continues throughout it. The play ends significantly with a shrieking head that has not been able to understand the "madness of God", indicating thereby that bafflement will be an integral part of certain other plays too, or at least will prevail in the next one to follow. Unlike *Yayati*, the source of this play is not to be found in myth but in history. However, there is a deliberate attempt at an 'ahistoricisation' of facts, similar to the attempts that sought to historicize myth in *Yayati*. Sultan Muhammad-bin-Tughlaq of 14th century India was a complex man. He could dream but he could also act. He appeared to be a godless man but was actually quite devout. He was a good man who could at times also be cruel. The action in Karnad's play ensues from these contradictions in the protagonist's personality and the unique position of power he held. They seem to have offered Karnad apt correlates with the action in the play and the disenchanting contemporaneity of Nehruvian India. Towards the end of his life, in the 1960s Nehru was, like Tughlaq, seen as a failed dreamer.

In *Yayati* Karnad had sought a resource from the realms of the self to make a play, in *Tughlaq* he has located the action in the larger political order. This is the first Karnad play that was translated into English by the author himself, *Yayati* having been translated by another and not published till date.

Tughlaq is a play in 13 scenes. The entire action is marked by a progressive degeneration of the public/political order. Karnad has located this process of degeneration in the significant five years of the approximate fourteen-year tenure of Tughlaq's reign. In this period the major changes that rocked his kingdom took place. Thirteen in Christian mythology is a number of betrayal and fourteen in Hindu mythology is the number of years that the god Ram spent in exile in a forest. Here again one can hear echoes of contemporary Indian politics and the conditions that had overtaken Nehruvian India, as much as one can relate the betrayal and exile to the life of Tughlaq himself.

There is another complex set of symbols here as the dramatist has woven in a network of selves and anti-selves into the play. One concrete example is the characterisation of the hero/anti-hero Tughlaq himself, who needs the historical Barani and the political Najib for completion of his self.

Creatively *Tughlaq* may be read as *Yayati*'s other. By extension then Tughlaq becomes Puru's Mask. In other words, in their togetherness they constitute a whole for they are two heterogeneous parts that bear the weight of particular homogeneous characterisations, and come together to validate each other by filling each others' silences and gaps. The dream that failed for Puru in a personal sense, is a dream that fails for Tughlaq in a public world. Moreover, it is not just a failed dream for Tughlaq but a dream that metamorphosed itself into a nightmare at both a personal and public level.

Even when the curtain falls at the end of *Tughlaq*, the audience is left with some unanswered questions. What was this national space that never seemed to offer solace and succour? Does it not need re-defining? In the 1960s, India though an independent nation from 1947 onwards, was still struggling to define itself as a modern nation. Nehru's vision of a modern Indian nation was at this time being challenged by counter political forces that saw it as too idealistic and impractical.

The strain of bafflement with God's purposes continues in *Hayavadana* (1971). We are instructed at the outset by the Bhagavata/narrator who begins the action in this play saying "...that the completeness of God is something no poor mortal can comprehend", even though the dramatist is bent on a new course in *Hayavadana.* This he does with the help of two definitive acts and a prologue, which though not scripted separately or entitled thus, is inscribed into the play. The Bhagavata has a counterpart in an orthodox Greek chorus, but there is a progressive blurring of edges when the three principal protagonists, towards the end of Act I, perform the strophe/antistrophe.

Contained within the pages of this text are two stories that though apparently independent in actuality are inter-linked. Indeed, the audience for the one become the actors of the other, and thus by extension the audience is made to become pro-active and complicitous, instead of being allowed to remain as mere spectators.

The shrieking head of Tughlaq is twinned here, even as the twin ideas of a conflict between mind and body vested in the protagonists of *Yayati* – Puru and Yayati – get substantiality through independent corporeality – Devadatta and Kapila. The nature of their togetherness finds a fit correlate in the twin-headed bird, the transmuted symbol, perched in the doorway of the house of the central female protagonist, Padmini.

The sources of this play are Thomas Mann's *Transposed Heads*, which itself seems to be inspired by the sixth story in Vidyasagar Jivanand's *Vetala Parichavimashti* (New India Press, Calcutta, 1873), which is in turn part of Somdeva Bhatta's *Kathasaritsagara* (Niranya Sagar Press, Bombay, 1930) and Kshemendra's *Brihatkatha Manjari* (Niranya Sagar Press, Bombay, 1931). Karnad is inspired at this stage too, by Brecht, Vatsayana, and Auden. In particular, he creates a complex array of types/archetypes and polarities of 'truncated' characters with the use of masks/puppets within a format that is Brechtian.

The first story begins with the interruption of the Bhagavata's forward reading of the course of action of the second story and to its subsequent effective insertion into the action of the first story. A protagonist with a horse's head laments his condition. Actors one and two of story one enact the roles of the two male protagonists of story two in the actual performance. This is the larger story of nation spaces. This story gets resolved when the half-horse, half-man which goes by the dictates of the supremacy of head over body turns entirely into a horse. He is born to a Karnataka princess and is sired by an Arabian horse –an obvious trope for land and lady. There is also an implication here of a curse that accrues on the progeny by virtue of the actions of the parents, a thought that links it backwards to *Yayati*. It is thus for Hayavadana ("horse-headed" in Sanskrit), to find a solution to his predicament. Since God does not enable him to overcome it, he rushes on stage to the Bhagavata. It is thus that the dramatist brings the case to court so the audience can judge it. As if to accentuate the point, he keeps slapping himself on the forehead, saying, "What a forehead! What a forehead!" Here Karnad is also alluding to the Hindu belief that when you are born, your future is already writ on your forehead, originating in action in your past life, just as future rebirths for their turn are dependent on one's present actions. *Hayavadana* is unable to circumvent fate inspite of traversing the length and breadth of the country for a solution and his deep sense of civic duty.

There are yet again three spaces in play here i.e., the private and the public ones, and the larger nation spaces, the first two serving as correlates for the third. The plot also dramatises the politics of the existence of the nation. Here too, consistent with the twin-headed bird that marks the entry of Padmini through the doorway, there is interplay of self and the wider other. Padmini, the woman protagonist of the play, is a bored and yawning presence in it. There are moments in the play where she exudes the stoicism of Chitralekha, the passivity of Swarnalata, the deliberate impetuosity of Devayani and the volatile sustenance of Sharmishtha – characters from *Yayati* discussed above. Evidently she has to negotiate between the politics of the body and the mind, between power and knowledge, poles represented by the main male characters Kapila (the body) and Devadatta (the mind). The action ends with her ritual suicide – *sati* – it being impossible for her to choose between the two.

The two stories – that of the horse and that of Padmini – overlap. The horse is at one level happy with its head since it has ironically beaten the human body to its required shape. At another level, the victory of mind over matter has resulted only in mortality. In the aftermath of the death of the three protagonists of the second story what is left behind are a boy and some 'androgynous' dolls. In other words dolls as art/drama and a boy as a symbol for life are veritably left behind. Even as the horse gently prances around with the boy on top of him, and the Bhagavata instructs the discarding of the dolls, and the actors walk away with them, one is reminded of them having borne witness to events not wholly comprehended. The question one is left with in this instance is why were the horse, the boy and the dolls left behind? The answer will be found in the *Naga-Mandala*, Karnad's next play, where the story moves from *anima mundi*, *anima humnis* and *deus ex machina* to flames, "that cannot singe a sleeve" in a movement perhaps from art to artifice

Naga-Mandala (1988) is a play with a prologue and two acts. It contains a story told by a story, which is clad in a song, and lighted by flames. The story and song are personified and are made to manifest themselves in accordance with the dramatist's requirement. The *Naga* of the title refers to a cobra while *Mandala* seems to refer to the circle in which it exerts its power, that is to say, a circle in which humans step in and get enchanted. The action takes place in the sanctum sanctorum of a ruined temple, defiled by a broken idol, within the partial darkness of a cracked roof and wall, there are flames exchanging notes. These flames come from different sources and different homes. There is for instance, a kerosene lamp flame, a *Kusbi* lamp flame and all of them carry images of the lives and homes from which they come. There is also a new flame, that has just joined the other flames and all of them try to save a dying man – a man shocked by the floating images. He is saved by the flame, which is manifested as a story clad in a song, manifested as a woman in a sari – a symbol that acquires a mouth which has breath.

The main story is of the 'innocent' Rani married to – Appanna – 'Anyman' – who keeps her incarcerated. A blind relative – Kurudavva – Kapana, helps her win back her husband from the 'other' one who is conspicuously faceless and nameless. The behaviour of the husband by day and by night is as different as light and darkness. Kurudavva gives Rani a couple of roots from an original bunch of three, so that she can make a magic potion to entice her husband back. The plan backfires when a frightened Rani empties the potion in an anthill where a King Cobra resides. Allured, the cobra takes the guise of the husband and discharges 'his' duties with such zeal that she has a child by him. 'Anyman', a non-believer in the stork story, slighted by the malicious denial of his patriarchal rights, screams for justice. Helped by the otherworldly knowledge of the cobra, Rani alters the conditions of her trial, succeeds and wins for herself respect, credibility, and the status of Goddess – all due to the test she devices: holding the cobra in hand, she swears to the truth as instructed. The resolution is a dramatic one and revolves around the oath she takes that she has held no other man in her arms, other than the cobra and her own husband.

The story is layered in innumerable ways. There are thus two endings to the play – one that makes it a 'play pleasant' and another a 'play unpleasant'. There is yet another sub-plot, through the blind relative and her vehicle – the spectral son who carries her on his back – that seems to hinge on her loss of mobility. Thus 'a ghost without even a ghost's substantiality' steals her mobility – so to speak. Though her knowledge too is otherworldly, the turn of events makes this knowledge suspect or at least unproductive.

One may see the conflict found in *Hayavadana* played out once again in *Naga-Mandala* as Padmini too was embroiled in the politics of the body and mind. The conflict that existed in the earlier plays may be said to now extend to doubles and spectral doubles. For after all, the cobra is at one level a husband impersonator and at another level from another world, one distinct from the human one.

The conflict between head and body typical of the Karnadian Play is played out again in *Tale-Danda* (1989) (literal meaning being punishment for the head but the title suggests beheading). As in *Tughlaq* the source of the play is history and ideological conflicts of caste/class and religion that threaten to rent apart the secular fabric of India are the focus of the play. In this play Karnad goes back to the year 1168 and the city of Kalyan to focus on Basavanna of the Veerashaiva movement, a movement dedicated to Shiva, the destroyer and the powerful. But the logic is that out of destruction is born construction, and the old order must be destroyed before a new one can emerge. Another concern of the play is that of caste and the importance of dismantling the barriers perpetuating it.

Three very interesting strains interlock to make three important statements in *Tale-Danda*. One is of a class group seeking reform, another of a class group that rules, and a third one of a class group that hegemonises. That is to say this last group exerts its influence on other social groups by virtue of having reached a position of power due to certain privileges that prevents it from being easily dislodged from this position. While certain homologies are possible between the first two none is possible with the third. The group that seeks reform has Basavanna at its head but it slowly looses its hold over the masses when it fails to understand that it may not circumvent historical time. The second group has a thinking and conscientious king in Bijjala but he lives a lie inspite of knowing the truth, due to certain compulsions rooted in caste. The third group consists of people who forsake their traditional intellectual status. Governed by self-interest and self-preservation instincts, these people turn absolute reactionaries and are masters at the art of intrigues through which they try to usher in unpalatable changes. It is in the interplay of tensions jutted by these class/caste groups that we feel the reverberations of the Mandal and Mandir issue that had upset the social balance in India in the 1980s and 90s. The Mandal Commission in the 1980s had raised a hornet's nest when it sought to widen the scope of India's extant policy of positive action *vis a vis* the lower castes, by including more castes and sub-castes in the original list of castes that would benefit from positive discrimination. The resistance to Mandal's report was from among the higher castes who felt that it further empowered the lower castes and eroded their own power base. The Mandir issue refers to the conflict between the Hindus and the Muslims over the Babri Masjid in Ayodhya, which at the time that Karnad wrote this play was beginning to come into public consciousness although the bloodshed that followed in the wake of its destruction in 1992, was still in the future.

Noticeably, the issue of gender is absent in this play and women are absent voices in spaces laid waste by masculine epistemology. The end too is predictable. There is a coming to nought yet again of all purposes, purposes wrapped in a shroud, and of bloodshed and mayhem, as the genuine king is killed farcically. The ever-hegemonising group triumphs yet again. A saint is martyred. The reformists lose a battle even before the action begins. The king who was a friend of the common man and who wanted to rid society of inequalities pays with his life. Not only do their dreams not come true, the people of the kingdom, end up worse than ever before. The nightmare of Tughlaq's aborted reforms is revisited here, tying beginnings to ends. The new king is immoral and doesn't know anything of kingship. This being the case he ascends to the throne with the help of that same powerful class/caste group whose hegemony his father, the king before him and the reformists or truncated revolutionists, had sought to dislodge.

Karnad had delved once before into history in *Tughlaq* where the protagonist had initiated mayhem and was the arch-exploiter. Here the protagonist is in a sense Tughlaq's foil, as he is the victim of the effects of similar mayhem. In both instances the stage is littered with blood and corpses that spell the failure of the masses to resist or to stem the flow of such events. Even as the power group crowns a dubious prince and propitiates him, the state of things to come suggests a nightmare and makes one want to see beyond what has possessed the world in such violent times.

Behind the propitiation are hidden cords, strings with which the puppet may be jerked and manoeuvred. Beyond the "urn of a thousand holes" that jets water into a thousand streams is the fire – tangential, symptomatic, and symbolic. Fire and water, one raging, one anointing, symbols pointing at the title of Karnad's next play, *The Fire and The Rain.*

The opening scene of *The Fire and the Rain (*1988) reveals a wasteland. Even mayhem and lost purposes are memories. A fire rages indiscriminately. Water is visible only as dried up tears shed in retribution or when it flows to wash the sin of the blood spilled of innocent people. As for *yajna* – the sacrificial fire – who could it propitiate but Indra? Indra, the King of the gods, is also the rain maker, that deity who could unify the two most powerful symbols that permeate the Karnadian aesthetic – fire and rain.

The play has as its source the *Mahabharata*, more specifically the story of *The Fire and the Rain* is drawn from the *Vanaparva* – the forest canto – of the *Mahabharata*. The plot is complex as are the characters. According to Karnad the play germinated in his mind for thirty-seven years. The format is dense, and includes a play within the play. Typically, thematically it is multivalent. The action is set in two places. In short, what we have is a dense mixture arrived at through at least three different strands.

Ostensibly, a play with a prologue, epilogue and three acts, the construction is such that the different parts are independent at one level, intra-dependent at another, mutually dependent at a third, and organically inseparable at another. For instance, the action of the prologue may be read as a foil to the epilogue and vice versa. Similarly, the active participants of the one become the passive observers of the other. The audience itself is built into the play by virtue of the very actors who enact it.

Relationships are presented in threes: Indra, Vishwarupa, and Vritra are the children of Brahma; Paravasu, Arvasu, and Brahma Rakshasa (a demon), the children of Raibhya. However, Indra and Paravasu, Vishwarupa and Arvasu, Vritra and Brahma Rakshasa may be paired, without affecting their tripled relationships. The women protagonists are also 'trined', for although only Vishakha and Nittilai are shown there are really two Vishakhas: one with a power to bring forth the death of Yavakri, who violated her faith even as he satiated her surfeited desire, and another epitomising desire, specifically the object of desire, for Yavakri. We could view Nittilai, as a symbol of desire too, the fulfilment of which could lead to knowledge and through it maybe even power. This yet again brings us within the shadow of the Karnadian aesthetic, an aesthetic that as seen in earlier plays, often has an inbuilt futility of purpose.

The story of Parvasu's yagna to propitiate Indra and bring rain to the parched kingdom, is interwoven with stories of sexual desire, betrayals and power-seeking. Vishakha's sexuality, exploited by Parvasu and his cousin Yavakri, is countered by the simpler passion of Arvasu and Nittilai, the tribal girl. Parvasu's betrayal of his brother Arvasu is at two levels – the personal and the political. In an attempt to seek political position, he lets Arvasu take the blame for the death of their father, but then betrays him by not telling the truth about this death. This also results in Arvasu being separated from his beloved Nittilai, as he could not meet her father at the appointed time to claim her hand in marriage.

What is of special interest is that these complex relationships ambiguously embody the indivisible presence of good and evil. In Karnad's world evil is something that is ever present and cannot be destroyed though it may be kept under control. Not surprisingly, then, the ending of the play mingles tears and rain. Retribution and liberation, absolution and the spectacle of people dancing with joy and rolling in the mud alternate with one another. At the end one see Arvasu clutching the dead body of his love, Nittilai, and exulting, "It's raining, Nittilai! It's raining!" *The Fire and the Rain* however, leaves one with a feeling of distaste at the sacrifice of youth and gender that had to be made in the cause of the progress of power and position. This links the play to Karnad's dramatic beginnings – *Yayati* – in which the youth was subordinated to age and power.

Bali, Karnad's seventh play opened in May 2002 at the Haymarket Theatre in Leicester and has been published along with *The Dreams of Tipu Sultan*, a radio play, in 2004. Here too, he has juxtaposed myth with events from history. Like his other plays *Bali* is about a ruler who has to juggle his personal emotions with his state duties. Interwoven into the tale of a queen's betrayal of her husband is the theme of non-violence – a central concern for Karnad in an India increasingly engaged in sectarian violence. *Bali* as Karnad has said in his preface, is a play that has emerged from several discarded drafts but the version put up at the Haymarket Theatre was re-written. The play is based on a thirteenth century Kannada epic, which in turn has drawn upon earlier Sanskrit texts of the ninth and thirteenth centuries. The moral choices the king has to make in this play reflect the choices before contemporary Indians.

The Dreams of Tipu Sultan was commissioned by the BBC to mark the 50th anniversary of India's independence and Karnad subsequently re-wrote it both in English and Kannada for the stage. In an interview with Bageshree S. in *The Hindu*, Karnad has said that he was attracted to the subject as at that time there had been a move by "right-wing fundamentalists, trying to picture him as a fanatic...Trying to paint an 18th century man in terms of 20th Century prejudices". *The Dreams of Tipu Sultan* brings to life a man who has been much maligned as a violent and ruthless warrior by British historians. Karnad's focus is on not just on the fighter but also on the dreamer – the man who meticulously noted down his dreams. Karnad's Tipu is therefore a complex character and in the play, dreams and reality often get blurred. Tipu has in recent years been presented as a Muslim fanatic who forcibly converted Hindus to Islam, but he was also the man who gave refuge to the Sringeri Swamiji when the Marathas had attacked Sringeri. Tipu was also a ruler who was imbued with notions ahead of his time. The English were his hated enemies but he also admired them. In a dream sequence in the play he tells his father: "The English fight for something called England. What is it? It's not a religion that sustains them, nor a land that feeds them. They wouldn't be here if they did. It's just a dream, for which they are willing to kill and die..." This is an interesting attempt at nascent nation building and national pride. Like in *Tughlaq*, Karnad has here taken on the task of rehabilitating a man who has not received justice from history.

So one can see that with increasing maturity Karnad's work is displaying a circular trajectory of going back to the beginning and his later plays have been engaged in tying up themes of the present with their beginnings in the past.

Karnad is the recipient of several awards and has been given the National awards of Padmashri and Padmabhusan too. He has also received the prestigious Jnanapeeth Award for his writing. However, his reception in the Kannada theatre world is rather ambivalent. C.N. Ramachandran has noted that Kannada critics hesitate to accept Karnad fully as according to them he is not really rooted in their culture. They think of him as an outsider as after writing his plays in Kannada, he quickly translates them into English thereby giving them an immediate high visibility in the Western world. As a result his plays are staged in the UK and the USA, whereas the plays by other Kannada dramatists do not even get a wider Indian audience. This places Karnad in a different category from most other Kannada writers. In fact his facility with English and his international audience puts him in the category of Indian writers in English, many among whom like Karnad enjoy not just a pan-Indian readership but also have access to a global literary world.

Such a critique of Karnad's plays or his access to a global audience need not detract from his importance to contemporary Indian drama. His position there is rather unique as his plays thanks to their hybrid nature and focus on class, caste and gender are different from the plays written by other Indian dramatists in Indian languages or in English. This makes it essential for scholars and students of Indian drama to take Karnad's work into account in their research/assessment of the practice of drama in India today.

References

Bageshree, S. "Visionary's dreams". *The Hindu*, 15th July 2004.

Bharata. *Natya Sastra*. Trans. Adya Rangachary. Bangalore: IBH Prakashana, 1986.

Dodiya, Jaydip Singh. Ed. *Plays of Girish Karnad. Critical Perspectives.* Delhi: Prestige books, 1999.

Karnad, Girish. *Yayati.* Translated from Kannada by Priya Adarkar, Unpublished, 1961.

—. *The Three Plays - Naga-Mandala, Hayavadana, Tughlaq*. Translated from Kannada by the author. Delhi: Oxford University Press, 1994.

—. *Tale-Danda.* Translated from Kannada by the author. Delhi: Ravi Dayal Publishers, 1993.

—. *The Fire and the Rain.* Translated from Kannada by the author. Delhi: Oxford University Press, 1998.

—. *The Dreams of Tipu Sultan/Bali: The Sacrifice: Two Plays by Girish Karnad.* Translated from Kannada by the author. Delhi: Oxford University Press, 2004.

Mann, Thomas. *The Transposed Heads.* Translated Helen T. Iowa-Porter. London: Vintage Books, 1972.

Mendonca, Allen J. "Breaking into the big League". *The Indian Express,* Bombay, 22nd August 1993.

Naik, M.K. *A History of Indian English Literature.* Delhi: Sahitya Akademi, 1997.

Pande, Sudhakar and Barua, Freya Eds. *New Directions in Indian Drama.* Prestige Books, Delhi, 1994.

Rajagopalachari. C. *The Mahabharata.* Bombay: Bharatiya Vidya Bhavan, 1971.

Ramachandran, C.N. Girish Karnad: "The Playwright in Search of metaphors". In Gupta, Balarama. Ed. *The Journal of Indian Writing in English,* Vol. 27, India, July 1999, pp. 21-34.

Saxena, Vibha. *Did the Andhaka see too much?: Redefining Girish Karnad in a Postcolonial Perspective.* Ph.D. thesis. University of Mumbai, 2000.

Valegar, Madhuri. "In Conversation, with Girish Karnad". *Sunday Observer,* Bombay, 4th September 1994.

Vatsayana. *The Kamasutra, Love precepts of the Brahman.* Preface and Introduction. Paris: Libraire "Astra", New Delhi.

11

Locating Bakhtinian Carnival in Girish Karnad's *Hayavadana* and *Naga-Mandala*

Sudha Shastri
Amith Kumar P.V.

Girish Karnad's much acclaimed plays, *Hayavadana* (1975) and *Naga-Mandala* (1990), both tend towards asking questions and problematising issues rather than making assertive statements of theme. Our paper aims to examine the questioning impulse in these plays, with a view to defining the spaces of ambivalence and subversion that it produces. We propose to use the Bakhtinian trope of the 'carnival' to read these plays in the light of the aim of this paper. We shall also consider the role of folk theatre in these plays, as the larger context in which 'carnival' finds its niche. A quick recapitulation of the two plays may be of help before we proceed to study them for their elements of carnival and folklore.

The central story of *Hayavadana* revolves around Padmini, Devadatta and Kapila. Devadatta, a renowned Brahmin, falls in love with Padmini and marries her. Their marital happiness proves to be short-lived as Padmini finds herself attracted to Kapila, who is Devadatta's close friend from childhood. Kapila reciprocates her feeling for him, but neither he nor Padmini is able to do anything about it, not even hide it from Devadatta. Meanwhile all three undertake a journey to

Ujjain, and on the way come upon a disused Kali temple. Devadatta sends his wife and Kapila away to a neighbouring Rudra temple and in their absence, goes to Kali and offers his head to her. When Kapila and Padmini return, they are unable to find Devadatta, so Kapila goes in search of him and finds his decapitated body in the temple. Torn by anguish and guilt, Kapila cuts his head off as well, leaving Padmini to come a little later and see the two dead bodies.

A frightened Padmini prays to the goddess Kali to restore the two men to life, and Kali does so by asking Padmini to join the two heads to the respective bodies. But in her hurry (?) Padmini mixes the heads and bodies, and brings back to life Devadatta's head with Kapila's body (which is the combination she desires to live with) and Kapila's head with Devadatta's body. The rest of the play then explores the outcome of such a mix-up.

In *Naga-Mandala* the protagonist Rani (Queen), is married to Appanna (any man), who locks her up in his house and visits only once a day for his midday meal. Rani suffers this cruelty for an indefinite period of time. One day Kurudavva, the blind friend of her late mother-in-law, gives Rani two root-pieces which, when served to her husband, would ensure his undying devotion to her. Rani first tries the smaller piece, which has no effect on her churlish husband. Hence she cooks the larger piece, but when it turns a blood red colour, she is frightened into throwing it out of the house. As luck would have it, the liquid falls on an anthill in which resides a king cobra (Naga). Predictably enough, Naga falls in love with Rani, and at night, after her husband goes away to his concubine, he assumes the form of Appanna and visits her. Startled at first, Rani gradually begins to accept her husband's schizophrenic behaviour, of being harsh to her at daytime and loving at night.

Things come to a pass when Rani becomes pregnant with Naga's child. Appanna, the 'real' Appanna, i.e., is enraged at what he sees as his wife's infidelity, and demands that she be brought to justice in front of the village elders. Naga, meeting Rani at night for the last time, advises her not to undertake the ordeal of the red-hot iron to prove her innocence (?), but to volunteer, instead, for the ordeal by the snake. For this Rani would have to hold the king cobra and speak the truth. Only if she spoke the truth, cautions Naga, the cobra would refrain from biting her. If she were to utter a lie, even in ignorance, the cobra would have no choice but to bite her. Rani tells the truth and yet proves her chastity, in the ingenious ending that Karnad gives his play.

How do we relate these spaces of interrogation to the Bakhtinian notion of 'carnival'? While attempting this, we shall also endeavour to show how 'carnival' and folk theatre have several common principles. The notion of 'carnival' in Bakhtin's writings appears in a set of interspersed ideas that share certain common characteristics like subverting and discrowning an established hierarchy, celebrating the grotesque and the profane, and foregrounding a laughter that parodies authoritarian discourse by emphasising the comicality of the folklore and the bawdy body. Bakhtin's concern in his writings on the carnivalesque has been to mock closed and finalised attitudes towards the word and the world, and cast them down. Bakhtin's 'carnival' puts forth an open-ended potential for life through laughter and parody.

And parody, as we shall proceed to discuss, is also intrinsic to folk-energy. Here is Karnad's comment on folk theatre:

> The energy of folk theatre comes from the fact that although it seems to uphold traditional values, it also has the means of questioning these values, of making them literally stand on their own head. The various conventions – the chorus, the music, the comic interludes, the mixing of human and non-human worlds – permit a simultaneous presentation of alternative points of view, of alternative points of view, of alternative analyses of the central problem. (Author's Introduction 14)

'The mixing of human and non-human worlds' is one of several intersections between folk theatre and 'carnival' as we shall show towards the end of our paper.

In the Author's Introduction to *Three Plays*, Karnad explains that the source of *Hayavadana* is from *Kathasaritsagara* (later adapted by Thomas Mann) in which the plot functions as a riddle involving the issue of identity. This story told by the Vetal to King Vikram, points to a moral dilemma regarding the identity of a human being. After the woman has transposed the heads of her "insecure and jealous husband and his friend" (12), she is faced with the question of which of the two men is her real husband. King Vikram's answer to the Vetal which poses this question, resolves the dispute in favour of the head. He unhesitatingly states that it is the head which is the distinguishing aspect of a human being. Thomas Mann who scorned this mechanical understanding of the head as superior to the body, retells the story to mock the concept that the head and the body can be different at all.

Taking this perspective forward, Karnad raises a related problem: that of completeness. The twin concerns, of identity as a hierarchically determinable entity, and completeness, become fused in the god of invocation, Ganesha, who is appropriately invoked at the beginning of the play. In the Sanskrit dramatic tradition, the Play proper begins with a Prologue or Invocatory Prayer. Using the standard and sanctioned figure of Ganesha to begin the play 'auspiciously', Karnad nevertheless infuses a subversive element within the self-same figure by asking what is – apparently – a rhetorical question of the deity:

> How indeed can one hope to describe his glory in our poor, disabled words? An elephant's head on a human body, a broken tusk and a cracked belly – whichever way you look at him he seems the embodiment of imperfection, of incompleteness. How indeed can one fathom the mystery that this very Vakratunda-Mahakaya, with his crooked face and distorted

body, is the Lord and Master of Success and Perfection. (*Hayavadana* 1)

The 'perfection' of the deity is already challenged at the outset of the play; as the play proceeds, doubt and protest against hegemonic social structures assert their presence progressively, especially when Padmini transposes the heads. The resolution of the play fittingly reaffirms the element of 'carnival', where completeness is determined in favour of the animal over the human. In short, Hayavadana (the man with a horse's head) attains completeness not by becoming a complete man but by becoming a complete horse. In his Introduction to *Hayavadana* Kurtkoti describes the defining folk paradigm of the play as follows:

> Karnad uses the conventions and motifs of folk tales and folk theatre – masks, curtains, dolls, the story-within-a-story – to create a bizarre world. It is a world of incomplete individuals, indifferent gods, dolls that speak and children who cannot, a world indifferent to the desires and frustrations, joys and sorrows of human beings. What is real is only the tremendous, irrational energy of the horse and its rider who move round the stage symbolising the powerful but monotonous rhythm of life. (vi-vii)

The folk identity of *Hayavadana* is traceable most in the spirit of subversion that the plot admirably executes, especially in the character of Padmini, which we shall return to in a while. Thus, Karnad's contribution to the story he has adapted is to invest it with a clearly folk flavour both in stage properties as well as in spirit, in the way that (above all else) the woman comes to be privileged.

Naga-Mandala's folk ethos is writ large in theme and plot, as it weaves two Kannada folk-tales together. The first comments on the paradoxical nature of oral tales which, despite existing independently, depend upon a story-teller to be passed on. Within this larger frame tale of Story, Man and the Flames, Karnad presents the story of Rani, Appanna and Naga.

It seems appropriate to recall Bakhtin on 'carnival' at this juncture. According to Bakhtin, 'carnival' is an indispensable part of folklore. To him carnival has emphatic and purposeful heteroglossia. 'Carnival' is opposed to official culture, and modes of hierarchy. "Carnival is not a spectacle seen by the people; they live in it, and everyone participates because its very idea embraces all the people. While 'carnival' lasts, there is no other life outside it" (Bakhtin, 7). It embraces all. And, while 'carnival' definitely has elements of Spectacle, well exemplified in the last scene of *Naga-Mandala* where Rani has to take her pledge – it is not one 'seen' from outside by the people, they live in it.

In an interesting modification of the Bakhtinian description of carnival-spectacle, in *Naga-Mandala* this spectacle is one imposed by official law, the law of the Panchayat, which says that a woman accused of adultery has to prove her innocence by taking a pledge. A huge crowd gathers to watch this. The element of carnival makes a furtive appearance here in a characteristically subversive manner, in Rani's decision to destabilise the sanctity and authority of truth, as opposed to the general Bakhtinian understanding of a universal overthrowing of values and structures. Thus the crowd at the end of *Naga-Mandala* itself consists of carnival players despite themselves, carnival players who do not realise their participation, who think they are only watching a spectacle, not that they are part of one where their roles are allotted to them. By an ironic inversion, their roles are assigned to them by the accused, who is also the goddess of the carnival, Rani. In a supreme moment of unwitting irony and unconscious parody, the Elders pay tribute to Rani's perceived chastity at the end of the spectacle by declaring her a "Divine Being" and a "Goddess" (39).

Without oversimplifying the issue, it seems possible to claim that a central factor that both *Hayavadana* and *Naga-Mandala* are concerned with is the questioning of authority. The privileging of the woman protagonist is one of the more obvious ways in which Karnad makes this point. The burgeoning female energy of Padmini in *Hayavadana* and Rani in *Naga-Mandala* directs the plots of the plays such as to overthrow structures of patriarchal authority at different points. Padmini's upper hand over Devadatta and Kapila becomes evident right at the beginning of her entrance. Her very anti-patriarchal desire to have both men at the same time, one man's intellect and another's body, in flagrant opposition to prescribed social convention, comes to be fulfilled against all patriarchal odds in the Kali temple (and it is perhaps not a coincidence that the deity is a goddess), even though the duration of the fulfilment is brief. In Rani's case, her feminine power takes a while to assert itself, but once it does there is just no looking back.

In both plays, it is the desire of the female protagonist that drives the plot onward from the complication to resolution. The goddess also conspires, in *Hayavadana*, by 'overlooking' Padmini's act of wish-fulfilment with grudging admiration. There is definitely divine condoning because Kali does see that Padmini's exchange of heads is wilful and not innocent. It is also Kali who points this out to the audience, saying, "My dear daughter, there should be a limit even to honesty. Anyway – so be it" (33), once Padmini has attached the heads of the two men on the 'wrong' bodies. It is to be noted that Kali's comment turns the issue to one of honesty rather than one of transgression or 'sin'. The subterfuge is observed, but not reprimanded nor corrected. It is allowed to pass.

In *Naga-Mandala*, Rani starts to get the upper hand of the plot after she seems to realise that Appanna is Naga. She becomes a loved and loving wife, from a bride who was tortured by her husband. But Rani's role has a more transgressional identity in the play, evinced in the pledge she takes with the King Cobra, which is a 'classic' case of equivocation.

Truth is monologic and absolute, it allows for no alternative interpretation. By creating two shades of meaning around her utterance, one prima facie and another a contradictory subtext, Rani succeeds in striping the face of truth with two layers. This double-voiced utterance becomes intelligible as an equivocating one only to the audience, whereby the play creates a divide between the characters on stage and those in the audience, the latter being the only ones who guess at the equivocation behind Rani's claim. Rani's predicament poignantly reflects the human need to live by fictions and half-truths, the need not to push for truth beyond the point where the structure of daily life may be threatened.

Padmini's desire to have both men is doomed to be fulfilled only for a brief duration, but Rani has a luckier fate. The first ending to *Naga-Mandala* has Naga strangling himself in Rani's thick tresses from despair. However, one of the Flames demands a happy ending to this story told by Man, and he substitutes an ending where Rani lives with her husband and son and Naga as well, who continues to live in her hair.

The riddle is an interesting presence in the cultural practices of folk communities, and one of the most obvious things about its paradigm is that it allows for double-voicedness and ambivalence. The riddle is structured as to allow room for conjecture.

Metaphor is the base of the riddle. "The riddle incorporates a question primarily and an answer secondarily. In the question a fact is concealed in the form of a metaphor, while in the answer the hidden meaning is revealed and the real purport of the implied sense is fully expressed. *Concealment thus becomes the most vital function of the riddle*" (Bhagwat, 1, emphasis mine).

Rani's assertion at the end of *Naga-Mandala* comes close to assuming the form of a riddle. Rani's entire experience with Naga is one that bemuses her, and leaves her pondering. Her puzzlement is itself expressed as a kind of riddle: "every night this conundrum must have spread its hood out at her"

(*Naga-Mandala* 41). Finally, it is the form of the riddle that saves Rani. Faced by a riddle, Rani tells the 'truth' in disguise, in a partial form, in a riddle of sorts whose 'true' meaning can be deciphered only through the recognition that her claim to have touched the King Cobra is not just literal, as the crowd thinks, but is metaphorical. She has known the touch of the King Cobra in a way that she ought to have known the touch of her lawful husband, whereas the truth is that her lawful husband has never made love to her, but the King Cobra has. This inversion lies at the heart of Rani's utterance.

It is noteworthy that whatever inference Rani makes of the puzzling phenomenon is protected from the audience's certain knowledge by the dramatist. Our question is thus also, 'Why does Karnad protect Rani's knowledge from us?' – meaning, Rani's ambiguous riddle-like answer is not only for the benefit of the Panchayat elders but also us, the reader/ spectator-group. Karnad cannot be protecting Rani in the interests of morality. The bipartite structure of the riddle keeps knowledge (here, knowledge is greater than truth) esoteric.

Among the various explanations given by anthropologists, historians, and literary to the riddle, one is that it is a device for mediating conceptual ambiguity and stimulating cognitive reexamination; thus riddles suggest the power of transgression. One of the effects of their playing with conceptual boundaries is to show that things are not quite as stable as they appear.

Traditionally, riddles are of three types: the "naming" riddle-session, the "waking" riddle-session and the "neck" riddle-session. Rani's riddle comes close to the third type. The "neck" riddle-session involves a condemned or imprisoned (wo)man seeking her/his "neck" or liberty, by posing questions which a judge or captor cannot guess, and thereby earning her/his freedom.

As against the official and the ecclesiastical life characterised by violence, discipline and authority, Bakhtin's concern is with the grotesque realism of the folklore characterised by laughter and mockery. Through an investigation of the medieval folk-humour, Bakhtin shows how laughter "discrowns" authority. The grotesque realism of the 'carnival' does not distinguish between gendered bodies. Nor does it prioritise the upper parts of the body that signify the heaven and the rational body. Rather, it is "the drama of bodily life" which celebrates the "lower stratum" (Bakhtin, 88). Thus, in the *Rabelais* book, the purpose of the carnival is not merely to parody but to discrown, debase and demolish the hierarchical constructions.

In *Hayavadana* and *Naga-Mandala*, we can observe the presence of a "second life" in the form of certain folk-elements like masks, flames, gods, dolls etc. These elements spring from the "realistic fantastic" imagination of the folklore to create a grotesque world - a world where body in the human form is turned upside down. They serve two important carnivalistic motifs. Firstly, these elements provide a comical background and critical intervention necessary for the plot. They are entrusted with the responsibility of attesting to human imperfections and incompleteness. To quote Hayavadana:

> I have become a complete horse - but not a complete being! This human voice - this cursed human voice - it's still there! How can I call myself complete? If I only could. What should I do, Bhagavata Sir? How can I get rid of this human voice?" (*Hayavadana* 68)

After some deliberation Hayavadana sings patriotic songs and the National Anthem as last-ditch measures since he is convinced that this effort will ruin his human voice. Here we have a mockery that discrowns authority, and a pungent criticism that exposes human imperfection and incompleteness.

The second carnivalistic motif concerns the prioritisation of the body over the mind. Karnad employs the folklore elements to describe grotesque bodies. The bodily functions are depicted through the flames in *Naga-Mandala* and the dolls in *Hayavadana* which create a "grotesque realism" in the

Bakhtinian sense. In *Naga-Mandala*, flame 4 describes a grotesque body: "My master had an old, ailing mother. Her stomach was bloated, her back covered with bedsores. The house stank of cough and phlegm, pus and urine" (3). Similarly, in *Hayavadana*, the dolls describe Kapila's body when he appears in Padmini's dreams.

Doll I: There he is again.
Doll II: In the middle of the day?
Doll I: (doubtful). I'm not sure this is the usual visitor. This one looks rougher and darker.
Doll I: It's him all right. Look at his face.
...
Doll I: (baffled). But he's climbing a tree!
Doll II: (almost a wail of disappointment). He's dived into a river!
Doll I: Is that all he came for?
Doll II: It's going...
Doll I: ...going
Doll II: Gone! Wretched dreams – They just tickle and fade away. (49-50)

Their conversation acquires a more sexually suggestive turn elsewhere in the scene. The rougher and darker body of Kapila and his actions of climbing a tree and diving into a river show a "bodily life" in the Bakhtinian sense, that offers Padmini a hope for an alternative "second life". The dolls enter Padmini's dreams and carnivalise the spectacle by being a part of the event that occurs in the human subconscious. Karnad effectively brings out the victory of the body over the mind in the psychological realm by making the non-human dolls comment on and bear witness to the operations of the human subconscious. The dolls also describe the "soft" and "sickly" shape of Devadatta whose body loses rigour and robustness within six months:

Doll II:	Why? What happened?
Doll I:	He touched me, and ...
Doll II:	Yes?
Doll I:	His palms! They were so rough, when he first brought us here. Like a labourer's. But now they are soft – sickly soft – like young girl's.
Doll II:	I know. I've noticed something too.
Doll I:	What?
Doll II:	His stomach. It was so tight and muscular. Now...
Doll I:	I know. It's loose. (47)

It is noticeable that the transposed bodies of Kapila and Devadatta symbolically convey regeneration and degeneration of the life force. Karnad brings to light the state of a constant flux in the two bodies, which provide a grotesque image signifying growth and maturity on the one hand, and death and decay on the other. As Bakhtin writes,

> The grotesque image reflects a phenomenon in transformation, an as yet unfinished metamorphosis of death and birth, growth and becoming. The relation to time is one determining trait of the grotesque image. The other indispensable trait is ambivalence. For in this image we find both poles of transformation, the old and the new, the dying and the procreating, the beginning and the end of the metamorphosis. (24)

Laughter is intrinsic to 'carnival', and is very closely related to freedom. And importantly, fear which "is the extreme expression of narrow-minded and stupid seriousness, which is defeated by laughter...complete liberty is possible only in the completely fearless world" (Bakhtin, 47). There is terror at the beginning of *Hayavadana*, with the actor running in fear at the sight of the half-horse and half-man. It takes the Bhagavata quite a while to persuade the actor to tell him and the audience what has been frightening him. In direct contrast, *Hayavadana* ends on a note of laughter, with the horse becoming complete only when its laugh becomes a neigh.

The laughter is an affirmation of all oaths redeemed. Padmini's son who has hitherto not laughed, bursts into laughter when Hayavadana comes in singing; Hayavadana himself, who is unable to become all-horse because of his human voice, starts to laugh and his laughter transforms his voice to the neigh of a horse. At last, laughter has endowed completeness, which he has been searching for since the play began. Laughter in terms of Bakhtinian carnival has a regenerative power. Carnival laughter is universal in scope, directed at all and everyone.

In this paper we have attempted to read *Hayavadana* and *Naga-Mandala* as enshrining the spirit of 'carnival' as explicated by Bakhtin. There is no doubt that the folk-tale identity of these two plays has been a major factor in aiding our interpretation of 'carnival' in Karnad-esque (if we may be pardoned the coinage) terms. In the final analysis, we believe that creativity transcends all definitions, even a definition that is carnivalesque in spirit.

References

Bakhtin, Mikhail. *Rabelais and His World*. Trans. Helene Iswolsky. Bloomington: Indiana University Press, 1984.

Bhagwat, Durga. *The Riddle in Indian Life Lore and Literature*. Bombay: Popular Prakashan, 1965.

Devika, V.R. "Naga-Mandala in Minnesota". *SPAN*. December 1993: 42-45.

Karnad, Girish. *Hayavadana*. Translated by the author. Calcutta: Oxford University Press, 1975.

—. *Naga-Mandala: Play with a Cobra*. Translated from the Original Kannada by the Author. Delhi: Oxford University Press, 1990.

—. Author's Introduction. Girish Karnad: *Three Plays*. Oxford University Press, 1994.

Kurtkoti, Kirtinath. Introduction to *Hayavadana* by Girish Karnad. Translated by the author. Calcutta: Oxford University Press, 1975: v-vii.

12

The Not-so-gay 'Gay' Plays of Mahesh Dattani

Nidhi Singh

Responding to a question in an interview published in *Sahara Time*, Dattani asserts, "My characters are simply personification of my perceptions. What moves me actually is an individual's struggles for identity. In fact more realistic view of things in life is my 'credo' " (34). In the light of this comment it is not surprising that Dattani chose to explore issues related to homosexual identity in his plays. To him goes the distinction of writing the first Indian play openly depicting the 'gay' scenario in India, an issue which has been pushed under the carpet as far as Indian drama is concerned. The path-breaking play *On a Muggy Night in Mumbai* was followed by other works which dealt extensively with different aspects related to gay identity as in the two radio plays *Do the Needful* and *Seven Steps Around the Fire*. Another work, *Bravely Fought the Queen* too has a gay character hounded by sexual guilt.

The major concern of Dattani in plays depicting homosexual situation is the identity crisis which results from being marginalised and oppressed. Identity crisis forms the basis of *Night Queen*, another work by the writer dealing with gay experience. Responses to rejection, alienation persecution and social conditioning are explored and highlighted. Dattani chronicles the struggles of character when faced with pressures from outside as well as from within. At one level the confrontation is directed outwards, facing the prejudices and rejection of the society, and at the other it is directed inwards where the confrontation is with the divided self, the product of social conditioning and sexual impulses.

What is it that has put the gay population on defensive? Was Indian society always closed to the issue? Is there a tradition of rejection of gay populace due to their gender preferences? Ruth Vanita and Saleem Kidwai trace the same sex love in readings from literature and history in the book *Same Sex Love in India*. Beginning from 2nd century ancient India to medieval era spanning 8th to 18th century, the book moves on to 19th century modern India. A trend of general tolerance if not approval has been traced till the closing of medieval times. In introduction to the section 'Modern Indian Material', Vanita and Kidwai define modern as 19th and 20th century India. They point out in their work *Same Sex Love in India*:

> Two significant phenomenon develop during this period – first the minor homophobic voice that was largely ignored by mainstream society in pre-colonial India becomes a dominant voice, and second, sexual love between women is depicted increasingly explicitly while such love between men is almost entirely silenced. (191)

In 1861 anti-sodomy law was passed which criminalized homosexuality in section 377 of the Indian Penal Code. Raj Ayyar in the review of *Yaraana: Gay Writing from India* holds, "not only did colonialism stigmatize traditional non-puritan sexualities, it also criminalized some of those behaviours..." (3). The law criminalizing homosexuals remains the same to date and is often used as an excuse to execute and silence the gay community.

The ensuing struggle is for visibility, voice and social space, not to be frozen into stereotypes but to have freedom of choice as individuals. Gay marriage too emerges as an issue challenging the sanctity of marriage with procreation as the natural and expected outcome. Love between same sex, since it cannot be procreative is seen as unnatural and carnal. Dattani in *Seven Steps Around the Fire* questions the stance which rejects the possibility of love, loyalty and dedication in a relationship between a eunuch and a homosexual. Using a 'who-dun-it' detective plot, Dattani skillfully brings out the petty jealousies and strong loyalties that regulate the 'hizra' community and the hypocrisy that permeates society at large. Uma, the scholar-detective with the help of Munaswamy, her reluctant aide, who also provides comic relief, unravels the mystery of murder of Kamla, a beautiful eunuch. Uma discovers that the murder has been perpetrated by Mr. Sharma, a rich and powerful Minister, owing to his disapproval of the secret marriage between Kamla and his son Subbu. In the climactic scene where Mr. Sharma is forcing his son into marrying the girl of his choice which he justifies saying "My truth is in ensuring he is on right path" (*CP* 37)[1]. Subbu shoots himself amidst marriage festivities and chanting of *muntras*. The futility of Mr. Sharma's machinations and his version of 'truth' finds reflection in futility of Uma's sleuthing for truth which becomes meaningless with the hushing up of the case and the realisation, "They have no voice" (*CP* 42). The irony arises from the fact that even she has no voice on the face of political clout of Mr. Sharma and her husband's complicity.

Hoshang Merchant in introduction to *Yaraana, Gay Writing from India* declares ".... most homosexuals get married due to social pressures. Some commit suicide. Most adjust to a double life, so do their wives" (xvi). Subbu commits suicide while Ashwin and Raghu from Dattani's *Night Queen* seek each other out for love, understanding and support. The play explores the identity crisis faced by Ashwin a homosexual character who learns to hate himself because his brother whom he loves, thinks of his preference for same-sex love as 'ugly and repulsive'. Ash cries out his fear to Raghu, "In his eyes, I didn't want to be so ugly" (NQ 68).[2] The pressure to conform can be strongest from within the family as in the case of Subbu where his father almost pushes him into arranged marriage and definitely into committing suicide. While in *Seven Steps Around the Fire* the coercive power of father leads to the crisis, in *Night Queen* the brother's disapproval combines with Ashwin's complicity. Dattani in this play questions this complicity on part of the homosexuals – the 'identitarian' unease they face is to some extent of their own making. Closely interlinked to the standing up for their right to be what they choose to be is the question of economic independence. Economic self-dependence of the marginalized serves as a great impetus towards empowerment. Ashwin rants at Raghu "...you have a secure job... you can tell the world to fuck off" (NQ 67-68). Raghu is definitely lucky to have a secure job and supportive sibling yet the insecurity comes through when he confesses to Ashwin, "I too am looking for help from you. Help me" (NQ 70). It is his bonding with Ash which finally enables him to laugh loudly and declare, "At last I am playing" (NQ 70). Dattani highlights the hypocrisy inherent in arranged marriage or marriage of convenience that homosexuals enter into due to their inability to take a stand against societal pressure. The victim in such marriage is the wife who either develops self-doubts if unaware of her husband's preferences, or is left with little option but to adjust. Dattani critiques the workings of personal and moral choices of the gay sensibility.

What is common to all the plays of Dattani is the elite urban milieu to which his characters belong. Bijay Kumar Das in his book *Postmodern Indian English Literature* holds, "Dattani's plays are about contemporary reality that one encounters in the metropolis of our country" (126). *On a Muggy Night in Mumbai* is, as has been pointed out earlier, Dattani's first play dense with a host of issues related to homosexuality. A gathering of gay characters, a lesbian and a hetrosexual provide multipohonic perspectives. They meet in the house of their host Kamlesh, the perfection of which is described by Dattani in detailed stage directions as an attempt on the part of Kamlesh "... at creating a world where he can belong" (*CP* 49) thus introducing the theme of alienation. In the introductory note to the play, John Mc Rae holds, "... it is a play about how society creates patterns of behaviour and how easy it is for individuals to fall victim to the expectations society creates" (*CP* 45).

Depicting characters who are diametrically opposed to each other, Dattani projects alternative realities about sexuality: Kamlesh the romantic riding the high horse of sacrifice and duty, Sharad the witty and the only character at ease with his gay identity, Guard the exploited hetrosexual with unacknowledged homosexual leanings, Deepali the lesbian feminist in command of herself, and Kiran is the only straight character projecting hetrosexual womanhood. Though a close reading of the play projects the essence of each character, yet the felicity with which Dattani portrays them prevents their emerging as stereotypes. John Mc Rae comments, "They are carefully balanced range of individuals with a depth of experience that exceeds traditional expectations" (*CP* 45). Through these characters, the writer explores the dynamics of personal and ethical choice made while focusing on interpersonal relationships and themes of friendship, love, deception and betrayal. M.K. Naik says about *On a Muggy Night in Mumbai*, "The play presents a group of well-to-do homosexuals in Bombay, their changing mutual relationships, their revelations, their self-delusions and self-discoveries" (51).

The plot moves around the dilemma Kamlesh is in owing to his sister Kiran's decision to marry Ed who had been his lover and whom Kamlesh still loves. Unable to resolve the situation himself, Kamlesh invites his friends over to his place. As his friends drift in and conversation begins various issues are taken up and discussed: lack of choice for women in hetrogenous marriage, extramarital affair, marital violence, exploitation of a person as sex object – be it male or female, the need for support group and bonding amongst homosexuals, stifling love relation between gays, hypocrisy of 'closet' gays, demonizing of homosexuality by religion, stereotyping homosexuals, gay-marriage, non-congenial Indian milieu in relation to homosexuals, the need to conform owing to social pressures, marriage of convenience to camouflage gay identity, and gays not at ease with their sexuality. In the course of conversation subtle shifts of perception take place. Kamlesh is able to get over his infatuation for Ed and learns to appreciate Sharad. Kiran on learning the truth does not break down or look for support rather emerges a stronger individual with decision taking power. The closet homosexual Bunny acknowledges, "I have tried to survive. In both worlds. And it seems I do not exist in either" (*CP* 103). He resolves to be true to himself and to his wife by confessing and asking for her forgiveness. Sharad and Deepali, on the strength of their conviction remain unchanged while Ranjit's decision to leave India gets reinforced, for to quote him, "I can't seem to be both Indian and gay" (*CP* 88). Ed emerges as the most pathetic character. Once the mask of masculinity slips a weak, treacherous and hypocritical character is revealed who in his machinations to conform to heterosexually, ends up becoming self-alienated. Homosexuality is not a matter of choice and so discrimination based on these grounds is questioned.

While the three plays discussed take up the issue of marriage of convenience in one form or other, the tone is serious – implicating the society as well as the homosexuals. The same issue is dealt with in *Do the Needful* but in a humorous way. The gay hero and the notorious heroine get into a marriage of convenience with a secret understanding that they will be free to follow their natural inclinations. The humour arises out of the honest-dishonesty of the situation yet there is also an undercurrent of fear whether their lovers will understand and sympathize with them or not.

Dattani's success as a dramatist lies not only in his successful portrayal of characters, themes and felicity with language, but also in his use of theatrical space, light-effect as well as sound effect. The two radio plays discussed make ample and effective use of 'sound-scapes' to create a sense of immediacy as well as atmosphere. In the interview in Anita Nair's profile, Dattani says "... I always direct the first production of any play I write. That enables me to put in more stage instructions which goes on to become a kind of blue print for other directors?" (3). This prevents any deviance in connotation of the play by subsequent directors. Dattani seems to demand the atmosphere that he had envisaged and the effect he wants through specific instructions with regards to sound, light and space. Creation of sense of simultaneity by juxtaposing the past and the present and the use of overlapping conversation demands subtle and specific manoeuvring. At such juncture linear time is given up for emotional or non-linear time also known as compacting time. The coexistence of past and present is used in *On A Muggy Night* to divulge and to inform as well as to compare and contrast.

There is a symptomatic use of sound in *On A Muggy Night* as well as *Night Queen.* The sound of wedding 'band' like the repeated reference to 'heat' in the former is a constant reminder of the world out there with its own set of hegemonic values undermining those of gay community. In *Night Queen* the old woman calls out to Raghu in short intervals underlining the presence of familial and social obligations beyond the premises of his room. Dantani uses sound to create a sense of outer world pressing in and impinging upon the private space of the homosexuals. Anita Nair in the aforementioned profile concludes, "He does not provide readymade solutions or fully resolved endings" (7). In the interview for the same profile Dattani asserts, "...the theatre is a collective experience and the audience have to finish in their own heads what the playwright began" (6).

Mahesh Dattani's job is done, ours has just begun.

Notes

1. The reference to *Seven Steps Round the Fire*, *On a Muggy Night in Mumbai* and *Do the Needful* are, from *Collected Plays* (*CP*) by Mahesh Dattani. All subsequent references to the plays are from this edition.
2. Dattani, Mahesh. *Night Queen* in *Yaraana: Gay Writing from India.* Ed. Hoshang Merchant. All subsequent references to the work are from this edition.

References

Ayyar, Raj. "Yaraana: Gay Writing from India". Book Review. Online. Available on Internet at Gay Today.com.

Das, Bijay Kumar. *Postmodern English Literature.* New Delhi: Atlantic Publishers, 2003.

Dattani, Mahesh. *Collected Plays.* New Delhi: Penguin, 2000.

Merchant, Hoshang. ed. *Yarana: Gay Writing from India.* New Delhi: Penguin, 1999.

Naik, M.K. "Cinderella Still: Recent India English Drama". *Littcrit* 27, June/December, 2001.

Nair, Anita. "Mahesh Dattani: A Profile". Online. Available on Internet at google.com/nair.htm.

Sahara Time, July 10, 2004.

Vanita, Ruth and Saleen Kidwai. *Same Sex Love in India.* Delhi: Macmillan, 2001.

13

Dramatic Structures in Mahesh Dattani's *Tara* and *Final Solutions*

Charu Mathur

Plays are always written in the expectation of a performance, and performance modes differ from culture to culture and from time to time. The late nineteenth century saw the emergence of Naturalism, which as a movement insisted that art should accurately reflect 'life'. Yet writers like Brecht insisted that Naturalism could only show surface appearances. They claimed that what mattered in 'life' were the larger structures of society and history in which individuals and collectives choose between one action and another. The audience should be encouraged to concentrate on these structures and their own relationship to them rather than become bound up with the fate of an individual. To evoke an objective response from the audience requires a shift from the naturalist style to one, which can be termed as a more 'realistic' form of theatre. A truly 'realistic' drama must delve beneath and beyond the obvious 'given' to the subtext inherent in it.

Mahesh Dattani, the well-known contemporary Indian playwright, director and filmmaker, effectively achieves an objective distancing by experimenting and juggling with theatrical devices. He manoeuvres dramatic structures in order to create an objective and panoramic reality on the stage. However he never makes theatre a propagandist soapbox but allows the dramatic form to hint at possibilities that are contextually alive.

Endings can be closed – that is – defined and predicted, or they can be open-ended, holding within them the potential of different possibilities. My contention in the paper is to demonstrate how the closed structure of *Tara* and an open-ended one of *Final Solutions* weaves a fabric that becomes a faithful projection of the play's thematic design.

Tara is a rivetting play that questions the role of society that treats the siblings with double standards. The plot revolves around the conjoined twins Chandan and Tara Patel. An operation to separate the twins at birth leaves Tara crippled for life. The fact that the injustice is perpetrated by the victim's own mother whose preference for the male child suggests the complicity of women in perpetuating patriarchal norms.

It is a confined world that Dattani depicts. The play begins at the end and the exposition is through the metatheatrical dimension. Dan, the older Chandan is a narrator figure who is writing a play about his twin sister Tara. The narrative is non-linear and the play is predominantly a recall of memory with a predetermined closure. It moves back and forth in time and arrives at the starting point. Old newspaper cuttings, telephonic conversations, snippet from a television interview with Dr. Thakkar who records the progress of the medical advancement with a self-assured indifference all build up the action. The doctor occupies the highest level of the multi-level stage. "Although he doesn't watch the action of the play", state the stage directions, "his connection is asserted by his sheer God-like presence" (*Collected Plays* 323). God-like he is instrumental in bringing about the misfortune that befalls Tara. The acclaim he deserves for the successful surgical separation of the conjoined twins is annulled by his unethical favouring of the boy, something that he succumbs to for vested reasons. The fixity of his position on the stage, demonstrates the limitations of a dehumanized hand of scientific expertise. Dr. Thakkar is conceived as a stereotype. His connection with the realistic level is established through Dan, the interviewer who is always located in darkness with the focus being on the doctor. The distribution of light here communicates a message – Dr. Thakkar gets fame while the twins suffer in the cloistered milieu of gender prejudice.

The next realistic level shows Dan making an effort to write. He has a typewriter and a sheaf of papers in front of him. The play begins with Dan addressing the audience and acquainting them with his intention of writing a play about his sister. He thus establishes a line of communication between the stage and the auditorium emphasizing the world of stage being continuous with the world of the audience. The end however sees him tearing up whatever he has written seeking to make Tara's tragedy his own. The effective progress of Dan, the playwright, therefore amounts to zero.

The character dynamics, or rather the lack of it, is very much tied up with the plot. The main action of the play, which is also a projection of Dan's memory is played out on the lowest level of the stage. It represents the house of Patels. The parents, Patel and Bharti struggle to come to terms with their guilt, vindictively accusing and punishing each other. Their character shows no progression whatsoever and are bogged down by social stereotypes. The neighbouring offstage fictional space of the kitchen is Bharti's 'lair'. It is there that she escapes to, in order to cook Tara's favourite meals and silence the prick of her conscience. Even the distant offstage fictional space of the hospital, where she recedes to during her last days is more a morbid and hopeless reminder of her diseased self, than a place associated with recuperation. Besides, the absent figure of the grandfather pervades the narrative making the characters relinquish control over their life and situations.

Tara who is sharper and smarter than her brother is doubly victimized – once at the time of birth and then again by her parents discriminatory behaviour. Her mother's apparent showering of love is the only source of strength in her. "I am strong" she claims, "my mother made me strong" (*Collected*

Plays 330). When even this nurturing fiction of her life falls apart, she "wastes away and dies" (319). All through the play Tara is seen within the enclosed space of the Patel household. The only contact she makes with the outside world is through the inquisitive and garrulous girl, Roopa. There is nothing natural about this relationship, either, as she has been bribed into it by Bharti. She serves a plot function and acts as a 'foil' to Tara. It is through her portrayal that Dattani explores the prejudices that our society has for the crippled. Every time Tara ventures to move into the outer space of the street she has to face ridicule that, in turn, jettisons her back to the confines of her home. Here she finds a compensatory closeness to her twin brother. Their dependence on each other for happiness in spite of the physical separation, invites the audience to examine the rigid gender system. "Maybe we still are. Like we've always been. Inseparable", says Tara. Their estrangement after Patel's revelation has a shattering effect on both.

Chandan tries to escape the pain by moving to London and shielding himself with one mask over the other. In order to write about Tara and confront her again, he needs to get rid of these masks. Though he fails, he at least puts in the effort to adapt to changed circumstances. It is for this reason that Dattani assigns maximum mobility to his character. Dan or Chandan is the only one who mediates between the three stage levels. His movement between the multiple 'foci' for action is effected by a cinematic cross fading between these spaces. This sets up a tension between these 'foci', an appreciation of which is crucial to the understanding of the ironic undercurrents. Since, reminiscence is the crux of the narrative, the flexibility of Dan's position also contributes to the fluidity between the present and the past and shifts from the virtual to the fictive space. The schematization of spaces and the use of levels and areas led by lighting is engineered in such a manner that the characters seem to be in the grip of something larger than themselves. A number of different 'foci' for the action within a single stage set assists plausibility and furthers the main project of limiting the action to a single oppressive environment.

This is also evident in Dattani's use of simultaneous action and overlapping conversations, when spaces are contrasted and the characters are not explicitly connected yet lead to and arrive at a common point of understanding. The scene gains in ironic strength from this simultaneity. The conversation between Tara and Roopa in the street about the practice of drowning girl babies in milk, and Bharti and Chandan, in the house about Patel's preferential treatment of Chandan have overtones of the same narrative. Again later, Roopa in the street calls Tara asking her to come out so that she can teach the latter a lesson. While in the house Patel narrates the incident of how Chandan was favoured over Tara with the common leg, which made Tara a 'freak'. The point of connection that links these two scenes dawns upon the audience when Roopa prominently places against her house, a poster that reads, "We don't want freaks" (378). Both the conversations are seemingly unrelated, yet each lends meaning to the other.

The dramatic structure thus works to produce a feeling in the audience towards something more intangible than the spaces themselves. But the effect also produces an attitude towards the relationship between person and place, the audience feel that if the characters were not so irretrievably locked into their specific places they could perhaps find a way out. The staging makes them long for a movement between places, for things to un-fix rather than fix. The play turns out to be what Howard Barker calls, the "theatre of catastrophe" (13). It presents a world that shocks the audience into considering their own.

While *Tara* is a play about gender bias, *Final Solutions* deals with the sensitive issue of communal prejudice. The play opens with the partition of India in 1947 and then shifts between the past and the present while negotiating the changing nuances of Hindu-Muslim relationships. This involves three generations of people who convey complex and abstract messages about guilt, tolerance, religious bias and cultural prejudice.

Though the play begins with a delving into the past, the main action is located in the present. The exposition is through young Daksha's diary. The audience is introduced to the convulsions of the partition through her disturbed reaction as she realizes that the "pooja room" was as vulnerable as any other part of the house and the "idol" she had grown up seeing her mother worship was "just another painted doll" (*Collected Plays* 167). The symbols of religious fervour right at the onset, assume connotative implications of violence, loss of faith and insecurity. The character-plot potential of *Final Solutions* moves towards an open-endedness and hints at the possibilities of a resolution. The oil lamp converted into an electric one on Daksha's desk itself is emblematic of progress and change.

The shifts in time and situations have again been portrayed through a multi-level stage. The cross fading of lights plays a vital role in transferring the dramatic space from one time and place to another. The main action is in the present and takes place in the house of the Gandhis. The name 'Gandhi' is significant, as it becomes a mock representation of the justice and non-violence associated with it. Hardika, the old Daksha occupies a place at the highest level. Unlike Dr. Thakkar of *Tara*, she is not a fixed entity. Assigned a flexibility of movement between the different levels, she is a living embodiment of the past with its attendant guilt and shame. Her presence undercuts the apparent naturalism and upsets the fragile frictions, which the characters had created. "Things have not changed much" she says when she opens her diary after forty years (167). True, the mob outside was as mindless as before. Its location on the crescent shaped ramp that dominates the stage is indicative of its pervasive presence providing the impetus to the action. The wearing of either Hindu or Muslim masks demonstrates the manner in which ordinary people get misled by the superimposed mask of religious fundamentalism.

The uniform black attire is also a visual signifier, for the blackness of heart has nothing to do with religion.

By contrast, the world of Gandhi is seemingly at peace. The intervention of Javed and Bobby who seek shelter in their house shakes the complacency of the family members. These two ambassadors from the space outside come and disturb the equilibrium within. The gesture of Ramnik opening the door to let the young men enter is a symbolic one, for he then also allows a peep into the hypocrisy inherent in his liberal views. He is as guilty of religious fanaticism as the aggressive Javed who is a hired "riot-rouser" (198).

Hardika, we come to know, too has her quarrels with the minority community. This was not so much because they were responsible for the brutal killing of her father, but more on account of the punishment meted out to her for maintaining cordial relations with the Muslims. She was "Confined. Never let out of the house. Like a dog that had gone mad!" (223). Dattani highlights the contrast between the intelligent and friendly young bride Daksha and the grudging and revengeful grandmother Hardika by an actual split in her portrayal. Time has transformed her into a very different person. In fact, none of the characters are static. All through the play there is a free flow of ideas with each character opening a window to newer perspectives, transforming and getting transformed in the process. Javed sheds his extremist stance to arrive at a more moderate understanding of the cultural forces at work. The apologetic Bobby learns to boldly confront the truth about himself and about God. "He knows His strength! I don't believe in Him but He believes in me. He smiles!" says Bobby, "He smiles at our trivial pride and our trivial shame" (224). Smita and her mother Aruna also, come to have a more honest understanding of each other, and discontinuity of the characters becomes a sign of hope.

However, the cloistered space of the pooja room that Aruna guards with ferocity, is something to be wary of. The ringing of the pooja bell recurringly, is projected as a signifier of religious fanaticism. In contrast, Daksha's love for the songs of Noorjahan express a longing for harmony. In the combative struggle between the two lies the conflict of the play. Similarly, home has been repeatedly depicted as a space of oppression, earlier in Daksha's confinement and later when Smita comments, "Maybe we should all run away from home like Javed. For five minutes everyday. So we can quickly gulp in some fresh air and go back in" (219).

Hope lies in the movement of Smita, Javed and Bobby from the limiting inner space of the house to the outer one of different options. They are the windows that open to the future and it is within their power to build bridges that past hatred had destroyed. The play, in the end, avoids a clarity of the fictional situation suggesting that the 'final solutions' are ultimately in the choices that people make.

As a socially sensitive playwright, Dattani makes use of the onstage fictional space to tackle the disturbing abstractions of society that he encounters in the actual world. Whether the closure of the narrative is open ended as in *Final Solutions* or a closed one as in *Tara*, his plays never really conclude because of their continued relevance to the reality around.

References

Barker, Howard. *Arguments for a Theatre*. London: John Calder, 1989.

Dattani, Mahesh. *Collected Plays*. New Delhi: Penguin, 2000.

Wallis, Mick, Simon Shepherd. *Studying Plays*. London: Arnold, 2002.

14

Building a Great Tradition

Chaman Ahuja interviews Girish Karnad

"It is easy to be a genius at twenty, but it's quite another thing to be a talent at fifty." Thus averred Girish Karnad, a genius who won the Sangeet Natak Akademi Award when he had written just a couple of plays and who, having given ample proof of his abundant talent through masterpiece after masterpiece, got at sixty-one the most prestigious literary honour available in India, viz., the Jnanpeeth Award (1998). Of course, his plays can still be counted on fingertips but each work has proved a milestone in the history of Indian theatre. It was with his works that set going that never-ending debate about the identity of the Indian theatre. The creator of *Yayati* (1961), *Tughlaq* (1964), *Hattina Hunja* (Sacrifice, 1967), *Hayavadana* (1970), *Naga-Mandala* (1988), *Tale-Danda* (Beheading, 1990), *Agni Mattu Male* (Fire and Rain, 1996), Mr. Karnad is even more widely known for his leading role in that "poem in celluloid", *Samskar*, for his acting in *Swami*, *Manthan* and *Nishant*, for his direction of *Bhumika* and *Utsava*, for his roles in serials like *Khandan*, *Malgudi Days*, *Apna Aasman*, as the Director of FTII at Pune, as the Chairman of Sangeet Natak Akademi. But although he has wandered long in the realm of the electronic media, he regards playwriting as his home and keeps coming back to it. In fact, he would wish to stay home and write more plays but, then, there is no money in playwriting and he has to survive.

Meeting GK in Bangalore in 1997, Chaman Ahuja found him a most articulate person. Here are some excerpts from the interview – his views about his own work and art, and about the theatre scenario in India today.

Although you claim to be quintessentially a playwright, in four decades you have written no more than ten plays; are you satisfied with the pace of your playwriting?
I would not like creative work to be assessed in terms of numbers. Ibsen and Satyajit Ray could never produce more than one play, or one film, in a year. In playwriting you just don't sit down and dash away a script; good ideas don't visit you every day. Observing, reading, thinking, researching, planning, writing, rewriting several drafts – all that takes time. It takes longer when you are dividing time with other things – as I have to do, because I have to look after a family. Hopefully, in a few years, when my sons go to college, I shall take to writing full-time – as I have always wanted to do.

With so many achievements, you have a right to be happy. Any regrets?
Of course; why not? Very often, I feel miserable when I realize that, instead of writing good plays – which I think I can do, and should be doing – I have to act in bad TV serials. In this connection, I should wish to add that although acting in films is quite remunerative, it is soul-destroying, too. That is why I refuse to be just an actor, I act just for money, for my livelihood. Mercifully, I have been able to save my soul by returning to playwriting whenever I can. Theatre has been my first love and remains a passion still.

One should have thought that the writing of poetry in English was your first love.
That was later, in my college days. Much earlier, in my childhood, I had fallen for theatre – for the Parsi theatre of the Natak Companies in the city which I saw with my parents, and for Yakshagana in the villages which I visited with the servants of the family. If the former yielded to me insights into the dramatic power of the historical events, the latter opened up the scope of the material in the myths – in the episodes of the Mahabharata. But for that background, I don't know what I could have been writing.

In the tempering of your genius, what other influences would you like to own?
In Bombay, once I saw *Miss Julie* directed by Mr. Alkazi. I was impressed by the cannibalism of the play and the way the lights faded in and out on the stage. On that evening, without being aware of it, I decided that I wanted to be a playwright. In fact, when I actually started writing plays, I did it without being aware of it. When I got Rhodes scholarship, my ambition was to live forever in the land of Eliot and Auden, but my parents wanted me to return to India and to settle down here. This created tension in the family and it was to ease that tension that I found myself writing *Yayati* while travelling by ship to England. Suddenly I realized that my talent lay not in poetry but in drama – and that too in Kannada rather than English. Talking of influences, I could perhaps mention Anouilh whose *Antigone* and *Euridyce* introduced me to the art of investing myths with contemporary relevance. Also let me not forget my association with the Madras Players: it yielded insights into the craft of theatrical production. Now, even as I write, I can visualize what the scenes could be like on the stage.

Didn't the British theatre influence you when you were at Oxford at that formative age?
All that I learnt there was that the Western theatre had nothing for me. The absurdists were repeating themselves, and I found

the drawing-room plays – interpreting people within narrow psychological limits – boring. I think, the western society being too individualistic, western theatre is hinged round individuals while we in India define ourselves in relational terms.

Who, then, were your models in India – Kalidasa?... Tagore?
Not at all. Kalidasa is too remote, too classical, too perfect for me. Tagore's plays are pallid – exactly like the figures in the Shantiniketan school of painting, his characters are staid, two-dimensional, totally bloodless. I respond better to my contemporaries like Vijay Tendulkar, Mohan Rakesh, Badal Sircar, but I would not call that influence.

How about your interest in mathematics: did it play any role in your playwriting?
Maybe, yes. It gave me a sense of structure. I was fascinated to note that changing an element in one half of an equation brings about a change in the other half, too. I approach each scene like a sum and try to resolve the problems as if I were solving a mathematical proposition.

Generally speaking, what is the process of your creativity in playwriting?
When a story excites me, I want to share that excitement with others. As I analyze the components of its fascination, the form of the play gets shaped. Often my final draft has little to do with the first. In the process of writing, as I try different things, I develop my technique.

Why always borrow stories from myths, legends and history – why not create own plots?
Maybe, I cannot invent plots. I go in for stories that are exciting. I think these are better stories than I will be able to botch up. At least in this want of originality, I am perhaps as good, or as bad, as Shakespeare. The only time I tried to invent, I failed miserably – that was in *Anju Mattige* – a play about an

Indian family enmeshed in the racist and class antipathies of the life in England. One thing more; I turn not only to myths, legends and history, but also to folklore. In fact, what attracts me most is the archetypal folk tale: with no fat already there, I find in it all the scope for flirting with ideas. What is more, in a folklorist framework, I find the great advantage of being able to subvert the traditional, even classical, beliefs. Since folk tales make fun on every body – rulers, priests, even gods – every thing is taken in good humour. Of course, I must hasten to add, my basic concern is with the human spirit and not with the folk *per se*, using folk as a mere aesthetic device with no further exploration of what it is to be human, does not attract me.

How about a play holding mirror unto life and showing the contemporaries their face?
And is that possible only if I talk about the present? Can't one make history reflect one's own time? Can't ancient myths serve as metaphors for contemporaneity? In the fate of *Tughlaq*, the people could hear the echo of post-Independence politics of India – the loss of innocence, the decline of idealism into cynicism, the rift between ideology and practice. Likewise, *Tale-Danda* might have been about Basavanna but it reminds one of the Mandal and the Mandir-Masjid controversies as well; the betrayal of Basavanna's disciples recalls to mind the betrayal of our intellectuals during the Emergency. Do *Hayavadana* and *Naga-Mandala* have nothing to say to our audiences about themselves? When has man ceased to be interested in the relationship between mind and body, in man's quest for completeness?

Can't this be done directly by dramatizing the contemporary situations or events?
I have never been interested in turning theatre into a newspaper. Distancing is pivotal if one wants to look at the present critically, it helps the audience experience something and, at the same time, think about the problem dispassionately.

Realism in theatre is actually a myth. Human problems are universal, eternal; only social problems are time-bound.

How about the role of art in bringing about changes in society?
Perhaps a journalist is more likely to succeed as a reformist than a playwright. At best, an artist can question values. Those who deal with social reality *per se* seldom go beyond description. Photographic impression of reality has no value unless you do something more with it. I want my audience to return with a sense of greater dimension of things.

Has your work in the other media proved advantageous to you as a playwright?
Not in the process of playwriting as such, but, maybe, in certain other ways, indirectly. It has kept me involved in the general flow of life – I keep getting ideas from outside. Many of my contemporaries either went dry after writing a few plays or started repeating themselves. One thing more: one learns from experience, whatever the field. For example, I have done fairly well as an actor, but I failed in *Vamsa Vriksha* – the movie that I had codirected with BV Karanth. After that, I made up my mind never to act in a film directed by myself. I have extended that lesson in the other direction: I never act in my plays nor do I direct them.

For decades, theatre people in India have been talking about going back to roots – to ancient myths, to folk forms, to classical tradition; and a lot has been done, too. How far has that movement succeeded in forging a new identity for the Indian theatre, and what is your assessment of your role in that movement?
The discussion of the productions of my *Tughlaq* and *Hayavadana* were perhaps the starting point of that controversy. Anyway, I have written long enough and am now old enough not to worry about the identity problem. I write just what I feel like writing. As for that so-called movement, well some good experiments did emerge here and there – a body of

beautiful works like *Ghasiram Kotwal, Andha Yuga, Johumarswamy* – but I wouldn't says that all this gave birth to any specific tradition as such. Seen in terms of a tradition, I think we have no theatre. I have been trying to create a tradition of my own, as has Tendulkar.

The movement stemmed at least the onslaught of the realistic theatre of the west...
Now, even the West has given up realism. In fact, they are moving towards us. In America, for example, no one does Tennessee Williams' kind of plays any more. Realism *per se* is more or less dead. His *Three Tall Women* is so different from the work of the person who had written *Who's Afraid of Virginia Woolf?* In England, too, Osborne and his angry youngmen who dominated the kitchen-sink plays are long forgotten. When I was young, the domineering figure was Shaw; not so today. And who are their playwrights now? Dario Fo, who has won the Noble Prize, comes from the clowning tradition of *commedia dell'arte* – not from the realistic tradition. Indeed, the cultural imperialism of the West need not bother us now. In fact, more and more, the playwrights are moving away from written plays towards theatre.

Isn't that true of India as well?
We have never had any real tradition of playwriting at all; after Sanskrit plays, where are the texts? As for our folk theatre, it has been a tradition of performance, not of playwriting. Only the west has had playwriting tradition, and that too now and then, off and on.

How about our Parsi theatre?
To have any value to all, drama must engage itself seriously with the contradictions that lie at the heart of the human situation in general and the society it addresses in particular. The Parsi theatre simply refused to acknowledge the very existence of any problem, existential or social. It had, therefore,

no great drama; its strength lay in music. When the talkies came to offer even better music, the Companies just vanished.

Going by what has happened in the Indian theatre during the last few decades, we appear to be moving towards a semi-classical tradition. Does this appropriation of folk forms by the urban theatre imply an aesthetic risks or artistic compromises?
Well, after my *Hayavadana*, I found myself being invited to all sorts of seminars related to folk forms, and then I was offered Homi Bhabha fellowship to work on the folk theatre of North Karnataka. It was all so educative for me and ultimately brought home the realization that there was no difference between the folk and the classical drama: the aesthetic principles are the same. The basic thing, I discovered, is that the subject of any play has to be the human spirit. Using folk as a mere aesthetic device – with no further exploration of what it is to be human – does not attract me. It is not the question of garnishing the plays with music, colour and dance – that is how some of our playwrights have tried to cover up their sloppiness. Of course, the folk forms do have certain intrinsic advantages. For example, the folklorist framework subverts classical notions about our holy cows; through the tongue-in-cheek irony, folk tales make fun of rulers, priests, even gods – without offending even the puritans.

Do you think that the experiments in modernization of myths, legends and history have yielded the desired results?
Whenever the re-location of the folk forms in the urban setting has worked, the results have been spectacular – in some of the works of Jabbar Patel, Chandrashekhar Kambar, Ratan Thiyam, BV Karanth, for example. But not always. The reason is that we have not been able to evolve modern theatre music idiom; our urban theatre has yet to find a way of expressing contemporary problems through musical forms – the way the American musicals do.

Is there no way of reconciling theatre East and West – into a new kind of realism?
European realism has become such a universal idiom that it is hard to imagine any other kind. Maybe if we started rebuilding along new lines – that is, if, instead of verbose, mind-oriented Shavian realism, we opted for Chekhovian realism where mind, body and spirit coalesce, where silence speaks, where even inaction is a form of action.

What worries you most about the theatre situation in India?
What worries me really is that there is no theatre – a theatre that may sustain a playwright and save him from drudging in films, bad serials, or whatever, to keep his body and soul together. One thing more about which no one is talking. For theatre there is no audience because, they say, it is fighting a losing battle against the television. I don't agree there. It is not that people don't want to see theatre; it is the problem of getting out in the evenings in most of the big cities. In Bangalore, for example, the traffic situation is horrible. You don't get autorickshaws easily; there is no dependable bus service, no local-trains system. Once people come back from work, they hate to go out again on their two-wheelers – with all that driving tension and pollution outside. One doesn't mind spending thirty-five rupees on a ticket but when one has to shell out as much, or even more, to an autorickshaw while going and then again while coming, how many middle class people can afford that – and how often? In Calcutta, theatre is thriving because they have metro trains, in Bombay they have train service and bus service in tandem.

As a playwright, are you not worried about the growing trend to underplay the role of the script – and to change the script in the name of interpretation?
I have no choice, there was a time when changes upset me but now I have learnt not to bother, *Hayavadana* and *Naga-Mandala* have been done so variously that I have come to

see great virtue in directorial interpretations. I take it as a compliment that the same play of mine has the potential of yielding such diverse levels. When they were rehearsing *Naga-Mandala* for the Gutherie Theater, they called me for discussion and the director, Garland Wright, asked me how he might do it. I said, do it as an American play – as an American director would do a Brecht or a Lorca for the American audiences. As you would never get the Indianness right, I said, don't make it kitsch by putting a little sitar here and a little *ghagra* there. So when Garland did it his own way, it was a different production – different from anything done here but great in its own way. So I just write without bothering about what might happen later. Maybe, I can make some fuss today, but what about tomorrow when I shall be no more to intervene. What can poor Shakespeare do about what the directors have been doing to his play – at times mangling them beyond recognition?

And what about the interpretations of the theatre critics: are they dependable?

If you invite a critic to come and review your play, it is his right to like it or not. But more often than not, I find our criticism vindicating Susan Sontag's rather cynical remark that interpretation is the revenge of intellect on art. Anyway, I have learnt not to bother about critics too much. I struggle with my plays; I expect critics to struggle, too.

15

The Fugue of Experience

Transcreating Poetic Metatheatre

Anju Dhadda Misra
Arti Sah

Translating and putting together these poetic expressions of the experience of theatre one has as if participated in a relay race – the baton of the dialogic experience of the conflict to be handed on with the same unabated urgent expedience as received. There seems to be in this activity a kind of a cyclicity of getting back to the same step whether you climb up or you climb down.

The experience of theatre is the keeping alive of a conflict and of confluence together. The conflict between the personal and the public, between the rational and the emotional, between the cathectic and the jouissance, the argument between the multiple personae within, inheres.

Somewhere between the ebb and the flow of the argument the dramatist freezes the play into a written script which the director makes fluid and freezes into a performative text, which again the actor makes fluent and freezes into an enacted text.

The rise and fall of the thought, the arrivals and departures of the arguments, the oscillations and the vacillations of the vicissitudes and the making and unmaking of attitudes continues to pulse and reverberate carrying over as well as leaving behind something at every crossing that the thought makes.

It is this leftover, the residual or the excessive overflow that condenses itself into metatheatric poetry – in the poet, in the dramatist, in the director, in the actor and in the auditor/spectator. Translating metatheatric poetry is like being soaked in the fluent moment as the play melts into its original conflict and confluence over and over again.

Anju Dhadda Misra

Translating metatheatric poetry is carrying the pulsations of the theatric experience a step further by transcreating them in another linguistic and cultural context while keeping its rhythms alive and vibrant. What is required is to sustain the dialectics of drama with its movements and counter movements, its ebb and flow soothed into the lull of poetry and this confluence of theatric experience and poetic form to be energised in another language and culture in the right blend of ebullience and repose. It is thus a straddling of experience and form as well as of languages and cultures.

The movement of the inner conflict between the polarities of the theatric experience whose external expression continues the dichotomy in its fluent and frozen forms, becomes representative of the throb of the cosmic pulse and the metatheatric also becomes the metaphysical. The dimension of the dramatic divide becomes panoramic as it reaches beyond attitudes, arguments, states and thoughts to existence itself. It takes on the nature of core ontological questions about the self and the other, being and non-being, the real and the unreal, the seen and the unseen, continuity and cessation.

Arti Sah

theatre physiognomy

anju dhadda misra

words wander away
when looked for
speech stumbles
falling into silence
arguments to be made
arise only as treppeverter
and disagreements never stand their ground

voice deserts eloquence
visors mask vision
silent stands
stretch end to end
dividual multitudes warble
rising to fevered pitch

furled winged chrysalis
eye-screen-cyke
awaiting a breath

agonised
silent
savage
still!

another guise

rajendra gupta*

why am I startled
to see myself in the mirror
though little has changed
not dreams nor nights
not this world
not my startled eyes
not this silence
nor the idle banter
why, then, reveals the mirror
today — this strange someone
staring at me
or else an actor
seeking his self.

translated by
arti sah

---

* Rajendra Gupta an eminent film and theatre director and actor.

wordless, in language

navin sagar*

something
the child wants to create
the child wants to make anew
a word

even as he is about to create his word
language displaces it
and the child
enters language
silenced
bereft of his word

will he remember his displaced word
when years later
he steps on stage
seeking his truth
in language

will it burst upon him
even if only once
will he ever create
or only step into the deep backstage alley
pre-formulated

the child who even now is
about to create

translated by
anju dhadda misra

---

* Navin Sagar (1948-2000) poet, critic, fiction-writer. His story collection *Uska School* and poetry collection *Neend se Lambi Raat* were published in his life. These are from his posthumus collection *Jab Khud Nahin Tha*

curtain raiser

priyadarshan*

chairs in place
lighting complete
mikes tested
now each whisper reaches
every corner of the theatre

ready stands
Kalidas
but for the costume
Mallika preens her cloud tresses
in the unclear mirror of the dark greenroom
restive Vilom
silently rehearses his dialogues
quailing
at his own impact
Ambika reconnoitres the empty theatre

the stage dark still
presently she'll be winnowing here
and Mallika rush in
but, later.

darkness yet
on stage
and the theatre deserted
slowly the spectators will arrive
the chairs, rattling, be filled
snatches of conversation swell
and suddenly sink
a man will inquire after someone
some woman let out a peal of laughter
and suddenly fall silent
abashed at her temerity
plays are enacted before the play

---

* Priyadarshan, poet, critic. journalist and translator.

with Kalidas' repeated retreats
on stage saunters Othello
put out the light!
put out the light!
Macbeth rants in despair
burn out forlorn candles
in the taut world of theatre
aeons come and go

above all flows time
all aglow with dialogue
all hands touch all others'
moist, trembling
Othello on stage
but who lurks within Othello
who watches him from the gallery
orbiting his own mind
does he recognise
the seed of jealousy within?

To each his solitude
within all
theatres
a backstage
a greenroom
lit with a dim lamp
a little dust on the mirror
all ready to enact their roles
within each an Othello
lamenting Desdemona
Kalidas evading Vilom

even the actors
oblivious
of the aeons the show has run
of the years that fold into three hours
when the curtain falls and the lights go out
several worlds collapse with a clash.

translated by
arti sah

dance

'ajneya'*

there is this taut rope
upon which I dance
the rope upon which I dance
is tied to two poles

what I do really
is a tight-rope-dance from one pole to another

upon the tight rope between the two poles
upon which I dance
falls a sharp light—
in which people see the dance

they see neither me, who dances
nor the rope upon which I dance
nor the poles upon which the rope is tied
nor even the light that makes the dance visible

they see only the dance

but I who dance
upon the tight-rope
between the poles
upon which falls the light

in that light
between those poles
upon that rope
am not dancing at all
I only flounder
from pole to pole

---

* Sacchidanand Heeranand Vatsyayan Ajneya (1911-1987), poet, novelist, writer, one of the most eminent and felicitous writers in hindi, author of one poetic play *Uttar Priyadarshi*. The chosen poem is one of his famous poems on the creative process.

to release the rope
from one or the other end
that the tension ease
and in it I find release
yet the pull never slackens
and I run
from pole to pole
and the pull persists
nothing yields
as I flounder
that is the dance
they see
not me
not the rope
not the poles
not the light
not the pull even

only dance

translated by
anju dhadda misra

the dance bond

nand kishore acharya*

ta dhin ta dhin ta thai ta thai ta dhin ta
jhanjhananananana jnanjhananananana
jhanjhanananjhananan jhan...

beats the tabla and the feet beat
and ankle-bells dance
quickening, mercurial, spinning
intent

—as though the dance was creation

she dances
becoming the dance
unaware
of being watched
devoured
by people
unconcerned with dance

a bead
breaks from the ankle-bells
is flung asunder
afar into a corner,

the dance continues
people watch
what can she
who has herself become dance
and the audience
watching unabashed her becoming the dance, know
what became of the bead
the bead from her ankle bells!

ta dhin ta dhin ta thai ta thai ta dhin ta......

translated by
anju dhadda misra

---

* Nand Kishore Acharya (1946), poet, dramatist, dramaturgist and theorist, author of eight volumes of poetry and over twelve plays on historical, mythical as well as contemporary issues. The chosen poems are about the artist's performing relation to his art.

between earth, sky

bansi kaul*

earth, sky—
somewhere between the two
the old tight-rope-dancer
has lost his balancing pole

the child dancer
fearful without the pole
and that in the middle of this —

his child glance
gauges the length of the pole

his glance
apprehends the end of the rope

between earth, sky
the father's eyes
entreat,
spur him upward

there is no refusing
for it is his destiny
to climb up to the very edge
to walk the tight-rope
to be caught in the iron hoop

pole lost in sky
rope lost at other end

yet father, son
eager for the show
eager
between
earth,
sky

translated by
anju dhadda misra

---

* Bansi Kaul, famous dramatist and theatre director.

theatre

alok dhanwa*

the bench in the park
unending
only stands in the park
its presence pervades
beyond the city

lights on the bridge
steadfast
fill my nights
and will beckon to me
even beyond death

the long-billed tiny woodpecker
I saw
barely a couple times
in the whole decade
I shall see
in theatre this year

theatre, eternal,
is not the building only.

translated by
anju dhadda misra

* Alok Dhanwa, poet and critic

in act

nand kishore acharya

rapt all
in my act
endless the applause
at the end of the play
and I, cowering in shame.

not diffident
but wondering
if this applause could sense
the hatred, the ambition
seething beneath lust
and compassion
and the deceit
which I am
recognising myself in my act...

what for them is my act
is the truth for me
if only it would also be their truth for them
if they would see themselves enact in my act...

would the applause be endless still
or would their heads
be buried in shame?

translated by
arti sah

the play

sanjiv misra[*]

curtain rose
actors appeared
and after the dialogue
the play ended

some character
remained
speechless
hesitating
within the actor

despite the dialogue
something inhered
unsaid

so much that could have been
upon the stage
remained unperfomed

that
only so much
now
lingers
huddled to the heart
rest — forgotten

that alone the truth
rest
witnessed by all
only play!

translated by
anju dhadda misra

---

* Sanjiv Misra (1961), poet, journalist and translator, has published renderings of Zen and Sufi stories and Katherine Mansfield's, *Garden Party and Other Stories* and two volumes of poems.

spectacle

sanjiv misra

in the dazzling light
on stage
witnessed by all
always the valiant hero

pivot of every applause
yet each time
after the act
as lights fade and the curtains fall

legs trembling
head bowed
I sink in the same dream

that I
feeble actor
one day will really become
the spectacle I enact everyday
for the spectators

translated by
anju dhadda misra

the night of the Rammat

giriraj kiradoo*

upon a taut rope between two terraces each time they fixed the lights. the stage reached out to meet the terraces and the courtyards. ancient women peered from terraces of tall and courtyards of the small houses and sank into the crimson fluidity of memory of dead actors and their departed youth. lights would shake as if they would fall upon the stage or upon the next morn into our sleep.

(the balloon-vendor-boy ignorant that he was selling balloons to balloonfaced boys, gave a blue balloon which wore his grandmother's face to the redballoonfaced boys. to the yellowballoonfaced old widow he gave saffron balloons that looked like her grandsons who were to get the mother goddess's blessing the next morn)

the story had a colour for which we had not found a name for generations.
then someone said in our sleep: crimson
and since then, the story is crimson. not only we, even our elders seemed to see the colour sprinkled upon our terraces

crimson was the colour of the tale
crimson was the colour of the wail
the blood the two warrior lovers of a woman shed
was crimson as well

(the youth looking for a spot for the camera asked us in desperation, why you keep coming for the same story, over and over again for generations. These youths often were taken to be outsiders and often got their tea free)

and then, as had happened often
past the spectators the actors paced to the stage
the eldest, enacting the same role for years, led the procession
on stage, they were still young
wearing crimson costumes, men also played women

---

* Giriraj Kiradoo (1975) poet, critic and teacher of English, and recipient of Bharat Bhushan Agarwal award..

(most of us could hear the dialogues only through rerenderings by grand-mothers who could sniff rain in the air and whose bodies had no hollows for age)

costumes same
same narrative
only the cuts of the clothes changed

and then as we had often heard
dead actors whisper from the wings in the same roles that they enacted in their lives

"wings, too, are foreground"
"the tale, too, is a stage"
"dead, too, are actors"

(our narrators lament that they got the right to narrate only on occasions like this.)

the colours of the festivals to come kept us awake in these nights. we went away alone to leave the courtyard dwellers alone, to be the caretakers of the forsaken stage and deserted courtyard.

the nightwakers
sank in their crimson sleep
and the image of the desolate tale flickered
in our sleep
like lights.

translated by
anju dhadda misra

so well do I impersonate myself

navin sagar

stepped out of the house
then stepping out of myself
began to follow myself
I kept falling so far behind
as to barely appear before disappearing

one day
on the way back home, disappeared
where does one follow the invisible
came back home
blurring, the walls seem to lean
the stairs ascending
descending

but he came not home
stepped out of the house
then stepping out of myself, vanished

I peer into the mirror
he doesn't look back at me
I repeatedly return
he doesn't

none suspects at home
mute objects know but inquire not of me
where
was he and who was I!
so well do I impersonate myself
as to look identical
doors open—
awake in the dusky motion picture of sleep
I lie in the forsaken bed!

translated by
arti sah

exode

priyadarshan

chairs empty
displaced
darkness on stage

Hamlet's soliloquies
now solitary
no one utters them
none listens
voiceless they wander in the cold theatre

now comes the first awareness of the night
the darkness outside
no one rants on stage
that ominous as death
can silence sometimes be

after the multitudinous din
after the strutting-sashaying shadows
and mellow, rapt applause
after the sorrow, which
the blue spotlight's caress
could not sweep away, is spent
there's darkness
sombre as death
silence
leaden as death

not a spectator
nor actor
no musician, nor orchestra
neither any time, nor any sorrow

simply inert
breath suspended lies the theatre
corpse-like,
awaiting
resurrection ?

translated by
arti sah

the unseen

bansi kaul

what if I were to find the unseen
suppose all were to find it
would lives be easier then?

between truth and falsehood
are there some matters
of joy and pain?

suppose joy and pain were true
suppose the moon were true
suppose the sun were true
what then would falsehood be?

is this the dream
before the long sleep....
better to lose oneself
in the boundless unseen.

translated by
arti sah

real unreal

navin sagar

way before my origin
is where I begin
and beyond my end
exists my continuum

there persists a fading memory of the delusion of life,
I recall its forgotten form
when I step within, without
sprawls my shadow
earth and sky
gather in my perception
creation
an unravelling of my mystery

wandering within
I get scattered amongst the stars

I unreal
real unreal!

translated by
anju dhadda misra

16

Absurdist Dilemmas

Sircar's *Evam Indrajit*

Preeti Bhatt

The play *Evam Indrajit* (1962) by the major Bengali playwright Badal Sircar is a landmark in the history of Indian theatre. In a period when Indian playwrights were writing conventional plays with a definite plot structure, dynamic characters and complex storylines, Sircar's play originally written in Bengali, challenged the strategies of traditional drama. In his play Sircar systematically attacked all the conventional rules of dramatic action, motivation and language. Drama critics in India hailed the play as revolutionary in structure and style, and the play enjoyed great popularity and appreciation when it was staged.

The present article examines the unusual structure, setting and character portrayal in the play and argues that *Evam Indrajit* exemplifies the characteristics of the theatre of the Absurd through its structure and ideas. K. Venkata Reddy in "Badal Sircar's *Evam Indrajit* as an Absurd Play" aims to study the absurdist features of the play but focuses primarily on the thematic concerns and does not convincingly bring out its absurdist traits. The present article attempts to do so by concentrating on the dramatic strategies employed by the playwright that highlight the element of absurdity in the play.

During the 1950s and early 60s some European and American playwrights wrote plays which expressed metaphysical anguish at the absurdity of human existence by focusing on the instability, meaninglessness and unpredictability of human life. Noteworthy among these playwrights were Samuel Beckett, Eugene Ionesco, Albert Pinter and Edward Albee. These dramatists agreed with the existentialist philosopher Albert Camus's assessment in his book *The Myth of Sisyphus* (1942) that the human condition was essentially absurd because humans continued to seek order and reason in a universe that was not based on these principles. Camus writes in the essay "Absurd Freedom", "these two certainties – my appetite for the absolute and for unity and the impossibility of reducing this world to a rational reasonable principle – I also know that I cannot reconcile them" (342). The existential writers in their works questioned the human tendency to analyse life on the basis of the theory of cause and effect.

This pessimistic vision of humanity struggling vainly to find a purpose of living as seen in the dramatic works of this period was a reflection of the overall feeling of defeatism and despair in the post-war world. After witnessing the destruction of the two World Wars, man realized that his idealist beliefs, his clinging to religion and his faith in the rationality of human beings could not save him. It was a world of pain and frustration, and offered no hope to the people. These playwrights wrote in a social context in which the traditional narratives or metanarratives of Lyotard "no longer inspire confidence, leaving society with a sense of alienation and loss" (Haney II, 39). The despair at the sight of the world and the loss of an ideology to depend on created the feeling of negativism that was evoked in the creative works of this period.

During the fifties, India was reeling under the shock and aftermath of the partition of the Indian subcontinent and the loss of life and property that accompanied it. The feeling of betrayal at the division of the country, the sense of helplessness at the poor administration of the country and its defense organization, and the rising unemployment of the educated middle classes, further caused frustration among the people. Badal Sircar's *Evam Indrajit* examined the existentialist dilemmas of the educated Indians who were trapped between the bourgeois contentment with jobs and a secure future, and the desire to break out of a mundane existence and make their mark in the world. The play departed from conventional realism through apparently illogical experiments with dramatic elements thereby reflecting absurdist traits in its construction and approach.

The ideas that generated the Absurd plays also dictated their structure. Absurd plays aimed to startle viewers, shaking them out of an existence that had become acquisitive and complacent. The notion of absurdity was reflected in the "disjointed, meaningless, or repetitious dialogues, incomprehensible behaviour, and plots which deny all notion of logical or 'realistic' development" (Drabble, 2). The theatre of the Absurd challenged the human faith in language as an effectual means of communication. The characters were shown to confront a world where language is an ineffective tool and man struggles in a vacuum, isolated from all certainties. These plays were often termed anti-plays as they openly rebelled against conventional theatre and seemed to be illogical and lacking a plot and conflict.

Sircar's *Evam Indrajit* is an experimental play, which follows the conventions of the theatre of the Absurd in both its structure and the ideas it conveys. It diversifies the simplistic performing mode that already existed in the Indian theatrical scene through formal innovations in characterization, plot and setting. The traditional elements of drama namely crisis, climax and denouement are blatantly missing in his play. Instead, the complex use of sound effects through chorus, poetry and music, and stylized actions through mime and gestures create a complete theatrical effect.

Chris Baldick explains that the term theatre of the Absurd refers to the playwrights of the 1950's "whose works evoke the absurd by abandoning logical form, character, and dialogue together with realistic illusion" (1). The anti-illusionist dramatic technique of Sircar's play is its remarkable feature. The principal character in the play is a character called the Writer who in the beginning of the play decides to write a play about four persons from the audience who have come to watch Sircar's *Evam Indrajit* (5-6). The very fact that the characters in *Evam Indrajit* are a part of the audience shatters the dramatic illusion of the play. As the play progresses, the conflicts experienced by the Writer regarding the theme, the plot, and the characters of his play become a part of Sircar's play. The Writer's comments draw attention to the complex process of the construction of his play. There is a constant interaction between the real world and the artificial world within the play. The Writer at three other junctures in the play addresses the audience as if directly conversing with them (15, 49, 53), and twice instructs his characters to wait before entering the stage (20, 25). The reader is made aware of the impact of contingency, coincidence and arbitrary decisions of the author in the creation of any work of art.

Sircar's play brings to mind the radically experimental comedy *Six Characters in Search of an Author* (1922) by the Italian playwright Luigi Pirandello (1867-1936). The play portrays six characters that have come to life since their author has left their story incomplete. As these characters invade a rehearsal of another Pirandellan play and sabotage it, they "challenge the ability of the theatre to portray their lives and relationships fully and accurately" ("Drama and Dramatic Arts" 3). Sircar's play, however offers a contrast, as the characters here are apparently real people whom the Writer casts into his play. The protagonist Indrajit in fact struggles to break free out of the play and goes to London for three years. The Writer expresses his helplessness and states about him, "The more I tie him up in a plot, the more he escapes; says it isn't real" (50).

Sircar disturbs dramatic illusion also through the role-playing of the characters and refuses to allow characters to be self-defining. The character called Manasi takes up several roles in the play – as the Writer's inspiration (her name literally translated as 'a creation of the mind'), as his cousin whom Indrajit loves, as another woman called Manasi whom Indrajit marries, as the wife of Amal, Kamal, and Vimal, and as Miss Malhotra who is a secretary in an office. Satyadev Dubey explains, "Indrajit has concluded that distinctive individual qualities are a fiction of the mind" (*Introduction* to *Evam Indrajit*). Similarly the Writer appears as an invigilator in an exam, as a peon called Hareesh and also as the boss in the office. Amal, Kamal and Vimal take up several different roles – as professors, as college students, as candidates facing an interview, as office staff and as husbands. Only the character Indrajit is represented consistently as a single person in the play. Identity thus becomes a problematic concept in the play as characters overlap and elude distinctive traits. Sircar's deliberate intermingling of identities foregrounds the absurdist contention that in a universe that is indifferent to human needs and suffering, the idea of the significance of man is a myth.

Similarly, Sircar's innovative use of setting in *Evam Indrajit* baffles the reader. At several points in the play stage-images of extraordinary concreteness are dissociated from the milieu that normally defines them. In Act I, the stage scene of an examination hall serves as a background for another scene when the Writer tells the audience, "Imagine that these chairs aren't here. Forget this bench. There's green grass here. That's a tree..." (20). A long scene follows with Indrajit and Manasi on the stage and the audience is expected to imagine that it is a public park. Act II opens with the stage setting of an office where all the characters are shown to be working. However, the same setting serves as a backdrop for all the scenes in the entire Act, which include dialogues between the Writer and Auntie, and between the three married couples. These techniques draw the attention of the audience to the makeshift world on the stage, and force them to be constantly conscious of its artificiality.

Absurdist plays express their distrust of language as a means of communication. Words fail to convey the essence of human experience, not being able to delve beneath its surface. The theatre of the Absurd drew attention of the people of the need to go beyond everyday speech, to communicate effectively. In Act III of *Evam Indrajit*, there are long passages of conversation between Amal, Kamal and Vimal (47-48, 53), which begin with meaningful dialogue but move on to dispassionate statements, phrases and words:

Kamal: Economics, politics, sociology.

Amal: Quotations, tender, statement.

Vimal: Report, minutes, budget (53).

In Act I, the speeches of the characters are evocative and contextualised and suggest a sharing of feelings and opinions between the characters. In Act II, dialogues become desultory and formal written language is satirized at one point to indicate the ineffectiveness of hackneyed expressions:

Writer: With reference to the above letter – in connexion with the above matter, I would request you – I shall be obliged if – forward us at your earliest convenience – let this office know immediately.... (33)

The mechanical exchange of arbitrary incongruous expressions between Amal, Kamal and Vimal in Act III suggests the increasing isolation of man, his emotional hollowness, and his inability to reach out to others.

As the Writer discusses with the characters the design of his play, Amal asks him, "What's the plot?" The Writer replies, "There isn't one" (13). Yet despite the apparent plotlessness of the play, a basic progression in the action and sequence of events can be discerned which parallels the development of the characters. Act I focuses on the student life of the characters

Amal, Kamal, Vimal and Indrajit and moves on to the stage in their lives when they are facing interviews for jobs. Indrajit in this Act is in love with Manasi, is optimistic and ambitious, and desires to go beyond the "world outside geography" (10). The Writer here discuses the characters, the plot, the theme, and the title of the play he intends to write. As he introduces the idea of the circularity, the repetitiveness of events in life, his own character and situation in life is revealed to the reader (27-29).

Act II portrays all the characters including the Writer as working in an office. Amal, Kamal and Vimal are later depicted as married to the same girl Manasi and in different stages of their married life. The Writer when talking to Auntie questions the nature of human existence – "who and what are human beings and why are they on earth?" (34-35). Indrajit is shown to have given up the idea of getting married to Manasi after having tried for a long time to persuade her to consent. He tells her later, "Who knows what marriage would do to us. Perhaps even our friendship would die" (45). The mundane existence of Amal, Kamal and Vimal is juxtaposed with the mounting frustration of Indrajit, his hopelessness and the Writer's dejection due to the meaninglessness of life.

In the final act of the play Indrajit foregrounds the idea of the pointlessness of life and the futility of faith. The Writer echoes the same idea when he states:

> You know I end here
> I'm dead.
> Within me.
> And yet why do I insist
> That I go on?
> For there is – Oh! yet there is
> No escape! (56)

Indrajit has married another girl called Manasi and acknowledges that he had wanted to do "something unusual, important, unprecedented" (58) in life, but couldn't, as he was Nirmal, an ordinary man. K. Venkata Reddy states, "Even when one is sincerely to be an Indrajit, one has got to end up as a Nirmal" (64). Amal, Kamal and Vimal are shown to be living a routine life, trapped in the whirlpool of family responsibilities, economic constraints and career pressure. Their trite speeches reinforce this idea. The Writer counteracts Indrajit's negativistic viewpoint and professes that Indrajit, Manasi and he himself is not a common man, and they "must live. We must walk. We know no sacred places. Yet we must go on with the pilgrimage..." (60).

Indrajit can be called an anti-hero due to his inability to wrestle with the challenges life offers him. Chris Baldick explains that an anti-hero is an important figure in the theatre of the Absurd and defines the term as "a central character in a dramatic or narrative work who lacks the qualities of nobility and magnanimity expected of traditional heroes and heroines in romances and epics" (11). In Act I Indrajit is a rebel who is deeply hurt by the misery and suffering in the world and hates the rules of society, which are biased and favour a power equation. But he is aware of the fact that his hatred for rules is "a pointless anger. It's blind. Powerless. It only beats its head against the wall" (23). In Act II he has lost some of his vitality and has realised that human existence is insignificant and trivial. In Act III Indrajit becomes very disheartened and believes that death promises a release from all pain and frustration. He tells Manasi, "So long as I couldn't accept my ordinariness I dreamt. Now I accept it" (58-59).

Indrajit's predicament is the predicament of the existentialist anti-hero. Ihab Hassan states, "The sad history of the anti-hero is nothing more than the history of man's changing awareness of himself" (66). Hassan elaborates that the anti-hero aspires for "freedom and self-definition" as a way to existentialist self-realisation(72). But due to the inherently meaningless nature of the universe, which is bereft of values, human beings suffer a sense of anguish or *angst* when they are forced to make their own choices. Religion, faith and love offer no solace to the modern man and freedom implies that human beings take the responsibility of their actions. Albert Camus states that human beings are aware of the finality of death and "What freedom can exist in the fullest sense without assurance of eternity"? (345). The anti-hero acquires an understanding of the futility of human effort and takes a stand by degrading himself and retreating, which increases his alienation and his sense of guilt.

Indrajit too after embarking on a futile quest for the meaning and worth of human existence, retreats and is depressed and exhausted, having lost the energy to think, to question any further. He tells Manasi, "I've thought a lot. Argued a lot. But I can't find an answer. I'm tired now" (45). Similar thoughts are echoed by the Writer immediately, "I am sick of reasoning now. Alone, in the depth of shadows let me just go to sleep" (45-46). One gradually realizes that Indrajit is the alter ego of the Writer, and through the struggles and travails of his character Indrajit, the Writer acquires an understanding of the absurd nature of human existence. The play thus focuses on "the tragedy of knowing" (48), the awareness of the meaninglessness of human endeavour, and the need to carry on, to "Walk! Be on the road!" (59) inspite of this painful knowledge.

The marked polarity between the two trios, the Writer, Indrajit and Manasi, and Amal, Kamal and Vimal is due to their contrasting aspirations. The former group represents a search for truth and a desire for spiritual, moral fulfilment while the latter a quest for material success. Indrajit's pain and frustration is intensified for he observes with surprise the smugness of Amal, Kamal and Vimal and causes self-doubt in him. While all the other characters are engrossed in routine office work, he asks the Writer, "Is there nothing except this?" (34). For both, Indrajit and the Writer, it is the need of the hour to "Deny that circle. Deny that going round and round" (26).

The refrain of numbers occurs repeatedly in Act One and carries great symbolic significance. It begins as a song being sung by the chorus in the background slowly in the beginning, then faster, "One-two-three/One-two-three-two-one-two-three..." (11). The Writer recites it soon after as "a short poem" (12). Later when Indrajit talks about the unchanging, repetitive cycle of events in life, the Writer speaks it out again followed by the song 'One-two-three' sung in the background with loud music(18). It continues as Amal, Kamal and Vimal talk to Indrajit as Professors and ends with the refrain, "Nine-eight-seven-six..." (19). The refrain is repeated by the Writer at several points in the first act and suggests the absurdity of our actions that are invariably performed by every human being, yet signify nothing. He states, "It's all a question of going round and round. The answer is a circle – a zero" (19). The recurrence of the song of numbers accompanied by music in the play underscores the mechanical repetition of actions in life, which are empty of meaning.

In the play Hindu and classical Greek myths are seen to merge bringing a new insight into the complex character of Indrajit. The Writer in *Evam Indrajit* can be seen as creating an fictional world in his play like Brahma, the Creator part of the supreme trinity in Hindu mythology. He states, "I have to put into language the drama of these atoms going round and round" (28). As he populates his play with characters, one of them is Indrajit (or Meghnad). In the Hindu myth, Indrajit was the son of King Raavana who performed rigorous penances and obtained many boons from Brahma. He led the armies of demons against the Gods and captured the God Indra and asked for the gift of immortality if the Gods wished Indra freed. In the play too Indrajit is a rebel who rejects the authority of the Writer. The Writer says for Indrajit, "The more lines I write for him, the more he stands outside them. Says they are not real" (50).

In the concluding part of the play the Writer compares Indrajit, Manasi and himself to the mythical character Sisyphus whose "wickedness during life was severely punished in the lower world, where he had to roll up hill a huge marble block, which as soon as it reached the top always rolled down again" (Smith, 392). The Writer states, "We are the cursed spirits of

Sisyphus. We have to push the rock to the top – even if it just rolls down" (59). Sisyphus symbolizes the victim who perpetually suffers injustice and exploitation and is incapable of resisting it. Yet Indrajit has been a rebel and it is only towards the end of Act II that he assumes the role of a victim.

The paradoxical concept of the anti-hero as a rebel-victim emerges in Ihab Hassan's discussion of the anti-hero, wherein he states that man attempts to overcome the challenges of his experience, its negative elements, by assuming the role of the anti-hero, the rebel-victim. According to Hassan, the anti-hero always bears the essential qualities of Prometheus and Sisyphus – "the eternal rebel and the eternal victim" (73). Human beings are a victim of an indecipherable supreme power, and are trapped in the cycle of life, which is beyond their control. They can only revolt against the social order, against the norms established in society, and their defeat is predestined. But, as Hassan asserts that the victory of the protagonist of the Existentialist novel "depends on the certainty of defeat, is the process of defeat" (71). Indrajit is one such enigmatic character, with which the reader identifies himself due to his courage to question the meaning of existence inspite of his ultimate defeat.

Badal Sircar's radical play *Evam Indrajit* sensitizes the audience/reader to metaphysical questions about the nature of human existence. His play brings out absurdist dilemmas by abandoning established dramatic techniques like realistic illusion, consistent characterization, or self-defining setting. It foregrounds the painful awareness of the futility of human endeavour and prudence through the confrontation between human reason and the inexplicable silence of the cosmos.

References

Baldick, Chris. *The Concise Oxford Dictionary of Literary Terms.* Oxford: Oxford University Press, 1990.

Camus, Albert. "Absurd Freedom." *Inquiry and Expression: A College Reader*. Eds. Harold C. Martin and Richard M. Ohmann. New York: Holt, Rinehart and Winston, Inc, 1963. 342-47.

Drabble, Margaret, and Jenny Stringer. *Oxford Concise Companion to English Literature.*1987. Oxford: Oxford University Press, 1996.

"Drama and Dramatic Arts." *Microsoft Encarta Online Encyclopaedia 2005*. 3.

Dubey, Satyadev. Introduction to Evam Indrajit. By Badal Sircar. *Three Modern Indian Plays.* New Delhi: Oxford University Press, 1989.

Haney, II, William S. "Beckett Out of His Mind: The Theatre of the Absurd." *Studies in the Literary Imagination*. Vol. 34.2, Fall 2001: 39. 39-54.

Hassan, Ihab. "The Anti-hero." *Inquiry and Expression: A College Reader*. Martin, Harold C. and Richard M. Ohmann. New York: Holt, Rinehart and Winston, Inc, 1963. 65-73.

Pirandello, Luigi. *Six Characters in Search of An Author*. Ed. Eric Bentley. New York: E.P. Dutton and Co., 1955.

Reddy, K. Venkata. "Badal Sircar's *Evam Indrajit* as an Absurd Play." *New Directions in Indian Drama*. Ed. Sudhakar Pandey and Freya Barua. New Delhi: Prestige, 1994. 58-66.

Sircar, Badal. *Evam Indrajit.* Translated by Girish Karnad. *Three Modern Indian Plays.* New Delhi: Oxford University Press, 1989.

Smith, William. *The Wordsworth Classical Dictionary*. Wordsworth Reference: Hertfordshire, 1996.

17

The Protean Self

Karnad's *Tughlaq*

Urmil Talwar

Karnad is one of the most vibrant playwrights of the post-independence period. He is a bilingual writer, writing both in Kannada and English, and has in addition to this translated several of his own plays. Besides this, he is also a director and an actor, acting both in films and on the stage. When his first play *Yayati* (1961) appeared in the early sixties, his work ran parallel in time to the innovative, off-Broadway American theatre and, one finds in his work, an awareness of both the western tradition and Indian folk theatre.[1] Karnad elaborates on the factors that influenced him and his technique in his "Introduction" to *Three Plays*[2]. All his plays in some way or the other explore the various aspects of Indian folk theatre.[3]

Tughlaq (1964), Karnad's second play, was an immediate success in Kannada and later in English (1970). He uses the historical character of Muhammad-bin-Tughlaq[4], the fourteenth century Sultan of Delhi, to depict the divided self, one who is torn between the ideal and the real. In his desire to be an ideal secular humanist he begins to manipulate, treat men as pawns in a political game of chess, resort to cruelty and bloodshed and ends up as a frustrated human being. This fractured plural self of Tughlaq reflects the contradictions and discrepancies in the Indian value system. Critics find the political disillusionment of the post-Nehruvian era reflected in the play.

Tughlaq is a tale of an over ambitious virtuous king whose dream and aspirations – of communal harmony, of shifting the capital to Daulatabad, of making copper coins equal in value to the silver Dinar – were all well-meaning. But the means he pursued to achieve these were cruel and violent and thus they failed miserably. Basically *Tughlaq* is a play based on this single complex character of Tughlaq and the other characters are bits and pieces of the same self. U.R. Ananthamurthy in his 'Introduction' to *Tughlaq* writes, "All the other characters are dramatized aspects of this complex personality" (qtd *Three Plays*, 144). The whole play is structured on this multiphrenic personality.

My endeavour here is to reveal that the subjectivity or construction of the self is not based in eternal values as the humanists thought and Tughlaq's subjectivity is constituted by his ever changing value system at different 'discursive locations'[5] constituted in his practices and discourses, in action and dialogue which interrogates the notion of a unified subject. It invites a postmodern debate on the concept of a unitary, autonomous selfhood and situates the subject in a multiplicity of cultural and historical contexts. The fission that develops due to cultural and historical contexts in the nuclear self raises questions on the subjectivity of the individual self. Karnad uses many devices to reveal this ever-changing protean self that leads to indeterminability of self-identity of Tughlaq. He foregrounds this multiplicity differently in every play, through the use of masks in *Hayavadana* (1972), through the cobra-man in *Naga-Mandala* (1988), and through the dream sequences in *The Dreams of Tipu Sultan* (2004). In *Tughlaq* he does not use any such overt design instead Tughlaq keeps on assuming one role after another to become a secular, social humanist while

Aziz keeps on masquerading first as Brahmin, then as a Khalifa in order to counterfoil his ideals.

In overt design Tughlaq appears to be an idealist but in his pursuit of ideals he perpetuates the opposite and there arises a discrepancy between the real and the ideal. The postmodernist premise is that the personae are the surface appearances of deep structures and the search for self or true being seems to reveal an endless deferral of presence, projecting in the process its multiple narratives/selves. Postmodernists may differ in their views on subject formation but what is common to all of them is that 'paramount self' can be understood only through the interpretation and rendition of the subject as a construct. And Tughlaq's persona works through multiple constructs. Religion, politics, history, law, morality are the various 'discursive locations' from which Tughlaq derives a sense of a multiple self.

In *Tughlaq* Shiekh Imam-ud-din, Najib and Barani are the personae of Tughlaq, with the Shiekh symboling religion, Najib politics and Barani both history and spirituality. The Shiekh Imam-ud-din "has a certain resemblance some gestures,...some mannerisms" (150) with the Sultan but they "don't think alike" (163). The Shiekh an orthodox theologician and a fanatic who inspired communal riots in Kanpur is "willing to do something for Islam and the country" (163). He believes that the Sultan has made "scores of transgressions" and "fails to understand what the Koran says" (164). The Sultan invites him to address a meeting to analyse his administration (sc iii) and claims that he has not "consciously tried to go against the tenets of Islam" (164). At the same time he believes that the Shiekh's criticism will help him complete his mission. This indicates the sincerity of Sultan's motives but soon it gives way to deceit and manipulation and in the fifth scene it becomes clear that the Sultan had laid the trap and the public was deterred from coming to hear the Shiekh. The Sultan acts on Najib's advice that "courage, honesty and justice do not count in politics" (sc ii, 158), "traitor's a traitor, friend or saint, and he must be crushed" (159). Taking advantage of the physical similarity he sends the Shiekh as a peace emissary to dissuade Ain-ul-Mulk from war for the sake of "the Muslims who will die at the hands of Muslims if there is war" (sc iii, 166). When the Shiekh begins to understand the trap laid by Sultan there is no way he can retreat. The Shiekh dressed in royal robe and head-dress, looking exactly like the Sultan, marches towards Ain-ul-Mulk's camp and gets killed. At the death of the Shiekh Tughlaq says, "They brought his body into my tent and I felt – as though it was I who was lying dead there... I should have been there – in his place" (sc iv, 170). It symbolises that politics has won over history and that Tughlaq has killed the fanaticism of Muslim religion in himself to become the secular ruler. He even justifies this stance, his secularism, "to live by the Koran" alone would be to kill "the Greek in me" and deny "the vision which led Zarathustra or Buddha" (165). Only Tughlaq knows that the Shiekh is got rid off by incidious planning. Later (sc vi) it is revealed that the Sultan's army had started the battle.

Shiekh Imam-ud-din the 'other' or the split self of the Sultan is but 'real' at the point of war thereby questioning the concept of personal self or the discrepancy between reality and truth. If the Sultan was secular why did he lay the trap for the Shiekh? It seems there is no essential understanding of individual personality only a plurality of possibilities. A particular situation or moment inscribes and reinscribes the subject in different ways underlining its coherence and discontinuity[6]. In *Tughlaq* Girish Karnad first installs the Sultan and then challenges the transcendental subject in a typical postmodern and paradoxical way. The more the Sultan wishes to become a unique personality the more diverse and fragmented he becomes. Liberal towards the Hindus, he revokes Jazia and wishes for a communal harmony among his subjects. A section of his subject appreciates that he "isn't afraid to be human" (147). In the contemporary context the Sultan invokes the image of Gandhi in the minds of the audience/reader who wanted peace and communal harmony at the time of struggle for India's independence. Moreover, the Sultan has publicly accepted the charge of a Brahmin that he is "guilty of illegal appropriation" of the poor man's land and granted "just compensation for the loss" (148). At the end of this scene the guard dismisses the crowd saying "What are you waiting for? The show's over! Go home" (151). These words suggest that the guard has seen through the performance staged by the Sultan to win support of his people. Tughlaq indulges in role playing not only in public but also in his private conversation with his stepmother. Like Ashoka the Great, the Sultan says:

> Come my people...Confide in me your worries. Let me share your joys. Let's laugh and cry together and then let's pray. Let's pray till our bodies melt and flow and our blood turns into air.... Come! I'm waiting to embrace you all." (155)

At this speech his stepmother bursts into laughter and says, "I can't ask a simple question without your giving a royal performance" (155). Is the Sultan giving a royal performance or is he really concerned about his subjects? The Sultan reply, "I'm only worried about my people" (155), is not borne out by his later actions. Similarly, his intention to shift his capital, is declared in scene one:

> this is no mad whim of a tyrant. My ministers and I took this decision after careful thought and discussion....Daulatabad is a city of Hindus and as the capital will symbolize the bond between Muslims and Hindus which I wish to develop and strengthen.... Only those who have faith in me may come. (149)

It is revealed only in scene five that of the Amirs and Ulamas, no one was consulted and it was the whim of a tyrant to shift the capital to Daulatabad, and was a manipulation of his subjects for retaining power. Aware of a growing dissidence and with a foreknowledge of rebellion, he still tries to appeal through his emotional theatricals. He questions them:

> What gives me the right to call myself King?
> *(The Amirs are baffled)*
> Am I a king only because I am the son of a king? Or is it because I can make the people accept my laws and the army move to my commands? (181)

He bows and kneels before them, picks up a copy of the Koran and wants to exhort from them an oath of support. Unable to achieve anything out of this, at the rebellion during prayer he gets the Amirs arrested and then kills Shihab-ud-din. Politics again overpowers him; to appease Shihab-ud-din's father he declares that Shihab-du-din "died a martyr's death" trying to save the Sultan. At this Barani questions him, "Aren't even the dead free from your politics?" (185). In his wish to realize his dream of shifting his capital he initiates a series of killings and cruelty.

In the same scene, another announcement is made that no one should remain behind in Delhi. Anyone who attempts to stay behind or go elsewhere "will be severely punished". Barani again questions him "... there was a time when you believed in love, in peace, in God. What happened to those ideals?... Why this bloodshed?" (196). In fact Barani and Najib are in a constant dialogue, reflecting the kind of inner conflict that goes on in Tughlaq's construction of self. After Najib, the politician is poisoned to death, Tughlaq becomes ruthless and orders that his stepmother be stoned to death. After killing Shiabh-ud-din all his actions are aimed towards the continuation of power and all killings are a means to it. This issue of self-realization is problematized not by the discrepancy between intention and outcome but by revoking the issue of knowledge "to recognize myself" (204). The self is variously addressed and its meaning assembled and assigned which every time seems provisional. There is no essential understanding of the plurality of the possibilities that one can be. 'Self' construction is never complete. There is only a relative stability of contextualizing which makes the occasional reality true. In case of Tughlaq each reality of self gives way to reflexive questioning and probing of yet another reality.

The world of Tughlaq is a diverse world of multiple selves exploring through a series of representations the real character of the Sultan. There is no way that Muhammad the tyrant can be separated from Muhammad the idealist. He is also a poet, a civil servant, a historian and, in the end, a self-pitying king. There is an overreaching aim of the Sultan to create history. Muhammad wanted to reduce history to a kind of autobiography, to reduce India to his own consciousness. He thought "one day I shall build my own history like this, brick by brick" (194). The historian Barani and the politician Najib both represent different sides of the Sultan. All these roles, although momentary, reveal the authentic inner self. The roles he is striving up to in any particular context explains the conception he has provisionally formed of himself that helps to determine his identity. These different selves reveal the underlying indeterminacy of self-identity.

Another way of deconstructing the self would be through the binary opposites, in splitting the 'self' as the 'other'. Girish Karnad achieves this in different ways in his plays. In *Yayati* it is through the father and son, through the split in body and mind in *Hayavadana,* through Appanna and the cobra-man in *Naga-Mandala.* In *Tughlaq*, Tughlaq and Aziz form the binary opposites. Aziz's success story runs parallel to Tughlaq's tragedy. Through the character of Aziz, Girish Karnad reveals how the compassion, generosity and bonafide intention of Tughlaq are reverted into selfish individual gains.

From the very beginning Aziz perfectly understands the political situation in which Tughlaq is trying to realize his ideals. He subverts each of his well-intentioned moves, upsets the apple cart. Taking life as a theatre Aziz keeps on changing his masks *sans* moral integrity. Aziz, a low caste Muslim, takes up the guise of a brahmin and wins the case against Tughlaq to reveal his "impartial justice", he is the civil servant who instead of helping loots the people on their way to Daulatabad. He mints counterfeit coins to counteract Tughlaq's faith in his people, and in the end he takes up the guise of the Khalifa who will bless the wilderness of the kingdom to restore peace, prayer and prosperity to the populace. The irony is tragic. How fake the Khalifa is! How fake the prosperity will be! Tughlaq and his empire are one in chaos. The Aziz-Azam plot is a parodic intertext and these masquerades of Aziz are covert interruptions in Tughlaq's metanarratives.

The paradoxical and ironic implications of the four major metaphors – prayer, the game of chess, the rose garden and sleep – reveal the frustrated attempts of the Sultan to achieve his idealism. The sacred prayer is ridden with disease and exiled later it is revoked in the presence of an imposter. The game of chess depicts Tughlaq's approach to life. Tughlaq who regarded other people as pawns and manipulates them to his own advantage becomes the same in the game laid by Aziz. The rose garden envisioned as a utopia is piled up with counterfeit copper coins and has become a "kitchen of death". The sleep that deluded Tughlaq in the beginning suddenly returns putting an end to all his scheming.

Tughlaq has been compared to Camus' Caligula and Eisentein's Ivan the Terrible. His complex existential[7] personality portrays the Indian experience of the sixties. Tughlaq wishes an immortal place for himself by imposing liberal humanist secular mindset on his people but he fails miserably. His idealism declines into cynicism. The ideal and the real, the fanatic and the secular, the political and the historical are the different selves or facets of Tughlaq. These are neither facades nor hyper real images but subjectivities as open-ended constructs. Their authenticity can be recognized only within their 'discursive locations' or contexts. In theatrical terms these multiple selves are the performances which he exists in and through which he exists.

Notes

1. After the Second World War a new Radical theatre was born which rejected the modernist dramatic form to experimental and exploratory postmodernist dramatic form i.e. towards spontaneity and irrationalism, freedom and anarchy. See Jasbir Jain "Introduction" to *Deconstructing Character*.
2. Girish Karnad in his Introduction in *Three Plays* elaborates on his use of space in *Tughlaq*. p.7-8. In the Parsi model it was required that the scenes alternate between shallow and deep. In *Tughlaq* I, III, VII, IX, XI are shallow scenes alternating with deep scenes II, IV, V, VIII, X, XII, XII. He adds an aside that E. Alkazi ignored this arrangement and placed the action on the ramparts of the Old Fort at Delhi and it worked very well.
3. Girish Karand spoke at 'Meet the Author' programme organised by Sahitya Akademi on Nov. 16, 1998 (*Indian Literature* No. 131, May-June 1989. pp. 85-99). He writes about the three kinds of theatre between which he swiveled and moved.
4. Karnad read the history of Kannada literature where a major critic Kirtinath Kurtkoti had made a categorical statement that no Indian playwright has been able to handle history like what Shakespeare has done with Richard III or Brecht with Galileo. All we have done is to produce costume plays. Karnad started looking for a subject from history and he hit upon Tughlaq, known for his revolutionary views on philosophy, religion, battle war-field and calligraphy (p.96).
5. Lyotard in *The Post Modern Condition* writes that the self is not a given; it derives from the situated contingencies and rituals or interaction. 'Self' is located at institutional "nodal points" and exists in experience to the degree that is variously constructed within a "mobile" fabric of relations and practices(15).
6. According to Derrida there is nothing that is just there, present durably identical to itself. The subject is not destroyed by this but only "reinscribed... within relations of forces that are always differential" and therefore "mobile" (146).
7. Karnad in 'Meet the Author' says, that during the sixties existentialism was very much in the air. To be considered mad was very fashionable. (96) Tughlaq is called "mad" in (sc i, 149), "honest scoundrel" (sc iv, 171), "I told you he's mad!" (sc vi, 182). "All I need now is myself and my madness... I have a companion to share my madness" (sc xii, 220). Most critics have built up on the existential hero taking a clue from Karnad.

References

Barua and Pandey. Eds. *New Directions in Indian Drama.* New Delhi: Prestige Books, 1994.

Bhabha, H. K. *The Location of Culture.* London: Routledge, 1994.

Das, Bijay Kumar. *Twentieth Century Literary Criticism.* New Delhi: Atlantic Publishers, 1992.

Jain, Jasbir. *Deconstructing Character.* Transformations in Postmodernist American Drama. New Delhi: Rawat Publications, 1997.

Karnad, Girish. *Three Plays: Naga-Mandala, Hayavadana, Tughlaq.* Delhi: Oxford University Press, 1995.

—. *Two Plays: The Dreams of Tipu Sultan, Bali the Sacrifice.* Delhi: Oxford University Press, 2004.

—. "Acrobating between the traditional and the modern". *Indian Literature,* Vol. 131. Delhi: Sahitya Akademi, May-June 1989. pp 85-99.

Leitch, Vincent B. "Deconstructive Criticism". In *American Literary Criticism from the 30s to the 80s.* New York: Columbia University Press, 1988.

Lodge, David. Ed. *Modern Criticism and Theory: A Reader.* Longman 1988.

18

Gurcharan Das's *Larins Sahib*

Pranav Joshipura

Gurcharan Das wrote his play *Larins Sahib* in 1968 when dramatic activity was at its peak. In India, during the Nehruvian and post-Nehruvian period, history was a major source of inspiration for assessing the contemporary situation. Gurcharan Das is a playwright of this period whose contribution to the growth of drama is significant. His three plays – *Larins Sahib* (1968), *Mira* (1970), and *9 Jakhoo Hill* (1996), – establish him as an important playwright. He is a managerial executive and served at important positions in top industries. Playwriting has never been his full time occupation. Despite all these, Das' treatment and sensibility for history of India is remarkable.

The play *Larins Sahib* was first produced at Mumbai in 1969. It also was performed at major Indian cities and at the Edinburgh Festival. The play opens in the 1846 Punjab province of the then Hindustan. It is exactly one year after the famous First Sikh War and seven years after the death of great king of the Punjab, Ranjit Singh. Henry Lawrence, popularly known as Larins Sahib, who knows the Punjab better than anyone else in the East India Company, is promoted and has been made the Agent of the British Empire in the Punjab.

Political hindrances, his attempts to win the faith of the people through welfare schemes, and his proximity to the queen all conspire to bring about his doom. At the end of the play, he is a dejected man, as he fails to meet the expectations he had aroused.

The defeat of the Sikh army at Sobraon (10 February, 1846) changed the entire history of the Sikh land as it was not a defeat on the battlefield, it was treason. This had many consequences. Large number of Sikhs were slaughtered, the entire army got demoralized, the Lahore Darbar had to pay Rupees One-and-a-half crores as war indemnity, the minor Dalip Singh was declared the Maharaja and Rani as Regent, while Henry Lawrence as the British Resident at Lahore. At the request of the cunning Wazir Lal Singh, the British army was to be stationed at Lahore for one year for the protection of the Maharaja. Later on, they shifted the Rani and Dalip Singh to another place so as to have a free access to the Punjab. The British constituted a Board of Commission to administer the Punjab and ultimately, to annex it.

The Queen of the Punjab, Rani Jindan, clearly foresaw, "...that the future of the Punjab is in British hands" (54)? There are, obviously, reasons for that. The Punjab, after the death of its great ruler, Ranjit Singh, could not produce a powerful leader, who could keep the large kingdom united, which was created by late Ranjit Singh. Henry Lawrence says:

> Since his (Ranjit Singh's) death there's been chaos everywhere and a fierce struggle for succession. The Sardars have been quarrelling like dogs. And understandably, Sir. For he not only created the Punjab from a mass of petty states – in fact his personality united the kingdom. He established no institutions which could live after him. When he died, the Punjab died. (32)

After the Sobraon war, the Khalsa, the united seat of the Sikhs, got shattered, butchered, beaten, and was at the receiving end. They took time to reunite. The Sikh leaders, who were in power to decide the future of the Punjab, proved to be traitors.

They contacted the British to achieve their own ends, not knowing that the British, too, will sideline them when their purpose will be fulfilled and that they will merely be pawns in the grand design of the East India Company. Further, Ranjit Singh's wife Rani Jindan was young and incapable of effective ruling. Her son, Dalip Singh, was still a minor. Lal Singh, the Wazir, and Tej Singh, the Commander-in-Chief, misled the entire Sikh community by making them believe that the Rani and her son were responsible for the Sobraon loss. So that, the entire Sikh community would turn against them. The entire Punjab leadership failed to foresee the grand design of the British, of usurping and exploiting them.

The British knew that the Sikhs are known for patriotism and bravery. To defeat them in battlefield would be almost impossible. Therefore, by unethical means they conquered the Punjab. Henry Lawrence fully knows this and objects to ugly remarks. He says, "...for a fairly fought battle would have resulted differently" (32). Ironically, unethical practice was the only practice of the British.

Larins Sahib is a play about the rise and fall of this "phenomenal" character, Henry Lawrence, viewed from the point of view of the Indian people. When the play opens, Henry is seen as getting promoted from a routine Revenue Office Clerk to the post of the Resident in the court of the Punjab, a very high stature. The sudden rise certainly does not mean any undue favour. This is owing to his great work done in the Revenue office. Elliot is of the view:

> I was saying, sir, that this man has built a phenomenal reputation. Just two years on the border as a minor clerk with the Revenue Survey, and he's become a legend. I believe he's on first-name terms with most of the nobility of the Punjab. They swear by him, and peasantry of the Ferozepur district think he's some kind of a saviour. (28)

These words of praise for Henry actually comment on his outstanding work. He was much impressed and influenced by the late Maharaja of Punjab Ranjit Singh, who died in 1839. Ranjit Singh's great work and statesmanship won him fame. When Sher Singh passes on a comment comparing Henry with Ranjit Singh, Henry says, "Don't speak like that about His Highness... We should be lucky if we can continue his work" (37). Now as Henry has been appointed as the Resident, he has a greater opportunity, greater power, greater scope to complete certain reformatory tasks left unfinished by the late Maharaja. But Henry knows that this is not going to be easy as the Punjab has been hampered very badly by the local feud. Moreover, indirect involvement of the British Empire in the affairs of the state may further infuriate the already angry Sikhs. Henry says, "What's written, or where it's written, I don't know. I do know that keeping the Darbar together and honouring the Treaty are not going to be easy" (36).

When Lawrence was working in the Revenue Office in the Ferozepur district, he saw the condition of people, he saw how peasants lived. He realized that amidst all rise and fall, only the peasant had remained constant. They have witnessed everything. So, in order to win sympathy of the people of the Punjab, one must win over the peasants. Henry says:

> Yes, the Punjab peasant will always be there. Isn't it reasonable then, that we win him in our side? To win him, we must work for him, for his sake. The memory of the British would rest in the peasant's heart, in his timelessness. (58)

To unify Punjab, to bring their faith back, to make them happy, Lawrence decides to bring certain reforms. He was sure that reform means abolition of certain evils and bringing of prosperity. Reacting to the incident of killing of cows by a British officer, he sees this as an opportunity to start with his idea of reform. He declares:

> To convince you of our sincerity, I have decided to waive one month's land revenue for the citizens of this district... We want to begin by listening to you, honoured citizens, rather than by

> ordering you about like 'Lord Sahibs'. We want to build canals, bridges, roads. We want to ensure as much justice as possible to each citizen. (60)

This not only pacifies the religious anger of people, but also restores certain amount of honour for the British. Unfortunately, waiving of revenue infuriates the Governor General's office, as they believe in not winning the heart of people, but collecting or to be precise, looting as much money as possible. On another instance, in his *Diwan-e-aam*, he attempts at bringing another reform. He announces:

> Sher Singh, we are issuing a proclamation: *Sati* is with immediate effect abolished in all provinces and districts of the Punjab. And the Hindu Reform Bill is with immediate effect extended to all parts of the Punjab. (72)

One may wonder why Henry Lawrence, being British, wanted to bring reformation for the people of the Punjab. Was reformation a part of "civilizing mission of the white races" (32)? Or had he certain other political benefits in mind? Had he no idea about himself becoming unpopular among the British think-tank? Or did he take reformation as a political device to become popular? Or was he genuine? All these possibilities may not be overruled. However, as history witnesses, Henry Lawrence's reformation won hearts of people to such an extent that during the 1857 mutiny, people of the Punjab stood by the British. This gesture is exclusively due to the generosity and good will created by Henry Lawrence. He tells Rani Jindan:

> Yes, yes, just as it was in the days of the Lion. We'll make it rich and happy. We'll build, build. Build roads, canals, and the land will sing with joy. (65)

This appears to be his dream. But in reality, his aim is something else. He is so much impressed by the late Ranjit Singh's personality that he wants to raise himself to that level so that people may compare him with the late Maharaja. Whether we call this an identity crisis or some type of complex, one thing is certain, Henry Lawrence's idea of comparing himself with the Lion is related to acquiring fame. He says, "Yes, they'll say that the Lion has returned! (65). Reform began very well. But it was not easy to keep up the process of development as the Punjab was reeling under tremendous political, social and economic turmoil and the land was torn by factions. Wazir Lal Singh and Tej Singh were unitedly making attempts to defame and thereupon dethrone Rani Jindan and Dalip Singh. The two camps had no choice but to keep close contact with the Resident. Rani Jindan, in fact, professes love for Lawrence, to save herself, Dalip Singh, and the kingdom.

The Rani passes on the famous *Koh-i-noor* diamond to declare her "friendship" and to strengthen her position. Whereas Lal Singh wants to use this gift of friendship to defame the Queen. He says, "I need the diamond to show the Darbar what kind of Queen they have – she's selling our country to the Angrez swine" (62). Lal Singh even tries to bribe Sher Singh by offering him the post of Wazir. Lal Singh and Tej Singh even plan to kidnap Dalip Singh. Henry Lawrence knows the internal bickering and detests all this. Irritated by these rifts, he starts using his authority. He says:

> That's the way to rule India... with dignity... Yes, Indians like colour, pagent, style. They respect it. That's authority for them... they liked to be ruled through the heart; we rule through head. They like to be dealt with at the personal level; our basis of administration is impersonal law. They respect tact; our laws and settlements are crudely blunt. (68)

Henry's transformation from being an imaginary reformer to a crude manipulator is not sudden and unthinkable. It is the British Empire's authority that makes him an insensitive ruler. The British Empire was in India not for any civilizing mission or charitable task. They had, in fact, very different objective for being in India. Currie says, "It's clearly a matter of racial superiority. Every pagan power, no matter how formidable in appearance, must succumb to the civilized mission of the white races" (32).

Therefore, Lawrence's reformatory actions appear unnecessary to Hardinge & Co. They rather instruct him to collect revenue strictly, tender an apology to Wazir Lal Singh and Tej Singh, to accept the authority and superiority of both, to behave politely and cordially with the fellow British officers even if they create trouble, not to employ and be friendly with native officers even if they are faithful, to separate Rani Jindan and her son Dalip Singh, to send the Rani to prison, and above all, to surrender *Koh-i-noor*, the symbol of friendship and loyalty, to the British Empire.

These instructions of the British Empire can be considered as the major cause in the change of attitude in Henry Lawrence. From Act three, Scene two, we have a different Henry Lawrence. All the fire, imagination, vigour, and enthusiasm have gone off. The Rani comments:

> You're just like the rest of them. I thought there was something different in you, Larins. You were simple, austere, single-minded. Now you're behaving the way the other *Ferangis* did when they got power under my husband. They became swollen. (64)

Except Wazir Lal Singh and Tej Singh, everybody fails to realize the sudden change in Henry. The earlier Larins Sahib orders to be addressed as "the Angrez Badshah". This transformation may be owing to his failure in handling the pressure created by both, the British Empire and the local community. The British Empire's orders compel him to take action against his dear fellows and honour those whom he and the locals hated. Moreover, he, now, would have to retreat from the promises that he once made to the people of the Punjab. The applauds that he once had won through magnificent reformatory announcements backfired. Locals, too, failed to look beyond his face, they failed in realizing that something else is responsible for the change in Henry Lawrence. Henry Lawrence was the last surviving hope for Rani Jindan, Dalip

Singh, and Sher Singh in restoring the glory of the late Maharaja and saving the throne from the traitors. Sher Singh says:

> I feel sad now. For you were our hope – our golden evening. You gave us a sense of life – to me, to the Rani, to Dalip. We returned it with the only thing we had: our love. But we were mistaken. (94)

With this, not only the Punjab fell to incapable British spies like Lal Singh and Tej Singh, but also the fall of Henry Lawrence became imminent. Once a rising star of the British Empire, a Ranjit Singh in making, a golden hope of the Punjabis, and a great reformer failed miserably owing to his inability to strike a compromise between the power and the people. This is very unfortunate. Lawrence's outburst is an example of his transformation:

> Bow down to the Angrez Badshah! Bow down, you Lal Singh's and Tej Singh's. You can kiss the jewel. The Punjab is mine, as surely as the *Koh-i-noor* is mine.
>
> Where is my Rani? In the harem, is she? So much the better.
>
> Where is my son? Asleep. Let him sleep. He needs his sleep.
>
> The tribes are restless? We shall teach the tribes. They are dealing with a great Badshah of a great land. Let's go on to a battle. The Lion has come. (83)

The play, however, fails in creating an effect of realizing the transformation of Henry Lawrence. His change is sudden and at times unacceptable. The psychological conflict that he faces is not revealed here. The struggling self behaves abnormally. The internal conflict is not revealed as in *Hamlet*. This is the only limitation of the play.

Lawrence's shift and unhealthy political announcements make his loyal friend Sher Singh and Rani Jindan angry. Sher Singh, who even risks himself by accompanying Larins Sahib, becomes angry. He says:

> You hypocrite! You never loved anyone. You don't deserve anyone's friendship. You turned into a hypocrite when you saw how powerful you'd become. You imagined that you had become Ranjit Singh. (93)

Lawrence's beloved, his idol's wife, the Queen of Punjab quite understands the reason of Larins becoming the Angrez Badshah. She says:

> God, now I understand your robes, your Darbars, and your 'Angrez Badshahs'. It all fits. And your obsession with my late husband. You're drunk, my friend. Power's gone into your head. And you've forgotten your friends. (90)

Though this is not the only truth, yet it is a part reality. With the loss of two of most loyal and faithful friends, Sher Singh and Rani Jindan, Henry Lawrence's decline becomes imminent. Without support from anyone, how can he rule? Under terrible depression he mutters:

> But I still have the Punjab. Let them go away. I don't need them. I don't need the Rani; nor Sher Singh. I have the Punjab. Angrez Badshah! The new Lion is here. I am the Punjab! (96)

Though he may have acquired total authority over the Punjab he knows fully well that his imagination is vanquished, his dream is shattered, and that he can never become the Lion anymore. What a pathetic degradation of a great person! History has witnessed it. In the end, when it is announced that he is no more the Resident of the Punjab, the dejected and tired Henry Lawrence says, "I'll take off the Lion's *chogah*. It's grown too hot for me". (96)

Henry Lawrence's ambitions and desire for power shows the play's departure from historical fact. History witnesses Henry Lawrence as a humble, visionary, progressive ruler. It is, however, up to an individual playwright to take liberties with historical episodes while picking up certain issues and leaving out the rest. According to historical facts, Henry Lawrence was demoted and shifted to Rajasthan, then a lesser important province while his brother John replaced him in the Punjab. Indeed, this play extends an excellent opportunity to have a fresh look into the historical perspective while throwing open various issues for debate. The play tells us the story of the rise and fall of a great person, Henry Lawrence, and the dirty political feud for power by local leaders. It has a neat structure and a smooth racy narrative.

For reasons inexplicable, Ranjit Singh, who was the most powerful and a brave ruler, never attacked the British Empire. He had a brave and well-trained army ready to attack any place, he also had an ambition of reaching far and wide, and he also was able to muster support of his contemporary kings. The British, on the other hand, were successful in keeping a safe distance from Ranjit Singh, yet they lost no chance to harass him by indulging in the affairs of Afghanistan, Nepal, Kashmir, etc. Ranjit Singh could easily have foreseen this as the British motive to enter into the Punjab, sooner or later. However, to a greater surprise, the great king never realized this danger. Ultimately, the British waited patiently for the Lion to die and then enter the Punjab diplomatically.

The play allows an insight into the *Koh-i-noor* diamond episode. There are numerous speculations about it. India makes a firm claim of the diamond. But history says that Shah Suja, grandson of Ahmed Shah Abdali and ruler of Kabul, was ousted by his brother Shah Mahmud in 1809. To recover the throne of Kabul, he solicited Ranjit Singh's help and came to Lahore. As a part of treaty, Shah Suja passed on the *Koh-i-noor* to Ranjit Singh in lieu of the latter's support. In the end, Shah Suja could not receive Ranjit Singh's help, as he smelled the latter's ill intentions, and ran away. What happens to him thereafter is an unimportant matter. The fact remains that the *Koh-i-noor* remained with Ranjit Singh. As the play suggests, this diamond was given to the British Agent as a token of friendship and loyalty. Rani Jindan says to Henry Lawrence, "This is a symbol of our friendship and yours for safe-keeping. It belonged to His Highness and I value it greatly" (56).

The play has, at its centre, the conflict of emotion as well as of power – a conflict in which racial boundaries are crossed, loyalties divided, the nation pushed into the background and power foregrounded. It provides an insight into palace intrigues that brought the state failure and defeat and the process which brought about an alienation in Henry Lawrence. The common man's hero is alienated by the leaders.

Larins Sahib has a lot of contemporary relevance. It reflects the ugly fight among political leaders to the advantage of foreign agencies. Political leaders, for their petty and selfish interests can undo anything, however great it may be. The recent issues of attempt to curtail the autonomy of a top-level management institute while trying to re-adjust its administrative structure is the best example of how a nefarious political motive can destroy anything. This issue is a classic example of crude political move under the false garb of 'privatization', 'modernization', etc. It seems that most of the political leaders utilize their energy in maintaining themselves. If they divert their energy for the betterment of people unselfishly, then that would certainly bring a positive change in the country.

There is an underlying sense of tragedy and a great deal of introspection into the causes of our past mistakes and failures. History is used to interpret contemporary reality and to project its message into the present. The making and breaking of great men is closely linked with the making or breaking of a nation. *Larins Sahib* thus offers a postcolonial reading of history.

References

Das, Gurcharan. *Three English Plays, Larins Sahib*. New Delhi: Oxford University Press, 2001.

Karnad, Girish. *Tughlaq*. New Delhi: Oxford University Press, 1972.

—. *Tale-Danda*. New Delhi: Ravi Dayal, 1993.

19

Transformation to Transcendence

Gurcharan Das's *Mira*

Madhuri Chatterjee

Gurcharan Das is a well-known novelist and playwright. He is also a columnist for *Times of India.* Das has attempted to combine the Indian legend of Mira with the sophistication of western total theatre in his play *Mira* (1970). The play explores the phenomenon of sainthood through the story of Mirabai, the sixteenth century Rajput poetess saint. Saints like Mirabai subverted the traditional ideals of Indian womanhood and challenged the social order. Mira's mystical love for Krishna challenged the social order and completely ruffled the conservative Rajputs.

The Bhakti movement arose in different parts of the country and had different idioms. The word 'Bhakti' meant 'devotion, and it sets out to work pedantry, ascetic withdrawal and emphasised the intense, mystical experience of personal devotion. The devotees cajole, chide, woo, rage against God, who is a personally chosen husband, lover to the 'Bhakt', imagined as a wife/lover and the mystic union is often imagined in sexual terms. "The Bhakts" argues Neera Desai "were not social emancipators but they were individuals trying to lead a liberated life. It is their individualism, that appeals to us" (212).

Priyadas' commentary on Nabhadas' *Bhaktamal* written in A.D. 1712, has shaped the historical work on Mirabai. There is only one indisputably known fact that is linked with her name, namely that as a woman Mira spurned her caste and family obligations in order to live out a life with Krishna. Nabhadas' began his entry on Mira in the *Bhaktmal* by saying that Mira left her class (Kul) and society and all notions of decorum in order to worship Krishna. Priyadas' account of Mira provided two other details which were missing in Nabhadas' – One that she was born in Merta; the other that she was married to the Rana of Chittor. Priyadas then recounted Mira's refusal to pay obeisance to the *Kuldevi* of Sisodiya clan (qtd Mukta).

Mira was a princess of the Rathore clan of Merta in Rajasthan. She was born in A.D. 1498 when the Muslim dynasty of the Lodhis ruled in Delhi, Babar the great Moghul invaded India in 1526 and established the Moghul dynasty. There has been much political turmoil amongst the Rajput clans which Mira witnessed. Mira's great grandfather was the Rathore noble Jodhaji who founded Jodhpur. The legendary Rajput hero Jaimal was her cousin and she married the son and heir apparent of the great Rana Sangha, head of the Sisodiya clan and the ruler of Mewar who ruled from the citadel Chittor. Rajput honour requires courage in men and chastity and obedience in women in an archetypal feudal patriarchy. Mira thus after matrimony entered a state of unquestioning duty, heavy marital responsibility and a rigid domestic hierarchy.

The legend of Mira includes folk patterns and folk techniques i.e. songs and folk motifs. The observation of *Natyashastra* techniques, styles are preserved through our classical dance forms. The storehouse of *Natyashastra* talks of emotions, costumes, jewellery, masks, music, dance, every conceivable object which adds to the theatricality of a work. Some of this classical rhythm, songs etc. percolates to folk theatre. The play *Mira* is in one act to be performed as per the playwright's instruction in one setting. All actors are on the stage all the time, there are no exit or entrances. When actors speak their dialogues on stage, they do not generally enact what they say. Action does not stop when a dance is indicated – the dialogue continues throughout the dance, as a visual and emotional aid to the actor's words. It's a brilliant treatise on body movements or space which are being talked today by Peter Brooke or Artaud. It combines the oriental theatre which inspired Artaud with the verbal theatre of the West. The play practices Brecht's *Verfremdung* which has been variously translated as "estrangement" or "alienation" which he later classified as a "mere shift in emphasis". The practice of distanciation or alienation is also reflected through the characters. The play is deeply emotional, it shocks the reader and distances, and also moves and converts us.

The action takes place in the early sixteenth century Mewar a princely state in the North-Western India. *Mira* succeeds as a non-natural theatre with lot of songs and dances. It practices the concept of theatre that exists in our country in the form of Tamasha of Maharastha, Yakshagana of Mysore, Bhawai of Gujarat and Jatra of Bengal. But as Gurcharan Das confesses and accepts "It needed a young Martin Benzell of La Mama to introduce me to the magic of theatre – to teach me that theatre could be created minimally with body movements of the actors" (16). So when Mira says in the opening lines "I am an ant on a matchstick lit at both ends" the playwright in the introduction says "the actors made such a picture with their bodies" (16). There are in all five characters representing Mira, Rana (husband), Jai (her cousin), Uda (sister-in-law) and Jhali (her maid).

In the production of the play, there is specific use of sound and colour – the use of wailing for mourning and songs and dialogues to indicate happiness. One is reminded of Antonin Artaud and his ideas on spatial language propounded in his concept of the "The Theatre of Cruelty". This is another way of enriching the language of theatre by non-verbal means – colour, songs, sounds. The folk and ritual elements inspire passion, jealousy, mutual rivalary, betrayal and in the process conveys a social message. *Mira* reflects the multiple dimensions of Das' theatricality, style, form and total theatre wisdom.

Aporistic dialogues holds the play strongly. The play's prologue expresses Mira's state of mind, her devotion, her pain, anguish, her bareness and the land's, and the beginning of a new journey – emphatically her marriage day. The marital incompatibility is revealed in "Isn't the Bed Small for the Two of Us?" (title of scence two) Gurcharan Das focuses on the evolving relationship between the husband and wife (Actor I and Actress I). Initially, there is novelty, the embarrassment of two young people discovering each other. As the novelty wears, the Rana becomes absorbed in the affairs of the state and in the imminent war with the Mughals. Mira feels frustrated without her husband. Her demands both physical and emotional are greater. She is "The Rainbird" (title of scene three) dying of thirst. When she discovers that her husband is not equal to her love, she becomes disillusioned with marriage. Mira tries to analyse and synthesise the socio-cultural activities of the Rajput tradition. Metaphorically speaking Mira's journey into traditional society is one of acculturation and assimilation but also of individualism. Various prescriptive exhortations are echoed by Jhali and Uda (other actresses). She is supposed to show restraint and reservation. She is expected to shed her impetuosity and become more regal and reserved. In the early scenes Mira tries to incorporate and imbibe, internalize the properties and decorum and the spirit of Rajput heritage. In the Rajput culture the mistress and maids cut across socio–economic barriers during festivities and bereavements. But Jhali (Actress III) is a constant companion of Mira instructing and safeguarding her.

For a woman a child is the medium of self-expression. "It is her motherhood that the traditional family values and respects; her wifehood ... is devalued and debased. It is through her Son (heir) that her self-respect is protected and she traditionally exercises her authority" (Nandy, 75). Mira's failure to produce a family heir further brands her as barren. She is disillusioned and also unable to pay obeisance to Kali. Mira finds solace in Jai's company (Actor II). She unconsciously turns to her personal God, Lord Krishna the dark erotic God of love and entreats him to give her a son – in a way she believes would bring her husband back. The sister-in-law Uda (Actress II) suspects her of infidelity. Mira confesses "I fell like a monkey with a snake in its paw" (121). Once again Mira transfers her love to the image of Lord Krishna and "I must have gone to sleep with you in my arm.... I had a baby in my arm. He had shining black eyes and a black dress and a black turban" (123) and she lives in a golden cage (sc x). Rana unable to understand her preoccupation with Krishna, thinks that she has a lover, "a snake's poison and a wasp's sting are better than an unfaithful wife" (128). Bisexuality in India has always been considered an indicator of saintliness and Yogic accomplishments. Perhaps it is considered an indicator of having successfully coped with or transcended one's deepest conflicts about feminity and masculinity.

The energy of folk theatre comes from the fact that although it seeks to uphold traditional values, it also has the means of questioning these values. The various conventions – the chorus, the songs, dances, aphoristic dialogues – permit the presentations of alternative attitudes to the central problem. The central theatrical device in the play is the effective use of all actors on the stage who form the chorus and sing the popular bhajans of Mira. As the play progresses, the actors instruct each other, from neutral commentators they also turn voyeurs who participate and condemn their acts. Music and dance also become the instrument of comment and analysis. Devotional tunes turn upon itself indulgingly and sometimes critically.

The play interprets the popular legend concerning Mira and how a royal conspiracy is planned to kill her but she is miraculously saved. Once a poisonous snake is concealed in a basket but when she opens it, the snake turns into a garland of flowers. On another occasion deadly poison is mixed with her drink but she swallows it, fully aware of what it is and emerges unscathed:

> Rana sent a cup of poison
> Mira drank it and laughed
> Bells on her flying feet
> Mira drank it and danced away. (130)

Public defiance rationalizes one's guilt provoking private defiance. It binds the moral anxiety triggered by defiance of one's internal authority and at another level, atones for that defiance. "My soul is the universe. The universe my Lord Krishna. I am he who I love and he who I love is I" (130).

In India there has never been a bourgeoisie with its faith in individualism as the ultimate value. Indians define themselves in terms of their relationship to other members of their family, caste or class. They are defined by the roles they have to play. In Sudhir Kakar's words they are themselves in "relational" terms in their social context. Mira's battle to master her insane attachment to God and her realization that she can master it, constitute a fulfilment. In her mastery is her sainthood(15). From a reality in itself, the image of Krishna has become a symbol of greater reality. She is transcended in this process of realization. She finds complete peace within herself, but detaches herself from the phenomenal world. However Kumkum Sangari chooses to differ:

> Though she is a rebel, once she chooses the divine Krishna for a lover, her spiritual idiom becomes that of a chaste and dutiful wife who observes in every minute detail her household tasks. A feudal order is her support, not her enemy and her concern is to find fulfilment through an ever more intense involvement in a spiritual recreation of the God's wife's temporal role.

But according to the playwright the transformation of a human being into a love-obsessed Bhakti saint has a different inner logic. As the actress chants and sings women of the world and goddesses of the heaven hear her call and leave their homes and husbands and honour go to him. And they love him(132). Mira abandons regal duties to attend the life of a wandering saint. The turning point was the bloody battle of Khanua in 1527, when the Mughals defeated the Rajput confederacy under the leadership of Mewar.

The last two scenes explore the tragedy of her husband Rana who suffers the misery and pain of his wife's loss and her transformation into Saint Mirabai. Gurcharan Das uses the historical material and substances it with dramatic diction. The scene "Don't ask the Blindman the Way" (title of Sc. xvii) focuses on Rana's poignant cry "The house is doomed. There will be no more Ranas, no more victories, no more Kali, no more Mewar. It is over" (137). The play opens and concludes with Mira as the bride - to Rana in the prologue and to Lord Krishna at the end. "I am free - free from life and death and time. Look at his light.... I am blinded. But how I love my blindness" (Sc. xviii).

The play is infected with aphoristic dialogue which gives it an exciting interpretation. It had been first performed by Martin Brenzell who brought equity actors who had been trained by Martha Graham and could also sing. There have been many productions including Alyque Padameese's visual enactment in Bombay and M.K. Raina's production with Jawahar Wattle's music.

Mira's myth is an embodiment of understanding of a people, an understanding often intuitive and dependent on the miraculous and the divine. Myth can be re-questioned and deconstructed to retrieve their lost bearings and identities. Interpretations like *Mira* provide a sense of continuity and impart a sense of tradition to the past. It helps to construct new epistemological and social frameworks, deconstruct patriarchal structures through individual questionings. Mira's devotion despite its positive aspects of single minded pursuit of the divine and self transcendence, and its subversive aspect of resisting patriarchy, can also be viewed as an escape from all womanly roles. Mira successfully clears a space where all forms of hegemony and domination are confronted and contested. The play in a way also deals with the construction of feminine self.

References

Das, Gurcharan. *Three English Plays.* Oxford India Paperbacks, OUP, 2001.

Desai, Neera. "Women in the Bhakti Movement". In *Samya Shakti* 1-2, 1983.

Mukta, Parita. *Upholding the Common Life: The Community of Mirabai.* OUP, Delhi, 1997.

Nandy, Ashis. "Women Versus Womenliness India: An Essay in Social and Political Psychology". *Women in Indian Society: A Reader*. Ed. Rehana Ghadially. New Delhi: Sage Publication, 1988.

Sangari, Kumkum. "Mirabai and Gandhi: Reformulating Patriarchies". Paper read at the Third National Woman's Studies Conference, Chandigarh, India, October, 1986.

20

Vulnerable Victims

Vijay Tendulkar's *Kamala*

Nishi Upadhyaya

Vijay Tendulkar's play *Kamala* (1981), continued the kind of socio-political engagement, the writer had displayed in his earlier work right from the late sixties. Tendulkar belongs to the group of writers who were part of the dramatic renaissance which took place in the post-Nehruvian phase and was parallel in time to the "Angry Young Man" movement of the British writers and the anti-establishment existentialist work of Albee and others. Vijay Tendulkar, Badal Sircar, Mohan Rakesh, Dharamvir Bharti and others like them were all part of this movement. Not only were they critical of the socio-political realities, but each one of them, in his own way, went on to experiment with the theatrical form and succeeded in dislocating it from the firm embedding in the proscenium theatre.

Kamala opens in an enclosed space – the living space of a Delhi-based journalist who has bought a tribal women from a flesh market in Luhardaga. Based on a real life incident, it exploits the incident in dramatic terms and locates the two women in opposition as well as commonality. In real life, an *Indian Express* journalist, Ashwini Sarin bought an adivasi woman for Rs. 2300/- from a village auction and exposed the kind of flesh trade which goes on all the time and is a sad comment on 'civilized' society with its profanity of modernity. But once this 'Strange' element is introduced in the drawing room of an educated man, the material aspects of the marriage institution are also revealed. Trafficking in women is not only an economic exploitation but also a sexual one. Middle class men deal with it under the garb of marriage.

In this enclosed space, the clash between human values and personal indulgences, the need to be righteous and the need to sink comfortably in a relationship clash with each other. As the two women occupy different physical spaces and different social spaces, but find themselves enclosed in the same house, tension gradually begins to build up. Questions regarding the definition of respectability, of equality, of dignity and freedom are raised as Jaisingh Jadav (the journalist)and his wife Sarita debate these issues.

Jaisingh Jadav purchases Kamala from the flesh market and treats her as an object that can buy him a promotion in his job and a reputation in his professional life. He is one of those modern day individuals with a single-track mind, who pursue their goal unquestioningly. Jadav never stops to think what will happen to Kamala after this exposure. The play questions the motives of Jaisingh. While he is a committed journalist, striving to expose the inhuman practice of women being bought at auctions and then sold into prostitution, he also knows that the story will make his career.

Tendulkar makes a jibe at the modern concept of journalism, which stresses the sensational. For this, he uses Kakasaheb, a journalist of the old school, who runs a small paper with his own resources. Kakasaheb provides the true ideals of journalism and in contrast to these Jadav's concept of newspaper reporting is shown in a critical light. That Kakasaheb edits a paper published in the vernacular while Jadav's medium is English, also helps to highlight the elitist nature of the journalism practised by Jadav. By introducing Jadav's colleague into the play Tendulkar is able to depict the true nature of the rat race that goes on in this milieu. As one proceeds through the play, there is a growing realization that relations within the professional community are far less supportive, generous and harmonious.

Another important aspect of the play is, it makes the invisible visible, namely Dalits and Adivasis. The ignoble practice of buying and selling women in the flesh market is poignantly depicted.

> The man who wants to bid-handle the women to inspect them. Whether they are firm or flabby. Young or old. Healthy or diseased. How they feel in the breast, in their waist, in their thighs and...[1](14)

How strange it is that even in the context of this most intimate relationship between man and woman, in which they both ought to be equal partners giving and receiving pleasure from each other, women are looked upon as mere instruments of joy judged solely on the basis of the extent to which they satisfy the man. Ironically while exposing this shameful practice Jaisingh himself indulges in it. He treats Kamala merely as an object who will enhance his professional prospects. He does not allow her to take bath, to sleep and takes her to press conference against her wishes in a torn saree.

This inhuman practice of buying a woman as one buys a hat or an umbrella is "a sort of concubinage permanently subjugating the female slave to the will of the master" (50), says P. Gisbert. In India, dalits and adivasis have entered a limited political arena but they still face poverty, gender discrimination, illiteracy, child abusement etc. Education, empowerment, equal rights, opportunities and access to resources can only bring India's marginalized societies into the centre. Only then can we move towards stronger civil society.

In the play, Kamala is not just a woman who is bought at an auction for Rs. 250/-, a price less than that of a bullock, but is also a lens through which Sarita discovers the oppression she faces in her marriage. The way Tendulkar sees it both Kamala and Sarita have been bought. Sarita, at the time of her marriage and Kamala, at the auction in Luhardaga. Tendulkar's script is crisp and successfully juxtaposes the characters of Kamala and Sarita to analyse the complex question of subjugation and discrimination that women face even today in modern India. Like Kamala, Sarita is also an object in Jaisingh Jadav's life, an object that provides physical enjoyment, social companionship and domestic comfort. Kamala's entry into the household reveals to Sarita the selfish hypocrisy of her husband and the insignificance of her own existence. Simone de Beauvoir's *The Second Sex* explores the nature of woman's life and status in society. Woman has always been, she says, "man's dependent, if not his slave; the two sexes have not shared the world in equality" (19). Man's domination over woman's body, mind and life is one of the many forms of colonizations that are found in the world. She puts at par different types of slavery – of a sex, a race or a class, and says, "Whether it is a race, a caste, a class or a sex that is reduced to a position of inferiority, the methods of justification are the same" (22). The Black or the Jew are reduced to a type, a fixed image, an "other" against whom the Master recognizes and establishes his achievement. The subjectivity, existential freedom of these persons comes into conflict with their subordination. But the "compulsions of the situation" enforce an "inessential" status and women, like other oppressed human beings, have been forced into inauthentic, inessential roles.

Naïve Kamala makes plans with Sarita, how both of them will keep their "master happy":

> We will make him prosperous. The master will have children. I'll do the hard work, and bring forth the children. I'll bring them up. You are an educated woman. You keep the accounts and run the house. (35)

In Indian society children play an important role in the lives of the parents. They are a source of solace and happiness to the parents. Ashis Nandy in his book *Traditions, Tryanny and Utopias*, says:

> A male child in patriarchal system may be seen as a means of ensuring the continuity of lineage. Even in the modern times parents see children as sources of economic security, old age insurance and as allies in the cruel world of competition, work and day to day politics. (67)

Sudhir Kakar in his book *The Inner World* makes a very fine point when he says,

> In daughterhood an Indian girl is a sojuvner in her own family and with marriage she becomes less a wife than a daughter-in-law. It is only with motherhood that she comes into her own as a woman and she can make a place for herself in the family, in the community and in her life circle. (52)

The wish to have children is symbolic of creating a space for themselves by the two women. Children will give a meaning and purpose to their lives. The dialogue between Sarita and Kamala at night is sensitively depicted. This is the only scene, which brings the two women physically and emotionally together and establishes a female bonding between the two of them. Through short and crisp dialogues the scene shifts the emotional focus of the play. Sarita realizes that not only Kamala but she herself is the passive victim of the unalterable male oppression.

At the end of the play Sarita realizes her precarious position within the institution called marriage, considered to be the holiest in our society. The play provides a completely novel point of view showing that women are still mere slaves to their male owners in Indian society in the latter half of the twentieth century. One should take note here that all three female characters in *Kamala* are in some way or the other subjected by the dominant male character Jaisingh Jadav, who occupies the centre of the frame. In much the same way John Stuart Mill in his book, *The Subjection of Women*, notes, "Marriage is the only actual bondage known to our Law. There remain no legal slaves, except the mistress of every house". The only difference is that in some cases bondage is defined by religion, as in Hinduism, in some cases by custom, and in some by interpretation of doctrinal texts, as in Islam. In all cases, women are considered, inferior to men and therefore the overpowering need to have a separate set of rights altogether for women. The setting of the entire drama is the drawing room. The other rooms of the house are merely mentioned but the characters are shown to be moving and interacting in the drawing room only. The husband moves in and out of the house but the wife is never shown leaving the house. Her physical periphery is restricted. She is allowed a limited space in which she has to fulfill her household chores. The continuous ringing of the phone in the drawing room is symbolic of the dull, insignificant, monotonous and mundane routine of a housewife. She is a wageless servant who looks after the house, answers phone calls, attends visitors and fulfills the wishes of her husband. The restriction of space enforced on a woman is again symbolic of the restraints imposed on her in a patriarchal system. Extreme restrictive lifestyle is stifling and self-denying. It is based on the principle of inequality and implies the dual strategy of control and exclusion. Women are viewed as weak, fragile and therefore need to be protected and guarded. The limited space available to a woman gives a limited scope for the development of her personality and talents.

Virginia Wolf as a novelist endeavours to comprehend the patriarchal structures of power and resents the forms of economical, social, educational and professional inequalities and the disappointments, deprivation and anguish that they inflict disproportionately on women. She stresses the fact that women should have more space with in the prevailing social structures and yearns to deconstruct the existing *status quo*. Lorne Sage in her perspective article, "Available Space," speaks about women on the margins of society, attempting to create their own space.

In the end, Sarita has just awakened and is going through self-realization. She is now determined and confident. She knows she will leave Jaisingh Jadav because she will not put up with the situation any longer. However because of her tradition and 'Sanskar' and her sympathy for her husband who has just lost his job and is in despair, she will stay with him for the time being.

Through *Kamala* Tendulkar raises certain cardinal questions regarding the value system of a modern success oriented generation who are ready to sacrifice human values even in the name of humanity itself and how in a success-oriented male-dominated society, women are often victims or stepping stones in men's achievements. The greatest quality, which Tendulkar can claim as creative writer and dramatist, is an ability to simultaneously involve and distance himself from his creation. This endows his work with infinite subtlety. On receiving the Katha Chudamani award, Tendulkar confessed, "I have been writing about life around me. When I feel the need to say or do something, I do it. Otherwise I will not be able to sleep" (8). He is utterly conscious of the bleak future ahead.

"Today, there is utter unpredictability around us and I, as a creative person, am as much concerned about the future as anyone else," he said. Tendulkar's plays are a lament over losses, which are disturbing, irrecoverable and final. "I am shocked more and more by the growing nightmare in the world outside my creation," he confessed in the Katha's festival. However he is of the opinion that a writer cannot bring about any substantial social transformation. "Earlier, literature did have an influence on society. Today, it is media persons and politicians who wield considerable influence and together they can do anything,"[2] he opines. Tendulkar's enduring appeal and contemporaneity across the decades is a proof of his multi-faceted creative genius which continuous to experiment and explore the potentials of the dramatic genre – his primary area of creation.

Notes

1. All text citations are from Vijay Tendulkar. *Five plays*. Trans. Priya Adarkar. Bombay: Oxford University Press, 1992.
2. "When writing is life itself," Interview with K. Kannan. *The Hindu* (New Delhi) 16 September 2001.

References

de Beauvior, Simone. *The Second Sex* (Le deuxieme sexe Paris), 1949, Trans. and Edited by H.M. Parshley. London: Jonathan Cape.

Gisbert, P. *Tribal India*. Jaipur: Rawat Publications, 1978.

Kakar, Sudhir. *The Inner World: A Psycho-Analytic Study of Childhood and Society in India*. 1981. Delhi: Oxford University Press, 1991.

Nandy, Ashish. *Traditions, Tyranny and Utopias*. Delhi: Oxford University Press, 1987.

Sage, Lorne "*The Available Space*", Women's Writing, (Ed.) Moira Monteith, Harvester Press, 1986.

Tendulkar, Vijay. *Five Plays*. Trans. Priya Adarkar. Bombay: OUP, 1992.

Tendulkar, Vijay. "When Writing is Life Itself". Interview with K. Kannan. *The Hindu*. New Delhi, 16 Sept 2001.

21

The 'Narrative' of a Play

Cyrus Mistry's *Doongaji House*

Jasbir Jain

To undertake the task of tracing or identifying the narrative in a dramatic text is, on the face of it, to seek a combination between two opposite elements – the 'telling' and the 'showing' – which the two genres are identified with or to attempt to place the subnarratives in focus. But the 'narrative' goes beyond this. It is not merely a telling of an event which is not being enacted. Instead, in a dramatic text, it often assumes the role of super-coordinator, as it brings together the story, the plot and the visual element in combinations which explore the different layers of meaning.

The enactment of a text is located in the present; it is 'happening' right before our eyes in an actual space as well as a created space. The meaning is constructed through dialogue, through the various acts of communication which the characters resort to – nuance, sound, silence, body language, movement – and the playwright/director arranges lights, setting, paintings, facades, and the entry and exit of characters. There are also the strategies which suddenly turn a monologue into a dialogue, or transfer the act of listening that the audience is involved in is shared by one or more of the characters. This 'listening' can also become an eavesdropping and lead to other complications, that is characters who ought not to know get to know and bring about a shift in the action.

The difference between a dramatic text and a fictional, written text is, as many a playwright has pointed out, one of space and the kind of dialogue which is used. What needs to be stressed is that it is also one of time. The three elements central to an act of storytelling are: *what* is told, *how* it is told and how *much* is told. The first is the story, the second the plot – linear or ruptured and full of surprises, causal or retrospective – and the last, how *much* is told is a matter of selection and elaboration, of omission and hidden reference, is the narrative. While the story is centred in a perspective, the plot in effect, the narrative stands outside these both and is double-faced. It links with the world outside and explores both the universal and the unique. It, through the processes of selection and framing, evokes meaning and brings together time and space. Paul Ricoeur believes that narrative is the human relation to time. It become a mode of intersection between the objective and the subjective, and brings the past and the present face to face. While on the one hand 'expectations' of the future surface, on the other 'memory' attempts to bring forth the past. This is slightly complicated. Actually both the expectations and the recollections are related and they overlap, even what one had hoped for is embedded in the past, and memory is of the past. But as the contrast between the past and the present – what one had expected and what has happened – is articulated, there is a double travelling of the self. One enters the past, transfers oneself to the six-year old or the twenty-year old and is absorbed in the glow of the moment thus extracting pleasure out of the whole exercise. Parallel to this runs the memory of the actual happenings which brings one a sense of loss.

Memory in itself is also unreliable. Furthermore it is selective. Different characters remember the past differently.

The total narrative is made up of these contradictions. And the play of memory feeds into the structure of the narrative. The dramatic text, because it is being performed, can bring about an heightened awareness of structure, provided we are sensitive to it. Thus the narrative can perhaps never be complete in itself. It needs a narratee, or a respondent, which is the basis of discourse. As such it is different from 'structure' or framework and is closer to 'action' as it works in a play. We often do not use the term 'narrative' for a dramatic text, and when we use it, we narrow down its meaning to the dialogues, embedded stories and structural shifts. But the moment a play is seen in its journey from text to stage and to the audience, one begins to see how narrative emerges. The enactment assumes a responsive audience that constantly interacts through speculation, expectation or withdrawal. The act of watching the performance, of responding to the nuances of speech and shifts in the plot allow the narrative to surface.

Cyrus Mistry's play *Doongaji House* (1991) was developed in 1978 by the author from a short story he had written in 1976. Though at that time it was awarded the Sultan Padamsee Award, the first production took place only in 1990. The negotiations of the author from story to play have made the narrative element very evocative. The 'dramatic' text is foregrounded through the visual element but the narrative acquires a multiplicity as the various happenings revelations, recollections, recurring dreams, build up a whole network.

It is a five-act play, set in the late 1960s, against the background of the 'Maharashtra for Maharashtrians' movement. The time sequence functions as follows:

Act-I	sc.1	Present
	sc.2	Continues in the present
Act-II	sc.1	Same week – may be after a day or so
	sc.2	Set changes to a restaurant but time is still the same – a parallel happening

	sc.3	Domestic setting, same night
Act-III	sc.1	Next day
	sc.2	The same evening
Act-IV	sc.1	A day or so later
Act-V	sc.1	Evacuation of the inhabitants, in quick succession.

The first act is located in the present and the rest of the action covers a period of a week or ten days. Except for a scene in a restaurant, all other scenes are enacted in the sitting room of the Pochkhanawallas, located in the collapsing building, built originally by one Farad and now known as Doongaji House. But memory expands this in various directions and moves out of the limits of physical space. There are Hormusji's memories of his childhood days and the dead man Dhanjishaa Bapasola, who was fond of dogs, loved by them but hated by people; there are Piroja's memories of her childhood in Lahore, and their common hopes of their children, two sons and a daughter. One of the sons has migrated to Canada, hardly ever writes home, yet the parents hope they'll join him at some future date. The other, Fali, has married an ayah and is a gambler and a no-gooder. Avan, the daughter works to support them, but she too leaves with her cousin Cawas, who is the son of Hormus's step-brother Sohrab. Space is expanded through the imaginative shifts to Canada, to Bangalore, to the riot-ridden streets, the race course and the memories of Lahore. Together these different spaces and memories work out a narrative with underpinnings of universal themes: dislocations both at a physical and a political level, loneliness and alienation, engagement of the young in individual pursuits, and acts of human betrayal. But then these narratives are held back and personalised as each character picks out a different set of memories. Hormusji is convinced his brother has betrayed him, has sold the business, walked out on him during Hormusji's illness. He has also managed to convince Piroja of this betrayal. But Sohrab's letters and diaries, which his son Cawas unearths later, tell a different story. Hormusji had already arrived at a state of bankruptcy, Sohrab had nothing to do with it. His move to Bangalore is motivated by his consideration for Piroja. He loves her but does not want to disrupt Piroja's married life and hence the self-exile. Thus a man who had been painted a villain, comes out finally as an intensively sensitive human being.

Hormusji's initial pretence to having been wronged and betrayed, and the later confidence of being independent and positive looking is finally exposed for what it really was – a sense of failure and a descent into nothingness. But the mere story does not say all this. Some of it is brought out by the dialogue and the turn of events but they also do not evoke the fullness and the multiplicity of the narrative in so many ways. The final meaning or meanings are evoked by the visual and through the body language of this man who had created for himself a false sense of having been betrayed, a belief which enables him to escape his failures.

The visual element is first of all located in the set. The living room is poorly lit by a kerosene lamp that has a 'long exquisitely-shaped chimney'. The rest is mouldy and dreary. The room is located in a building which shows 'alarming signs of age and degeneration'. And the windows are shut, shutting out alike the breeze for this fanless room and the dust outside. The opening scene reinforces this impression with its drab domesticity and a building full of an ageing population. One by one Perin – the bride rejected by their son Fali – and Piroza lay open the various strands of the narrative followed by a monologue by Hormusji which simultaneously lays down the parallel narratives of betrayal, personal failure, self-deception and self pity. His passive indulgence in self-pity is contrasted sharply with the hustle and bustle of the cooking which is in progress. Words are extremely powerful in building up an atmosphere. Perin is interested in the Deaths Column, while Hormusji's feels 'brittle' when he thinks of old times. Fali, who has married a woman outside their community and Rusi who has migrated are both equally lost to them.

Dhanjishaa Bapasola is a recurring ghost figure (in Act I, Act-II sc.i). Thinking and talking about him provides Hormusji with an emotional release as well an existential reality. Throughout this scene there are emotional shifts to match the quick transition from life to death, from love to hate and self-hate, from fear to fearlessness and from seriousness to non-seriousness. Fali's single entrance triggers off a whole series of events as the play progresses. Hormusji robs his daughter's pay, convinces himself of 'high returns' in the betting, loses the money as well as his worked-up optimism. Introduced in the first act, the consequences of Fali's entry have a long way to travel.

With an unusual obstinacy Hormusji resists meeting Cawas and later resists the evacuation from the dilapidated building. Resistance is his only way of preserving himself. He views Cawas as evil, as the 'other', who is intent on working out his displacement. In the end he wants to be literally buried under the debris of the falling building', "I will stay alone ... shutter the doors and shadows, drive nails through them... I will not see the light of the day again" (59). The next two pages are full of images of descent – falling, falling endlessly, through space. Significantly, it is only when Piroza gives him the assurance (however falsely), that she did not believe a word of what Cawas had told them, that he consents to the evacuated and admits that he needs Piroza's help.

In order to get the full impact of the narrative, one may imagine the play in its showing and realise the limits of action. This is not to undermine the dramatic element of the play, which as it sucks in the reader/viewer's attention and emotional response also goes on to sharpen the image of collapse. The play opens at a leisurely pace. But even as Perin and Piroza are engaged in cooking, they convey a sense of haste. They are always pressed for time. And then with a quick change of scenes and shifts the tempo rises. Initially dramatic tension is built up through the dialogue, which is confrontational. The husband and wife think differently and are at opposite ends. They have different attitudes towards life, one is practical the other lives in a world of unrealistic hopes and unacknowledged failure. But then the conflict is given a human face: the dead Sohrab, the living Cawas, the quick to abandon Avan, and then the inanimate objects like diaries, letters and stone walls.

Conversely, read the play without imagining the visual impact. None of the two will hold. The background music, La Marseillaise, the litting Viennese waltz, the song Hormusji hums every now and then, the recurring symbol of the violin, all go to form the narrative as do the setting and the drabness, the memories and dreams of Dhanjishaa Bapasola the double self of Hormusji. The riots in the background, the collapsing building as a frame, and the exodus of all their children place Hormusji in the centre. These frames work from larger questions of politics and nation towards existential ones of the individual capacity to face reality. Doongaji House with its concrete stone walls raises the question of the nature of reality which neither the showing nor the telling can capture.

A dramatic text is neither limited to the page nor to the performance. It asks for a more immediate response and for a greater degree of visual imagination than a novel. Different categories of plays exploit the narrative in different ways. That is why the setting and the interpretation play such an important role in eliciting the meaning. The 'immediacy', which a stage performance acquires through performance, can not be done away with through mere enactment. Film and the television both use setting and directional interpretation but the heightened atmosphere, which a good play generates, is not reproduced through those mediums. It is the 'live' connection that makes all the difference.[1] The narrative has a life outside the page and the performance in its demand to establish this live connection.

Notes

1. 'Understanding' a play is not enough. Even when it has to be read in class, it should evoke the stage, the setting, the ghosts, the interaction and simulate the experience of a live audience.

References

Cobley, Paul. *Narrative.* London: Routledge, 2001.

Mistry, Cyrus. *Doongaji House.* Bombay: Praxis, 1991.

22

The Potential and the Real

Dina Mehta's *Brides are Not for Burning*

Neelam Raisinghani

Brides Are Not for Burning (1993) is a play based on the grim social reality of violence against women by those who are in power, or by the powerless in retaliation against coercion by others, to deny their powerlessness. The play won the first prize in a worldwide playwriting competition sponsored by the BBC in 1979. It was broadcast from London on their World Service and later by All India Radio. The play has been performed on the stage several times in Chennai, Bangalore and Mumbai.

Dina Mehta tells the story of her women's journey towards gender equality in the context of changing social realities, but this journey places her audience in space and time. The play consoles them, making their lives meaningful by placing them in something bigger than themselves. The play is not merely the story of a particular lower middle class Gujarati family but it refers to a meaningful and larger narrative lying outside the closed spaces of the Desai tenement room, Sanjay's living room, Vinod's office, Tarla's kitchen and the in-laws' living-cum-dining room. Its threads are related and extended to the tragic and pathetic tales of countless Indian women, whose sufferings arouse Mehta's greater sensitivity. She looks at the domestic violence against women in Indian Society.

Suma Chitnis in her essay "The Concept of Violence" blames: "the hierarchical system of social organization, where there are categories of dominant groups and subordinate groups, is inevitably accompanied by the victimization of the latter through various means – subtle pressure, through the power of ideology, through mechanisms of socialization that reward compliance and punish noncompliance and also through open force" (12).

Although the value system in urban, educated, relatively well-off and partly conventional lower middle class, is less harshly patriarchal than before, but gender discrimination and oppression still continues. The undesirability of daughters still remains deeply entrenched in the Indian psyche due to the demands for dowry before and after marriage. Harassment and torture of the bride for extorting more money and consumer goods resulting some times in death(either through suicide or outright murder by burning camouflaged as an accident while cooking), continue on a large scale inspite of relatively stringent legal provisions. The culprits are rarely arrested and even more rarely convicted (Kosambi, 23-24).

Dina Mehta explores the dowry system that prevails in India despite the legal sanctions against it. She perceives dowry harassment as a form of violence where in the garb of following the traditional custom of presents Laxmi's in-laws use the demand for dowry to enhance their social status. When Laxmi does not cater to their greed, she is punished through insults, forcing her to commit suicide and giving it the colour of an 'accident'.

The play is embedded in a network of complex relations, "part of the general process of representation which takes place in human discourse" (Cobley 3). She compels us to think about the ever-increasing number of cases of violence against women for not bringing 'adequate' dowry. She plunges her audience into the heart of a mystery by these words:

Malini: What was the coroner's verdict?
Amit: What we expected?
Malini: Murder?

Several questions automatically raise their heads – who killed her? How did Laxmi's saree catch fire? Who provoked her to commit suicide? Who prevented help from reaching her? She deliberately delays in giving answers to these questions to arouse suspense. This two-act play consists of eight scenes. Though Mehta moves from this beginning point, she impedes the progress of the play by including several 'diversions', 'detours', and 'digressions' (Cobley 12). Mehta selects some events to be shown and highlighted, and omits others like Laxmi's final predicament which is simply narrated.

Paul Cobley in his work *Narrative* observes, "The progress of fictional narrative must necessarily be impeded, and this is the key point...diversions, detours and digressions can yield a certain amount of pleasure for the reader" (12). In between the narration of the crisis and its resolution lies the narrative space. Cobley refers to the five codes that Roland Barthes in *S/Z* (1974) discusses. Of these the fifth code, the "hermeneutic", is of interest to the discussion of this play. It performs two functions in establishing the narrative 'space'. It pushes the play forward towards disclosure and at the same time delays the progress of the narrative by way of 'equivocation', 'snares' and 'false replies'.

The narrative 'space' of the play begins with the coroner's verdict and Malini's resolution to "have a breathing space" (I, i, 22) but the key events like Malini's discovery of Laxmi's murderer and her resolution to come out of the constricting patriarchal spaces, are delayed towards the end of the play. Mehta builds up the narrative in between these two points with the help of many 'detours'.

Malini refuses to believe that her sister Laxmi's death was simply an 'accident' (15). She argues: "Laxmi was never clumsy...There were people in the house when it happened.

Couldn't anyone have prevented it" (15). She blames her father for whom "Marriage is 12 tolas of gold, Rs. 2,000 for a hall, utensils of steel, sarees of silk" (13). She blames him for Laxmi's silence. Old Mr. Desai believes, "To be born a female...is to be born into servitude" (90). Laxmi had to give up her schooling because her mother was always pregnant and ailing. She had to baby-sit for her siblings though she was the brightest of them all. Malini's bitterness about gender discrimination is quite evident from her question, "What right had Father to hold her back?" (17). She further exclaims, "A pity you had not heard of contraceptives, father!" (14).

Mehta highlights another feature of Laxmi's transitional membership in her husband's family in Act I, scene i. Laxmi's living in the new setup depended upon her 'proper behaviour', efficiency in household work, and the pleasure of her in-laws. She tells her brother Anil:

> ...in five years her in-laws reduced her to – what? A cook? A menial – with all the heavy work they got out of her? A nullity, her nerves and pride shot to pieces? A stunt woman, her hurts and bruises a daily routine till finally they succeeded in.... (17)

They blame Laxmi for being a sterile woman. She has been made to go through all the tests – while doctors have found fault with her husband Vinod. He has tried all "the doctors and the tests and all the medicines – allopathic, ayurvedic, homeopathic" (81). Even her father holds Laxmi responsible for this. "She has no children. After five years!" (14). Vinod "plays the endless farce of dragging Laxmi from one holy man to another" (81). Malini suspects that her in-laws tormented and humiliated her because the dowry she brought them was not what they had angled for.

Malini's disillusionment with regard to law is justified. She questions the unjust verdict of the coroner concluding that Laxmi's death was an "accident". The prosecution fails to establish beyond reasonable doubt that Laxmi committed suicide because of ill treatment or cruelty by Vinod or his family members. She expresses her anger, "I spit on law courts! Playthings in the hands of exploiters and reactionaries, they deal out one kind of justice to the rich, another to the poor" (18). She is aware of the lacunae in the law itself.

Another baffling issue addressed by Mehta in Act I, scene i, in relation to violence is the 'silence' or succumbing to acts of violence not only by Laxmi but her father and brother Anil as well. Their mentality remains unchanged even after Laxmi is burnt to death. Anil tries to hush up Malini because neither his financial conditions allow him to pursue the matter legally, nor does he have any time to help Malini in exploring the case, as he has got a new job to get on with. Laxmi will not come back to life. "She is gone now. Let her go. She is beyond pain, beyond redress – what can we do?" (18). Moreover they are emotionally and physically exhausted in the nexus between Vinod's family, lawyers and the police.

Another 'snare' used by Mehta in Act I, scene i is Malini's distraction from her ultimate goal of being "up against a smooth wall of deception" (48) and find cracks in it. Malini has a great sense of betrayal. In her growing frustration, she is attracted towards Roy, an extremist who leads an aggrieved and politicized group of unemployed ex-students, who are wedded to a radical ideology. They foment violence on campuses and outside. The shock of Laxmi's violent death and the callousness of the social and judicial system push Malini into embracing their extremist ideology, where guns seem to offer a solution.

> But for centuries we have taken up battle positions on either side of the great divide – the haves, a mere handful, arrayed in all their strength and splendour against great numberless ragged masses of have-nots – and I know where my place is! (87)

She thinks of bringing an improbable utopian revolution, "which will unite the whole human race" (89). In Act I, scene ii Anil's Professor Palkar warns him about Malini's involvement with a discontented group of students, whose number is escalating. They are dissatisfied with the overcrowded educational institutions – "ballooned far beyond their capacity to educate – and at the end of it all, where are the jobs?" (37). Palkar tells Anil about Roy's flat being raided by police to find lots of pistols, shot guns, hand grenade and advises him to dissuade Malini to stay away from Roy. To his utter dismay Anil finds firearms in a locked trunk. He throws them into the sea and advises Malini to stay away from Roy.

Another 'detour' entailed by Mehta in the next scene delays the progress of the narrative but also reveals the first crack perceived by Malini in her investigation of her sister's murder case. Sanjay, a rich industrialist flirts with Malini, while she is quite serious about this affair. For Sanjay Malini's body is more important than her feelings. He intends to marry a girl of his own class and offers Malini the job of his secretary, "As my secretary, we can travel everywhere together" (51). But Malini retorts back angrily, "You couldn't hold me back with a mule's harness" (51). Sanjay makes fun of Malini's concern for her sister Laxmi's predicament. He defends Vinod and praises his kindness for his neighbour Tarla's husband, whom he got reinstated in Sanjay's factory. Malini comes to know how Vinod had obliged Tarla, and thus bought silence.

The complicated web of relations helps to build up the narrative and provides audience with a crucial site. Cobley refers to Russian Formalists, who discuss two concepts 'fabula', the chronological sequence of events; and 'sjuzet', the discourse which delays the movement towards disclosure. 'Sjuzet' and detours are bound to an end point by a 'binding' process (15).

Act II, scene i fills up the narrative space by digressing to Prof. Palkar's illness. Anil, here, meets Dr. Ram Lodha, who had been called after three and a half hours after Laxmi's death by her in-laws. The Professor is beaten up by Roy's men and as a consequence suffers a heart attack.

All these events are somehow linked and depicted by Mehta in relation to each other. The chain of causation takes the audience back to Act I, scene i, where Malini shares the secret with Anil that Vinod had insured Laxmi for eighty thousand rupees. In Act II, scene ii Anil investigates the matter further and blames Vinod, for not procuring proper medical attention to her sister. When Anil threatens him with dire consequences, Vinod offers him a bribe of ten percent of the Insurance Policy amount to keep his mouth shut. Anil's silence scares him so much that he calls his mother to be vigilant.

Next scene takes Malini out of her own tenement room to investigate the murder case. She goes to Tarla and gets her doubts confirmed. In Scene iv, we see Malini in Laxmi's in-law's house. Where her suspicions are confirmed a cold-blooded murder. She blames Laxmi's mother-in-law "Yes! You destroyed my sister. You she-devil! And it's better for you that we never meet again. Because if we do I shall be tempted to kill you...You murdered my sister as surely as if your hand had sent her up in flames. You are a murderess!" (82-83).

In the last scene the suspense is retained up right to the end raising several questions. What would be her next step once she has discovered the truth? Will she be able to triumph over the villains? Will she exchange one servitude for another? Will she emerge as a strong individual?

Malini escapes her grisly end due to Anil's tenacity as well as her own evolution. She realizes that Roy stands for another hegemonic structure, which would not allow her to grow up. Finally Malini is able to move out of these closed spaces. The playwright's solution to the crisis is Malini's resolve to fight back. She questions the patriarchal structures and finds the strength to move out of them. Realizing that she has to work for her self-preservation and personal dreams, she decides to study law and work for justice.

Beginning from a domestic 'accident', the action of the play moves outward to interrogate the social system that does not value its women and treats them as possessions. Overpacked with issues the action does move very fast. But as they are all relevant to feminine identity and as the play caught the mood of the nation at a particular time by showcasing the dowry death. Through this the family structure, the institution of marriage, man-woman relationship, need for education and a career all are brought in, constructing bit by bit the identity of a woman who can cross the boundaries which hedge her in. The two sisters are like two parallel case histories; Laxmi who falls a victim to her own passive indoctrination of patriarchal values internalized through the socialization process and Malini who realizes the pitfalls awaiting her and rises to protect herself. The potential is embedded in the actual.

References

Chitnis, Suma. "The Concept of Violence", *Violence against Women: Women against Violence.* Eds. Shirin Kudchedkar and Sabiha Al-Issa. Delhi: Pencraft International, 1998.

Cobley, Paul. *Narrative.* London and New York: Routledge, 2001.

Desai, Neera and Thakkar, Usha. *Women in Indian Society*. Delhi: National Book Trust of India, 2001.

Kosambi, Meera. " 'Tradition', 'Modernity' and 'Violence' against Women", *Violence against Women: Women against Violence*. Eds. Shirin Kudchedkar and Sabiha Al-Issa. Delhi: Pencraft International, 1998.

Mehta, Dina. *Brides Are Not for Burning.* Delhi: Rupa and Co.,1993.

23

Meaning in Abyss

Dattani's *Seven Steps Around the Fire*

Venkat Ramani

An attempt is being made in this paper to examine Dattani's play "*Seven Steps Around the Fire*" (1999) in the context of modernism and postmodernism. The use of these terms is strictly limited to literary criticism. Moreover, the pother over postmodernism being a logical extension of or a revolt against modernism has been avoided so that the reading of the play may be done in an impartial and judicious manner.

To begin with, the very title of the play is ironic and is in paradoxical reversal to the story. The story itself is a conglomerate of paradoxical and ironical implications and episodes inhering in itself polysemic and semantic "warping", juxtaposing contradictions, which at a close perusal, point to a higher unity judged by the standards of modernism or to an annihilation of its own meaning evaluated by the tenets of postmodernism. The latter view is basically deconstructionist, which holds any sort of binarism suspect and robs the creator of his creation, which the creator had decentered while creating it. The point of emphasis is that in the various forms of deconstruction, whether it is the grammatology of the rhetoric interfering with the rhetoricity of grammar or the writer's

Oedipal conflict with the works of his predecessors, or mere interplay of words denoting "differance", meaning and signification become a casualty and the primacy of the linguistic medium is upheld.[1]

Consider the paradoxes and ironical juxtapositions in the play. These are at the level of words and thoughts, incidents and episodes. The "tension", the contradictory placement of "she", "it" and "they" at the beginning of the play tends to balance the theme of potence and impotence, the human and the "un-human" and resolves the existing antagonism into a higher unity, designated and symbolized by "it" the eunuch. The stage properties and stage directions which portray mantras being swallowed by the fire; the portrayal of "chanting" of mantras against "screaming" are paradoxically juxtaposed. Fire which is a significant part, a *sine qua non* of practically every Hindu ceremony and ritual (particularly marriage) a symbol of purification, a totem of things sacrosanct etches out as a menacing image of desecrating all things consecrated.[2]

The ironical inversions associated with the fire are obvious: fire at the beginning of the play is a harbinger of death; at the end is the tocsin of death. Just as "fire" loses its traditional significance so do the Sanskrit mantras which harbinge death both at the beginning and the end. The theme of death as a vindication of love is ironically reinforced by the theme of love being a vindication of death. Subbu commits suicide for the love of Kamala who is burnt to death for "she" loved him.

A close reading of the play reveals that the story is built upon a host of incongruities and oppositions that unravel both psychic and social conflicts and antagonism. The instances quoted above from the drama are intended to illustrate how linguistic "legerdemain" operates to collapse semantics into polysemy.

Consider how Anarkali is variously addressed: the constable calls her "it"; Uma, "she" and Suresh, "they". The human and the "un-human" are co-existent. The transformation of "it" into "She" and then to "they" is a psychic transformation of the ego into the "feminine" a symbol of sacrifice and devotion and thence into selflessness. The portrayal of Uma as one torn between the demands of her thesis and her inadvertent "collapse" into social work thus serves as a foil to the projection of self and the selfless. The opposition between the self and the selfless is striking; while Uma is on a struggle to selflessness, the selfless self is already crystallized in Champa, Anarkali and Kamla. Thus what has been traditionally labelled and treated as potent and human, and what has been defined impotent and "un-human" are reversed and placed in contrariety. The eunuchs are shown to be rational, emotional, human and selfless; the human beings are displayed as irrational, stony, inhuman and selfish. What prevented Subbu from falling in love with a girl? or What forces him to fall in love with a eunuch?

And here exactly the playwright places Suresh. The positioning of *hijras* is significant when we come to him. The story moves by indirection. It places Suresh not in the biologically correct but amongst the biologically defective. For meaning and signification is latent not in the former but in the latter. Uma speaks at random about Suresh going for a medical check-up, for a sperm count. The contradiction lies in the apparently productive and fecund being barren and sterile. The story posits the opposition between the seminal and the sterile. There is a subtle indication in Uma of her infatuation with the sexless, the neuter, the infertile. In Suresh's case the male libido has failed; phallocentrism has been overcome by a kind of deconstructive feminism. A tension is generated by valorising the eunuch over the human, underlining the sterile over the seminal. But the question that arises is that do they get valorized?

And here we are back to the questions we raised a little earlier about Subbu's choice of a eunuch. Granted, love involves no choices but inversely, sometimes choices are guided by considerations of love. Fear inhabits the mind of Subbu; the fear of surrendering his phallocentrism to feminism. The play starts with the death of 'feminism' and ends with demise of 'phallicism'. Consider how meticulously the whole story is worked out. Deconstruction of feminism begins at the start of the play and ends up in 'reconstructing' it: for Subbu's father, his son's marriage to a girl signified meaning, fertility and reproductivity; for Subbu this union meant quite the reverse. For him meaning lies in the dry and the barren, in emasculation and castration. The conflict generates a negation of meaning; meaning is in conflict with meaning; a nihilism at semantic and the social level; a kind of "textual subconscious" subverts the obvious, the apparent, the visible leading to an aporia. An example is the methodical use of "carnivalisation". It is used to show that even in the binaries' hierarchy, privileging of the one over the other is ironic. We may state some:

human being/eunuch

man/woman

love/hatred

life/death

marriage/dissolution

chanting/screaming.

innocent/criminal

fertile/barren.

In the play the 'textual subconscious' reverses the hierarchy. It requires a little critical and closer reading to discover the endless deferral in the play.

Carnivalisation debunks not only the hierarchies but also the social and cultural beliefs and practices. *Seven Steps Around the Fire* is the promise of a happy marriage but fire is marginalized in the deaths of Kamla and Subbu.

The above analysis does not call for a 'readerly' or 'writerly' approach. It is a question of treating the text as 'readerly' or 'writerly'. But once that is admitted, the reader discovers clashing connotations and denotations the juxtaposition of opposites, the congruence of the disparate. The modernist reader going through these contradictions looks for the achieved unity in the text. The postmodernist counterpart would rather calmly point out that the very act of looking for that unity has decentered the center, destabilized the text. It is not a question of indeterminancy of meaning; it is challenge of meaning yet to be determined.

Notes

1. The basis of this argument is constituted by the deconstructionist and poststructuralist approach of theorist like Derrida, Paul de Man, Harold Bloom.
2. Burning, burning, burning I came to Carthage" (T.S. Eliot's *The Wasteland*). From the structuralist point of view' 'fire' that purifies and purges travels through the literary tradition and consumes and destroys all that it was supposed to grace and make holy.

References

Dattani, Mahesh. "Seven Steps Around the Fire". In *Collected Plays*. New Delhi: Penguin, 2000.

Derrida, Jacques. *Of Grammatology*. Trans. Gayatri Spivak. Baltimore: The John Hopkins University Press, 1977.

Bloom, Harold. *The Anxiety of Influence*. New York: Oxford University Press, 1973.

De Man, Paul. *Blindness and Insight*. London: Oxford University Press, 1971.

—. *Allegories of Reading*. New Haven: Yale University Press, 1979.

—. *Resistance to Theory*. Minneapolis: University of Minnesota Press, 1996.

24

Countering Darkness

Manjula Padmanabhan's *Lights Out*

Sonu Shiva

Manjula Padmanabhan's play *Lights Out* is based on an incident of gang rape that occurred in a compound amidst a middle class community in Santa Cruz, Bombay, 1982. The play unveils the presence of crime in the society, where the acts of sexual violence occur frequently and no one comes to the aid of the victim. The people living in the neighbouring three buildings, all through this incident, due to fear, keep their lights off as everyone with their lights on had their windows smashed. They hesitate to initiate solving this problem as 'no one wants to do it alone' all the more they think that as it does not 'hurt' them, so it is no use indulging. Their apathy is due to their individualistic approach towards life based on personal interests. The title *Lights Out* is suggestive in itself; depicting the darkness of fear and ignorance that requires contemporary concern. Padmanabhan, through this play, wishes to convey that humans are basically social animals. If they really wish to find solutions to such problems, they cannot do it effectively until and unless they cease to pursue their personal interests and look for remedies for those with whom they live. It becomes crucial for the society if one limits oneself to only those people with whom one shares interest and obligations and not others whom one does not see every day. This tendency results in a break-up in the society.

This play readily facilitates the readers an interesting study of an individual's behaviour, that is to say, how the individual responds when one finds oneself in a particular situation. If an individual is directly questioned about one's behaviour or intentions at the time of being an eyewitness to such act of sexual abuse or violence in the society, it would be difficult to know one's actual response in a given situation. Padmanabhan through her six characters, who cease to be individuals at length and are rather stereotypes of middle class, foregrounds their actual response when they witness such act of brutality. At the end of the play brief messages are projected on the curtain over the window that I would like to mention first, before I begin my discussion. 'This play is based on an eyewitness account. The incident took place in Santa Cruz, Bombay, 1982. 'The characters are fictional. The incident a fact. 'In real life, as in the play, a group of ordinary middle-class people chose to stand and watch while a woman was being brutalized in a neighbouring compound. 'In real life, as in the play, the incident took place over a period of weeks. 'And in real life, as in play, no-one went to the aid of the victims' (53).

After the projection of these slides, there is silence, the theatre lights come on abruptly and there is no curtain call; suggesting the unveiling of a problem before the audience, through which Padmanabhan's deliberations of spreading awareness in the society can be well understood. The play also foregrounds the widespread disillusionment among people with regard to police and law. The cast of the play consists of three male characters – Bhaskar, Mohan and Surinder and three female characters – Leela, Naina and Frieda. It begins with a conversation between a couple Bhaskar and Leela who are joined at intervals by other characters. The maid Frieda remains constantly in sight on stage. The setting is drawing-dining area of a sixth floor apartment in a building in Bombay and there is a large window in the rear, its curtains drawn back. The décor is unremarkably upper-middle class. The brutal act of gang rape is being committed in the neighbouring compound from where the screams of a woman for help can be heard intermittently.

The reaction of these six characters to this act of gang rape is noteworthy, as they do not come forward to extend any help to the victim. Manjula Padmanabhan seems to portray not individual characters but stereotype characters that represent the society. In my discussion I have tried to delve deeper into the psyche of these characters, countering their attitude in such a situation.

A difference in the approach of the male and female characters in a given situation can be observed in the play by Padmanabhan, that has its roots in human psychology. Helen Bradford Thompson, the first psychologist to undertake an extensive and systematic experimental examination of the psychological characteristics of the sexes in her work *The Mental Traits of Sex* concludes that:

> The psychological differences of sex seem to be largely due, not to the difference of average capacity, nor to difference in type of mental activity, but to difference in social influences brought to bear on the developing individual from early infancy to adult years. (qtd Milar 617)

The social conditioning in the process of socialization of individual is responsible for the individual behaviour. In Indian middle class society the difference between male and female psyche depends mainly on social expectation and upbringing. The way the feminine role is emphasised in the society surely has an everlasting impact on their personality and identity formation. Quite early in their lives women are taught the need for flexibility, adjustment and submissiveness. Perhaps this is the reason why women hesitate in forming any strong opinion or taking initiatives. Women are mentally conditioned to obey their husbands and not to take initiative in any case. Either they are ignorant or they do not wish to resort to the police or law and they are intimidated by the facilities provided against any harassment by law, administration or police. Male is expected to take initiatives in the play. Leela throughout the play can be seen nagging her husband to call the police. As for herself she does all possible things to prevent the voice of a screaming woman entering her house by keeping the window shut, curtains drawn and plugging her ears. She is so much enveloped by the fear that she dare not go near the window to find out what is happening outside. She has some faint idea about the problem outside the window of her house, but she dare not acknowledge it to herself or openly in front of others. Perhaps she believes in what her neighbour Sushila says, "that by watching it we are making ourselves responsible" (6). She is much disturbed by the screaming that can be heard in her house, but her concern is not the victim rather her own life that she wants undisturbed. Leela's comments very aptly portray the individualistic way of life that has slowly crept in Indian society, where people weigh their relationship to a particular problem according to the direct influence it has on their lives in terms of profit and loss. Leela says:

> I don't care what they do or who they are, or what they are – I just want them far away out of my hearing ... out of my life. (44)

At another place she comments:

> Their sounds come inside, inside my nice clean house and I can't push them out. If only they didn't make such a racket I wouldn't mind so much. Why do they have to do it here? Why can't they go somewhere else. (8)

Through Leela we come to know that other neighbouring women Kummu, Picky, Tara, Mrs. Memon, Nini etc. talk about this incident among themselves to which Bhaskar comments, "And what they are doing about it? ... Right! wringing their hands and nagging their husbands" (7).

The banding of the women together to face this problem is missing. Bhaskar has invited his friend Mohan for dinner, who soon joins this couple on stage. The dialogues of Mohan and Bhaskar appear complementary to each other and can be seen as a response of the typical male world towards the acts of violence against women that prevails in the society. The passivity of Bhaskar and Mohan towards this sensitive issue is a result of apathy of police on one hand to which Bhaskar says:

> You never know with the police these days. They may say it's none of our business what goes on in the next-door compound. (9)

Bhaskar does not want to 'Stick his neck out'. On the other hand, perhaps there is a presence of fear of getting physically harmed by the victimisers; an expression they need to hide in order to maintain their self-esteem before women. This fear prompts the urge in them to flee from the situation. This is the 'defence mechanism' which R.F. Baumeister et. al. discuss in their study of Freudian defense mechanism from the point of modern social psychology:

> This research provides evidence for the use of defense mechanisms in situations where there is threat to self esteem ... Psychologists in the field of social psychology have continued to (re)discover the existence of the process by which humans deceive themselves, enhance self esteem and foster unrealistic self illusions. (Cramer, 637)

Bhaskar and Mohan both are curious about the crime but are insensitive towards it. They enjoy watching it because they are 'Just far enough not to get involved, just close enough to see everything clearly'. It's their own safety that matters most to them. They don't feel connected with the happenings outside. Their passive behaviour finds its expression when Mohan says, "Who said anything about help? I'm talking about looking that's all" (16). Mohan and Bhanskar's insensitivity is visible, as they discuss among themselves in detail about the kind of screaming, whether it is high-pitched or hysterical, genuine or not. To cover up their quiescence and hide their timidity, both these characters build up illusionary interpretations to the reality. They keep Leela in dark and try to give all sorts of deceptive arguments against it. They reason out saying, 'perhaps the screaming is for sheer pleasure'. They give it a name of domestic fight in which it is not proper for them to intervene. They suggest that it is a torture for fun because its too exhibitionistic. They unnecessarily try to confuse the whole matter saying, "perhaps it's the victim who smashes the windows of the onlookers". They even suspect the victim whether they are same or different victims every day. They justify their passivity and also create a class division by saying:

> Well as long as it's the poor attacking the poor ... you know how it is ... they live their life and we live ours. (24)

Kohut in his *Analysis of the Self* calls 'human connexion' as a psychological oxygen (353) which Lacan in his work: *The Four Fundamental Concepts of Psychoanalysis* describes:

> The disconnexion characterising human relationships; our experience of each other and of ourselves is radically alienated by the unconscious. Lacan's unconscious is structured like a language revealing its complexity through symbolic forms. (qtd Hamburg 360)

The disconnexion of these two characters towards this sensitive issue can be noticed in the way they give it a name of 'religious ceremony', 'sacred rites' which does not require any interference. 'Someone else's religion is someone else's business' (25). They justify it in the name of being secular. They try to dilute the matter by calling it barbarism, some new cults that are violent at the outset, and by judging them they would be showing their prejudice and intolerance. Their spiritual barrenness is reflected when they dine and listen to the woman screaming for help simultaneously.

When Leela's friend Naina enters the scene they try to hide the matter calling it "... some sort of religious ceremony, the local dwellers putting up a programme" (33). Naina has the courage to accept and give words to the reality, although Mohan and Bhaskar try to mislead her by calling it a ritual and then exorcism. First they try to reason out that it is not a gang rape, but afterwards they accept before her that this was really something they didn't want to talk about. Manjula Padmanabhan through these characters tries to project the innate fear that leads a person to approach a problem in a negative way and how men betray the exaggerated sensitive matters to small disappointments that they experience in the society.

When Mohan and Bhaskar are unable to give any justification for their passivity they try to transfer the blame on victim by calling her a whore. They try to polarize the issue creating a dichotomy between their women and victim. Sheba George in her article has tried to draw attention towards the fundamental weakness that lies in banding of women towards the issues that are directly related to them. She says:

> The recent tendency that is particularly dangerous to women's movement, the tendency of women themselves to become polarised in terms of community, setting up a dichotomy between our women who are sacred and there women who are fit targets of attack. (qtd Kudchedkar 4)

Though Naina can be seen arguing in favour of women rights but soon she too can be seen falling into the trap of fear. As for initiative, she too looks at the male world to do something about it and asks them to call the police. When her husband Surinder enters the room, realising the sensitivity of the issue, becomes enraged and desperate to take immediate action, Naina is seen preventing his involvement for his safety. Mohan and Bhaskar realising that as Surinder was ready to take initiative it wont be possible for them any more to hold themselves back. The maid servant, being a woman, belonging to the poor section of society that is most exposed to all types of violence, throughout the play can be seen performing her duties in a mute undemanding way. Perhaps she is well aware of society's response in such matters and feels frustrated. But when other characters engage themselves in planning various strategies to cope up with the situation, she can be seen on her mission, bringing things even before she is asked. Lazarus and Folkman in their work *Stress Appraisal and Coping* state that:

> Problem-focussed coping refers to efforts directed at solving or managing the problem that is causing distress. It includes strategies for gathering information, making decision, planning and resolving conflicts. It includes instrumental, situation specific, task oriented actions. (qtd Folkman and Moskowitz 650)

All these characters plan to use knives, petrol, acid bulbs, run them over by car, gun, electrocuting, public lynching, setting fire to their huts and taking pictures etc. Mohan and Bhaskar can be seen stooping low as to make money by selling authentic pictures of gang rape whereas Surinder sticks to his idea of beating the victimizers. Although one can notice positive approach of these characters engaged and focusing their attention to solve the problem outside yet they are unable to give it a shape of organised action plan. Their 'problem focussed coping' lacks the promptness required in decision making and they waste a lot of time in resolving their conflicts regarding their line of action. In the end they unanimously choose the safest way of coping with the problem; first by taking photographs of gang rape and then beat the victimizers if possible, but due to fear of self-safety, they ruminate for a much longer period. Soon everything is over and all their planning turns futile. Padmanabhan wishes to convey that presence of few men like Surinder in the society doesn't make much difference to the existing violence, and therefore the result is that, 'in real life as in play, no one went to the aid of victims'.

Padmanabhan's use of light effect on the stage is equally significant and symbolic in itself. Slowly the last slide fills over with red indicates that this attitude is most dangerous to the society. There is no curtain call and the theatre lights come on abruptly shows Padmanabhan's intention of bringing whole society from the darkness of ignorance to the light of knowledge. Perhaps, she intends to focus the point that our society has failed to cope up with the problems faced by women or the incidents of violence that happen every now and then. She through her play demands for an urgent need of social concern towards this decline as well as an awareness that is necessary for the people to follow new social laws. A spotlight here or there is insufficient, as it has happened in the play. Presence of awareness in the society shall instigate it to take prompt actions in such sensitive situations. Thus Manjula Padmanabhan intends to minimize the negative approach of society and favours to produce positive outcomes through her play *Lights Out.*

References

Cramer, Phebe. "Defence Mechanisms in Psychology Today". In Journal *American Psychologist*, June 2000, Vol. 55, No. 6.

Folkman, Susan and Judith Tedlie Moskowitz. "Positive Affect and the Other Side of Coping". In J. *American Psychologist*, June 2000, Vol. 55 No. 6.

Hamburg, Paul. "Interpretation and Empathy: Reading Lacan with Kohut". In Int. J. *Psycho-Anal.* 1991, 72.

Kudchedkar, Shirin and Sabiha-Al-Issa. Eds. *Violence against Women: Women against Violence.* Delhi: Pencraft International, 1998.

Milar, K.S. "The First Generation of Women Psychologist and the Psychology of Women". In J. *American Psychologist.* June 2000, Vol. 55, No. 6.

Padmanabhan, Manjula. *Lights Out*. Calcutta: Seagull Books, 2000.

Contributors

Amith Kumar P.V., Research Scholar, School of Humanities, I.I.T., Mumbai.

Anju Dhadda Misra, Poet, Department of English, Kanoria P.G. College, Jaipur.

Arti Sah, Department of English, Kanoria P.G. College, Jaipur.

Bandana Chakrabarty, Department of English, Government College, Gangapurcity.

Chaman Ahuja, Drama critic, formerly at Punjab University, Chandigarh.

Charu Mathur, Department of English, Maharani's College, University of Rajasthan, Jaipur.

Jasbir Jain, Writer and Critic, formerly at Department of English, University of Rajasthan, Jaipur.

Madhuri Chatterjee, Department of English, Subodh P.G. College, Jaipur.

Neelam Raisinghani, Department of English, J.D.B. Government College, Kota.

Nidhi Singh, Department of English, Maharani's College, University of Rajasthan, Jaipur.

Nilufer E. Bharucha, University of Mumbai, Mumbai.

Nishi Upadhyaya, Department of English, Government P.G. College, Dausa.

Pranav Joshipura, Department of English, Uma Arts and Nathiba Commerce Mahila College, Gadhinagar.

Preeti Bhatt, Department of English, Sant Jayacharya Mahila College, Jaipur.

Ranbir Sinh, Theatre Artist, Writer and Director.

Ravi Chaturvedi, Theatre Director, Associate Professor, Department of Drama, University of Rajasthan, Jaipur.

Shaila Mahan, presently posted at Directorate, Rajasthan College Education, Jaipur.

Sonu Shiva, Department of English, Government College, Bikaner.

Sridhar Rajeswaran, Faculty of Arts, University of Hodidah, Hodidah, Yemen.

Sudha Rai, Department of English, University of Rajasthan, Jaipur.

Sudha Shastri, School of Humanities, I.I.T, Mumbai.

Supriya Agrawal, Department of English, Shri Khandelwal Vaish P.G. College, Jaipur.

Tanuja Mathur, Maharani's College, University of Rajasthan, Jaipur.

Urmil Talwar, Department of English, B.G.D. Government Girls College, Shahpura, Jaipur.

Venkat Ramani, Department of English, R.L.S. Government College, Kaladera.